P9-EEU-045

Fundamentals of Law
and Security Administration

Mark Rohlehr

2005
EMOND MONTGOMERY PUBLICATIONS LIMITED
TORONTO, CANADA MLG

Copyright © 2005 Emond Montgomery Publications Limited. All rights reserved. No part of this publication may be reproduced, stored in a retrieval system, or transmitted, in any form or by any means, photocopying, electronic, mechanical, recording, or otherwise, without the prior written permission of the copyright holder.

Printed in Canada.

Edited, designed, and typeset by WordsWorth Communications, Toronto. Cover design by Celina Fischer, CBC Art Department.

We acknowledge the financial support of the Government of Canada through the Book Publishing Industry Development Program (BPIDP) for our publishing activities.

The events and characters depicted in this book are fictitious. Any similarity to actual persons, living or dead, is purely coincidental.

Library and Archives Canada Cataloguing in Publication

Rohlehr, Mark Anthony, 1956–
    Fundamentals of law and security administration / Mark Rohlehr.

Includes index.
ISBN 1-55239-096-9

    1. Private security services—Management—Textbooks.   I. Title.

HV8290.R64   2004   363.28'9'068
C2004-907215-3

For my wife and family for their love and support.

Contents

PART IV   OPERATIONAL PRACTICES

PART V   SECURITY DEVICES AND SYSTEMS

PART I

Introduction to the Security Industry

1 Origins and Development of the Security Industry

INTRODUCTION

Security is not a new concept. The role of security guard existed in the earliest human societies, where certain individuals were charged with protecting themselves, others, and property from wild animals and rival tribes. Cave drawings and archaeological digs provide evidence that ancient nomadic peoples developed and enforced social and regulatory codes similar in purpose (though of course, not in complexity) to the modern-day justice system. Certain individuals were designated to maintain order and to enforce rules through tribal customs and practices passed down by word of mouth from generation to generation.

Since the beginning of modern history, the needs of society's property owners, business people, and political rulers have shaped the evolution of security. In medieval England, for example, landowners were required to clear brush, large rocks, and tall grasses that might conceal highway robbers on either side of the king's roads. Land was also cleared around military establishments and castles for the same purpose. Around the same time, businesses and landowners began employing night watchmen to protect them against thieves. These rudimentary measures find their modern counterparts in today's cleared areas adjoining borders, in security patrols, and in intrusion alarms.

The notion of "security" suggests a stable and predictable setting in which people can go about their normal activities while feeling safe from intrusion or harm. Because the level of threat varies widely depending on a person's location or the nature of a person's business, the scope of modern security needs vary from situation to situation, reflecting not only our changing social structure, but also our economic conditions, our perception of law and crime, and our sense of morality.

Since the middle of the 20th century, the evolution of high-tech systems and computers have had a profound influence on the work of security professionals. Now, in the 21st century, security services must be prepared for future challenges; but it's important not to forget the roots from which the field grew, and to study the evolution of security, which now affords a wide array of professional opportunities.

Chapter Objectives

When you have completed this chapter, you will

- have a basic knowledge and understanding of the origins and development of the security industry in general, in North America and, more specifically, in Canada.

- be able to discuss the historical foundations of modern security.

- be able to identify the trends that currently influence the profession.

EARLY SECURITY INITIATIVES

Feudalism and the Middle Ages

feudalism
medieval social system based on an exchange of military protection for protection and labour

vassal
person who exchanged labour and loyalty for protection in feudal society

In early England, **feudalism** provided a very high degree of security for both the individual and the group. The Anglo-Saxons brought with them to England a culture of mutual responsibility for civil and military protection of individuals. They also brought the concept of the feudal contract, an arrangement by which an overlord provided arms and guaranteed the safety of **vassals** and their property in exchange for the vassals' assistance in administering the working of the lands.

In a world of constant warfare between men of power, the peasants' best chance at security was through this form of feudal allegiance. Though the gulf between rich and poor was incredibly wide, with little or no opportunity to change one's station in life, the system provided the stability necessary to permit the working of the land. The value of a peasant's allegiance depended on the power and cleverness of the overlord. Group security lay in group solidarity. The more formal systems of security that developed during the Middle Ages were largely refinements of this earlier system.

Post-Norman England, beginning with the rule of King John (1199–1216) saw the introduction of the idea of the rule of law through the negotiation of the Magna

Focus on Technology

Primitive Alarm Systems

Since the beginning of time, inventive humans have devised ways to detect intruders or threats and warn their allies of danger. Some simple examples include:

Canary Martyrdom

Miners traditionally brought domesticated canaries with them underground. The canaries, more sensitive than humans to deadly carbon monoxide fumes, would lose consciousness (or die) and cease singing if fumes reached dangerous levels.

Snap, Crackle, Pop

The following recipe for a natural alarm system, posted on iComm.ca (an Internet community for non-profit organizations) is credited to R. Lance Hill:

> Once you have found a suitable dry and wind protected area to sleep, lets say a suitable rock outcropping with a mat of dried moss and an unobstructed view of approaches from the road or whatever you want to watch, simply place around it, a wide circle of dead twigs.
> They will act as a primitive alarm system. Anyone or anything walking on the dead twigs will make a good enough racket to warn you ahead of the incoming troubles.

> Source: http://www.icomm.ca/survival/140-tips.don/alarm-on.htm.

What's the Flap About?

To communicate with each other on the open seas before the invention of radio, seagoing armies and merchants developed an elaborate maritime flag system. By flying a particular flag, a vessel could alert other traffic of its intentions or needs.

Carta (great charter). In a nutshell, this idea provided that a neutral system of laws was to have supremacy over the arbitrary edicts of whatever ruler was in power at any particular time. The Magna Carta was born out of a tax revolt that threw into high relief the people's desire to have continuity in the social and political system and its institutions. It incorporated a formal declaration of the individual's rights and of responsibilities between the state and its subjects and among subjects themselves.

Judicial reforms during this era included the emergence of local juries, circuit judges, coroners to restrain the power of local sheriffs, and justices of the peace appointed to hear and determine criminal cases. The movement also began the complete separation of courts and the exercise of the rule of law from the whims and power of the king.

Related measures were specifically aimed at the enforcement of public order. The **Statute of Winchester**, enacted in 1285, was the first Police Act. It established local law enforcement and reorganized the old institutions of national police and national defence. The Act described the "duty of watch and ward," which enlisted every man to pursue and bring to justice felons whenever a "hue and cry" was raised. Every district was made responsible for crimes committed within its bounds. The gates of all cities were required to be closed at nightfall, and all strangers were required to give an account of themselves to the magistrates.

Statute of Winchester
legislation passed in 1285 that established local law enforcement in parishes throughout England

To control vice and crime at the local level, boroughs enacted their own ordinances (regulations) since organized agencies for the enforcement of such laws were virtually non-existent. However, these efforts had limited success. Privately established night watches and patrols were often the only protection citizens had against direct assault.

1400–1750: The Emergence of Security Forces in Europe

Security was one thing in a largely rural society controlled by kings and feudal barons; it was another thing entirely in a world swept by enormous changes. From about the 15th century, European explorers opened new markets and trade routes, creating an increasingly important merchant class whose activities came to dominate the port cities and trading centres. By 1700, the social patterns of the Middle Ages were breaking down. Urbanization of the population (migration of peasants into city settings) and related poverty had led to increased crime that primitive public police forces could not contain effectively.

Different kinds of solutions evolved into attempts to deal with the problem. Individual merchants hired men to guard their property. Merchant associations created the merchant police to guard shops and warehouses. **Night watchmen** were employed to make rounds. **Agents** were engaged to recover stolen property, and various church parishes hired **parochial police** to protect their property and parishioners within major city districts.

In 1748, Henry Fielding, a magistrate and an author, proposed a permanent, professional, and adequately paid public security force. He refined a system of foot patrols to make the streets safe, a mounted patrol for the highways, and created his famous "Bow Street Runners"—a group of amateur police volunteers or special investigators. During his jurisdiction, legislation was refined to include common rights to property, and the receipt of stolen goods became an offence.

night watchmen
guards hired by merchants in the 1700s to patrol their properties at night and to protect their shops and warehouses from thieves and vandals

agents
first private detectives hired by merchants and private owners to recover stolen property

parochial police
regional guards hired by clergy in the 18th century to protect church property and parishioners within major city districts or dioceses

DEVELOPMENT OF SECURITY IN THE UNITED STATES

Across the Atlantic in the United States, security systems were also developing. In the West of the 1800s, the heroes of the day were Wyatt Earp, Bat Masterson, Pat Garrett, and "Wild Bill" Hickok. The Texas Rangers brought their own brand of vigilante order to the frontier. In the East, cities were growing rapidly under the influence of industrialization. By 1844, New York had its first police department.

Alan Pinkerton introduced modern-day security in Chicago when he opened the country's first private detective agency in the late 1880s. Originally from Scotland, Pinkerton became a deputy in Cook County at the same time as Chicago formed its first police force. He later became a special agent of the US Post Office Department, and finally Chicago's first and only public police detective. It was while in that role that he conceived the idea of a private detective agency, originally constituted to protect railroad companies from train robberies. His agency provided investigators and trained guards for railroad companies and industrial organizations. The Civil War provided Pinkerton with a new opportunity: he was engaged to send agents into the South to spy for the Union. As well, he supplied personal protection for President Lincoln.

Around the same time, Henry Wells and William Fargo founded a freight company they called Wells Fargo and Company. In the 1850s and '60s, Wells Fargo boasted a line of 1,500 horses and 150 Concord coaches. When gangs of thieves robbed their stagecoaches and bands of Indians terrorized their passengers, they hired their own detectives and security guards to **ride shotgun** to protect their shipments.

ride shotgun
job of riding atop Wells Fargo stagecoaches to protect passengers and cargo from robbers during the late 1800s

In 1859, Perry Brinks and his wife Fidelia opened a freight and package forwarding company in Washington. In 1891, Brinks made his first payroll delivery and the Brinks armoured service was born. By 1900, Brinks was transporting bank shipments, and in 1904, he put his first gasoline-powered vehicle into service. Between 1918 and 1932, branch banking led to the establishment of Brinks' offices and services in another 48 cities. In 2004, Brinks Inc. celebrated its 145th anniversary in business.

In 1909, William J. Burns, a Secret Service investigator for the president, challenged Pinkerton's monopoly service when he established a rival private detective agency. The American Banking Association hired this service to become its investigative arm. George Wackenhut, a former FBI agent, formed a security company in 1954. Today, Wackenhut is the second-largest security company in North America, while Pinkerton, Brinks, and Burns have remained big names in the security industry in both the United States and Canada. Until the founding of the Federal Bureau of Investigation in 1932, private companies (primarily Pinkerton and Burns) were the sole non-military providers of security and investigative services for the US federal government.

The demand for security services in the United States has shown consistent growth over the past 150 years. In recent years, security services have represented over 1 percent of the entire American gross domestic product (GDP), and the market is projected to carry on growing at an even faster rate through the next 10 years.

As in other industries, mergers have influenced the makeup of the security industry. After Pinkerton evolved into a full-service security company with over 60,000 employees and Burns International grew to over 38,000 employees, a Swedish security company, Securitas AB, bought and merged these two well-known North

American services into its multinational family, making Securitas the largest security company in the world.

DEVELOPMENT OF SECURITY IN CANADA

Pioneering in the Canadian prairies did not parallel the American's wild vigilante brand of law and order. In 1873, to avoid mounting violence associated with American trade expansion into the Canadian prairies, Prime Minister John A. Macdonald created a paramilitary force of mounted police to stop the pillaging of tribal lands. The mission of the North West Mounted Police (NWMP), now known as the Royal Canadian Mounted Police (RCMP), included orders to gain the respect and confidence of the native peoples, to collect customs due on traded goods, and to enforce law and order. Within months of the creation of the first police outpost at Fort Macleod, the NWMP suppressed the growing lawlessness in Canada's western frontier.

The next challenge to Canadian security came in the form of railroad development. When the Canadian Pacific Railway (CPR) sought to build a rail line from the Pacific Coast to Eastern Canada, it encountered problems with theft, workers' strikes, and vandalism. In response, CPR began hiring its own security guards.

In 1885, after government surveyors threatened the Métis people with eviction from their lands if they tried to block the railroad's progress along the North Saskatchewan River, Louis Riel led his people in rebellion against the federal government. Outnumbered, the NWMP recruited Canada's first private force of 43 Prince Albert volunteers. When hostilities erupted, 12 of the 99-man volunteer police force were killed. Riel's victory was short-lived, however, when the railway delivered army reinforcements to crush his rebellion.

The use of volunteers to supplement the public police force and the introduction of railway guards marked the birth of private security in Canada. As the United States security market became saturated with security companies, established organizations such as Pinkerton, Brinks, and Burns looked north to sell their security systems and services to Canada's growing manufacturers, banks, institutions, and building developers.

THE SECURITY PROFESSION IN CANADA TODAY

By 1954, security services in Canada had grown significantly. Security officers banded together to form the Security Officers Association of Ontario; later, a national association was created in the form of the Canadian Society for Industrial Security Inc. (CSIS).

CSIS is a professional organization consisting of individual and corporate members representing industry and business in and outside Canada, and all levels of government and law enforcement agencies. A national board of directors meets four times a year to discuss policy issues and problems relating to commercial, industrial, and institutional security. The Society encourages members to air their concerns as it seeks to set high standards for security education and nationally accredited training programs. The organization also lobbies the federal and provincial governments for legislative changes to benefit the security industry. One of

CSIS's specific goals is to help provinces form security advisory committees mandated to set standards for the security industry within their respective regions.

CSIS provides a certification program leading to a number of different types of professional accreditation for security professionals. The three initial types of certification are Certified Security Officer (CSO), Certified Security Supervisor (CSS), and Certified Security Professional (CSP). In general, certification depends on proof of completion of education and/or training programs that meet learning objectives set out by CSIS.

Certification/accreditation is intended to identify the recipient, within the marketplace, as a person whose training and knowledge in the area meets recognized professional standards. Maintaining CSIS certification requires payment of an annual fee, and recertification if the original certification is allowed to lapse.

Central to CSIS's emphasis on education and communication is its shared ownership of a national magazine, *Canadian Security*. Each edition of the publication has "how-to" articles, information on the rapid development of more and more sophisticated security technology, and case studies of developments in the industry.

REASONS FOR GROWTH IN THE SECURITY INDUSTRY

Several factors are responsible for the current dynamic growth in the security industry. These factors reflect the cultural, industrial, political, social, and financial influences of our time.

1. Growth in the Private Sector

Our economy is growing. Retail and manufacturing numbers are up. Building starts are up. Real estate is booming. Small businesses—especially in high-tech fields—continue to be formed. All of these require physical security and contingency planning.

2. The Technology Boom

Technology has allowed smaller companies to compete with large, established organizations. With the benefits of computer technology come risks associated with the exposure of sensitive personal and corporate information. In addition, the ability to manipulate and transmit large quantities of sensitive material increases the potential for industrial espionage. The need to protect corporate and government information has led to the rapid development of a security sub-industry dedicated to information security.

3. Crime Rates and the Perception of Security

Despite conflicting evidence—including statistics suggesting that the contrary is true—there is a prevailing public perception that the crime rate is increasing. This perception is heavily influenced by trends in media reporting, but regardless of accuracy, it tends to provoke fear. As we suggested earlier in this chapter, "security" requires not only actual safety, but also the perception of safety. A perceived gap in security has a negative impact on both quality of life and productivity and leads to increased demand for security services.

4. Law Enforcement and Judicial System Gaps

Because funding for public policing is subject to political control, the level and quality of policing varies. Recent cuts to policing budgets have left some individuals and businesses feeling insecure about the ability of public law enforcement to maintain an expected level of service despite decreased resources. This insecurity leads to increased demands for private security.

When offenders are given light sentences for hard crimes and criminal cases are dropped because of legal technicalities or lack of investigative resources, the public doesn't feel safe. Criminal court caseloads are backlogged. The perceived burdens on the justice system stimulates demand for increased private security.

Step Aside

Security is a large and growing industry in North America. It exceeds 1 percent of the American GDP. In a 2002 paper for the Canadian Department of Justice, Trevor Sanders analyzed Statistics Canada data and came to the preliminary conclusion that

> employment in the field of Investigation and Security Services has increased by more than 60 percent during the 11-year period from 1991 to 2001. This figure is contrasted with an increase of less than 1 percent in the number of public police officers over the same time period.
>
> From: Trevor Sanders, Department of Justice, abstract for "Rise of the Rent-A-Cop: Private Security in Canada, 1991–2002" (2002) (available online at http://www.lcc.gc.ca/en/ress/conf/conf_flyer/speakers_abstract/sanders.asp).

In 1998, there were approximately 55,000 police officers—and 125,000 security guards—working in Canada.

5. Cultural Changes

Increased diversity in the Canadian population and the incorporation of foreign cultures and business practices into the broader Canadian culture can lead to conflicts between individuals and neighbourhoods. These conflicts sometimes manifest in criminal activity. Clashes between culturally identified gangs (for example, Asian "Triad" gangs) lead to flare ups of violence, especially in urban centres. Increased security can help business owners in these neighbourhoods feel safer.

6. "Cocooning"

With the advent of new entertainment technologies and the home office, many homeowners have embraced valuable technologies (computers, entertainment systems, etc.), which make their homes more vulnerable to break-ins. Security can provide protection for the owners of these new consumer goods.

FAST FACT

After the events of September 11, 2001, the Canadian Nuclear Safety Commission (CNSC) hired officers from Globe Risk Holdings Inc. to provide immediate and effective armed security intervention at the Bruce nuclear facilities. Globe Risk was the first private security company in Canada to develop and train an armed tactical response unit in accordance with the CNSC mandate. Supplemented by tactical support from the Ontario Provincial Police (OPP), Globe Risk filled the gap until Bruce Power could train and implement its own rapid deployment team.

7. Threats of Global Terrorism

Since the terrorist attacks in the United States on September 11, 2001, people and businesses feel more vulnerable to violence from international sources and may look to security services to conduct threat assessments, minimize the risks, and guide them in preparing and implementing more effective security strategies.

SUMMARY

Since the first humans lived in caves, there has been a role for security. Security became more formalized in the feudal era, when a lord's protection was offered in return for tenants' work. The Magna Carta, signed in the Middle Ages, introduced the concept of social rights and protections.

Through the 17th and 18th centuries, escalating urbanization and trade growth increased the demand for protection of ports, ships, houses, and businesses. New security innovations of this period included merchant police, night watchmen, and agents to recover stolen goods and parochial police to protect parish property.

The 19th century brought the birth of the modern security industry in North America. While the industry developed later in Canada, factors increasing demand for security services are now common to both Canada and the United States.

KEY TERMS

agents

feudalism

night watchmen

parochial police

ride shotgun

Statute of Winchester

vassals

PERFORMANCE APPLICATION

1. How did the feudal socioeconomic system meet the security needs of both lords and vassals?

2. Why was the Magna Carta significant to the development of the concept of personal security?

3. The Focus on Technologies feature in this chapter describes three simple but ingenious early security systems. Give three other examples.

4. Describe two security challenges in the United States during the 1800s, and explain what solutions were developed to address them.

5. This chapter discussed the evolution of both the private security and, to some extent, the private investigation industries. What is the relationship between these two industries?

6. In what ways did the development of security in Canada differ from the development of the industry in the United States?

7. What is the principal professional organization for security professionals in Canada? What is its mandate?

8. Research and list five security companies in your local areas. What kinds of services do they provide? What kinds of clients do they serve?

9. List four factors that have stimulated growth in security in the last several decades. Do you anticipate that these factors will continue to influence public demands for security in coming years? Why or why not?

10. What do you anticipate will be the primary challenges facing security in the 21st century? How are these challenges different from those of the previous two centuries?

The Security Profession Today

INTRODUCTION

The role of the professional security provider and the duties commonly associated with the security industry have been changing constantly over the last 10 to 15 years. Today's security professionals protect both people and property, serve both individuals and corporations, and are becoming increasingly involved in the provision of specialized services, including the protection of information, neighbourhood-based crime prevention, and emergency response.

Despite growth in the market's appetite for security services, public law enforcement resources have stabilized and, in some areas, are even in decline. This situation has led to a high proportion of private security providers in the overall security landscape. It has also made it essential that private security providers understand how to integrate their functions with those of the public police in the common interest of crime prevention and reduction.

TYPES OF SECURITY SERVICE PROVIDERS

Security service providers include contract security companies, proprietary (or in-house) security providers, emergency response specialists, and private investigators.

Contract Security Companies

Contract security companies provide a diverse cross-section of security services for their clients. These include, but are not limited to:

- uniformed guard service;
- mobile vehicle patrols;
- K-9 sentry and dog handler teams;
- alarm monitoring and response;

Chapter Objectives

When you have completed this chapter, you will

- have a basic understanding of the duties of a professional security officer, a private investigator, and an emergency response specialist, and other functions within the security industry.

- be able to demonstrate basic knowledge of the organization and the role of the public police forces in Canada.

- have an understanding of the appropriate interactions between security officers and the public, the public police, and the media.

- electronic countermeasures;

- polygraph and integrity testing;

- crowd control and special event security;

- bodyguards and safe transport services;

- labour dispute management; and

- security consulting.

Proprietary or In-House Security

Proprietary or in-house security is a service provided by company employees. In other words, security is a job function within the organization. The duties of in-house security officers are often the same as those of contract services. Organizations that employ their own security include major retail chains, utility companies, transportation companies, and tourist attractions and museums.

Federal and provincial governments also maintain proprietary security forces charged with a diverse range of security tasks. At the federal level, the Canadian Security Intelligence Service (CSIS) (not to be confused with the Canadian Society for Industrial Security, also CSIS) is charged with protecting the security interests of Canadians from a wide range of physical, political, and economic security threats.

At all levels of government, proprietary security officers are charged with the protection of public works and utilities, Parliament and other government buildings (including laboratories and corrections facilities), and politicians and government personnel. Some government security forces (for example, prison guards and public utilities guards) are quite specialized, and are subject to special rules. For example, some public security personnel have the powers of a peace officer in the course of carrying out their duties.

Emergency Response Specialist

A new breed of security professional has been emerging, especially since the terrorist attacks in the United States on September 11, 2001. These professionals specialize in coordinated emergency response. Private companies and public services have recognized that, in addition to responding to traditional local emergencies and minor natural disasters, there is a need to develop expertise and resources to recognize and safely respond to larger-scale emergencies, such as acts of terrorism, nuclear, biochemical, explosive or incendiary disasters, and total infrastructure failures. Emergency response, as a specialized area of private security, is discussed in detail in chapter 26.

PRIVATE INVESTIGATORS

Private investigators have stricter licencing requirements (and often more training) than do regular security personnel. Some work for agencies; others establish private practices. They usually work in plain clothes. The role of private investigators is, for the most part, outside the scope of this book. However, the following section provides a basic overview of the primary functions of these service providers.

The clientele of private investigators may include governments, large corporations, lawyers, insurance companies, and private individuals. Clients often hire private investigators to uncover information and evidence that falls outside the mandate of the public police or that police don't have the resources to access.

Some functions performed by private investigators are as follows.

Background and Credit Checks

A private investigator may be hired by employers, lenders, or other clients to determine whether prospective employees or clients are everything they claim to be. For example, the private investigator can confirm personal information, such as a person's residence, determine whether an individual actually has a designation or degree that is claimed on a résumé, or determine whether a client has undisclosed debts.

Insurance Fraud

Private investigators working for commercial insurers may be hired to uncover asset misrepresentation or fraudulent property damage claims. Such investigations often require significant cooperation with public agencies. Alleged **arson**, for example, requires a forensic investigation, in which the fire department, the police, and the private investigator work together to uncover the felony.

arson
illegal act in which someone sets fire to a building or property

Internal Theft

Internal theft can range from employees taking home office supplies for personal use, to "creative accounting," to large-scale fraud. Private investigators may be hired to uncover internal theft of many varieties, using various methods. They may be hired to audit company books or to pose as employees to monitor theft of goods and cash.

Divorce Settlements

Private investigators are commonly hired to find evidence of extra-marital affairs, property hidden to avoid a 50–50 split in a divorce settlement, polygamy, undisclosed child support, or whether a person who claims to be single is married.

Missing Persons

While missing persons cases are often handled by the public police, missing persons other than small children must be missing for a minimum of 24 hours before the police will take action. Private investigators are sometimes hired to expedite a search, especially where foul play is suspected. On a cold case, where police have begun to withdraw their resources, it is not uncommon for the family to hire a private investigator to continue following up leads.

FAST FACT

Not Just a Fellow Shopper?

The retail industry often contracts people who are trained and licensed as private investigators and security guards. Being licensed allows them to wear civilian clothing, such as the clothing worn by the clerks in the store or the customers and shoppers. By blending into the store's environment, they are able to make arrests to recover stolen property and reduce theft. Every major retail outlet in Canada employs private investigators for this purpose.

Criminal and Civil Cases

While criminal cases are generally handled by police, private investigators may be hired by a defendant's law firm to uncover background information. In civil cases, private investigators play a much more significant role and may be hired by both sides to uncover a wide range of information.

Bodyguard Services

The image of the bodyguard has been distorted by movies and television. In Canada, there are no armed thugs in dark suits guarding VIPs. Bodyguard duties are limited by the constraints of the law, which in 99 percent of cases prohibits the carrying of weapons. There are some narrow exceptions; for example, in a situation where the police have been unable to offer the same level of service to protect a threatened citizen, a private investigator hired as a bodyguard may be authorized to carry a firearm in the course of duty for the period of time in which the person being protected is considered in harm's way. (For the rare circumstances in which a security guard might be permitted to carry a firearm, see s. 20 of the *Firearms Act* and ss. 2 and 3 of the regulations made under that Act.)

Courier Services

Courier services are especially important to gemstone merchants and dealers who travel internationally. They hire private investigators either to act as couriers on their behalf or to accompany couriers carrying jewels or uncut diamonds from province to province or country to country.

Industrial Espionage

industrial espionage
secretly accessing or collecting unauthorized manufacturing, business, or trade information from a company

electronic counter-measures (ECM)
art of locating and disabling unauthorized transmission, recording, and listening devices

Private investigators involved in preventing **industrial espionage** or information theft are one of the prime users of **electronic countermeasures (ECM)**. They use electronic devices to locate recording and listening devices and disable unauthorized transmission. ECM has been employed successfully in labour situations, where negotiations between a company and its union have been penetrated electronically. It has also been successfully applied in other areas such as pinpointing stock market leaks. Canadian private investigators do extensive work in this area.

Electronic countermeasures are also heavily employed by CSIS (the Canadian Security Intelligence Service). CSIS's mandate is to provide advance warning to Canadian governments of threats to the security of Canadians. Because CSIS does not have police powers, addressing those threats is the responsibility of other agencies (typically public police forces and the military). At the time of the Cold War, CSIS was very involved in investigating military and political threats, but its role has since evolved:

> In response to the rise of terrorism worldwide and the demise of the Cold War, CSIS has made public safety its first priority. This is reflected in the high proportion of resources devoted to counter-terrorism. CSIS has also assigned more of its counter-intelligence resources to investigate the activities of foreign governments that decide to conduct economic espionage in Canada in order to gain an eco-

nomic advantage or try to acquire technology in Canada that can be used for the development of weapons of mass destruction.

(From "The CSIS Mandate" at http://www.csis-scrs.gc.ca/eng/backgrnd/back1_e.html.)

CONTRACT VERSUS PROPRIETARY SECURITY: DISTINCTIONS

One key difference between contract security and proprietary or in-house security is that the security officer who works for a contract security provider must be licensed under the *Private Investigators and Security Guards Act* to carry out security assignments at different locales. This permits the contract security company to assign its employee officers to premises of any contracted client as it sees fit. As a result, a security officer who works for a contract company can work at different locations from one day or week to the next.

In-house security personnel, by contrast, do not require licensing under the *Private Investigators and Security Guards Act*. They can be trained in-house at the employer's expense. However, they are limited to working on the employer's premises. This limits their availability for certain investigative or transport/escort functions.

SECURITY AND PUBLIC EMERGENCY FORCES

The varied duties of private security officers often bring them into contact with public emergency forces such as police officers, fire fighters, bylaw enforcement officers, and ambulance/paramedic personnel. On any given day, a security officer may be involved in the arrest of an individual, responding to a fire alarm, investigating a client complaint, dealing with lost or found property, evicting trespassers, or assisting paramedics with a patient.

In carrying out these duties, security officers must have a clear understanding of the scope of their own responsibilities, and of the factors requiring the involvement of public emergency response forces. Once outside forces become involved, private security must be prepared to cooperate and communicate effectively with public personnel.

Whenever security officers are required to provide assistance, exchange information, or request the presence of emergency forces on site, they should remember that all parties share the same goals. Police and other public officers should be treated with respect and tolerance, so that both forces can work together for the good of the client, the property, and the public. The intimate knowledge security officers have of the site will assist outside personnel in an efficient and timely manner to ensure success.

SECURITY AND THE MEDIA

Discretion is a key duty of security officers, whether they are contract or in-house workers. While members of the media may be keen to question you about security-related events, it's important to remember that it's up to the client or employer to decide what, if any information will be disclosed. As a rule, security officers should

What Would You Do?

Contract or In-House?

How to handle security needs is an issue that faces all major retailers and many other organizations. The most important challenge is probably making the decision whether to employ in-house or contract security services. Each approach has strong proponents and opponents. Yet, both ways of handling security continue to flourish in the market. Some of the advantages of both types of security service are shown below.

Advantages of contract security

Lower Costs: Contract costs on a per-guard basis are usually less expensive than paying salary and benefits for a full-time employee.

Reduced Administrative Burden: Eliminates having to train employees, select, supply, and maintain uniforms and equipment.

Easier Management of Personnel Levels: Extra guards can be obtained quickly by calling the contract company.

Fewer Union-Based Conflicts: A source of guards during a labour dispute. Although some security companies are unionized, care is taken to ensure that personnel do not belong to the union that represents the workers at the client's facility.

Expert Management: Security management resources are available for specific tasks.

Impartiality: Working at different locations, security guards rarely form attachments to one site or group of workers.

Advantages of in-house security

Quality of Personnel: Officers often get superior training, more needs targeted, better pay, and company benefits.

Control over Performance: As company employees, officers are subject to company performance standards as well as performance reviews.

Loyalty to Management: Knowing management has the power to hire or fire, officers are motivated to perform well at all times.

Prestige and Trust: Pride in the company that employs them may enhance trustworthiness.

Familiarity with the Environment: Officers gain a familiarity with the employer's premises, which better equips them to manage recurring issues or deal with particular quirks.

Familiarity with Other Employees: Officers have a better opportunity to gain the trust of other employees, making them more approachable at the early stages of a security problem.

Assignment: Review and discuss the advantages and disadvantages of each approach above. Then consider the security needs, as you would identify them, of the sample "clients" listed below. Recommend either in-house or contract security, defending your choice.

Sample Clients

- a nuclear power plant
- a two-week neighbourhood jazz festival
- a botanical garden that licenses its grounds for weddings
- an electronics store
- a major exhibition
- a conference centre that hosts trade shows of varying sizes
- a public transportation system
- a university campus

not disclose information related to security incidents to the public, the media, or **non-stakeholders**; not even to a spouse.

Often, the only security worker who may be authorized to release security-sensitive information is the Director of Corporate Security or the director's delegate. It is the company's responsibility to communicate with the public, media, stakeholders, and employees during potential or actual emergencies. To facilitate this, most clients or employers have a policy governing emergency communications response.

Typically, the company issues information in one of four ways:

- **press releases** issued by corporate management;
- **public statements** made by company spokespersons or other commentators;
- interviews conducted with individuals involved in a reportable event; and
- **documented research**.

While all Canadians enjoy the right to freedom of speech, it is important that security officers understand the consequences of discussing corporate issues with the media. It takes a highly qualified and well-trained media spokesperson to properly handle media interviews. Otherwise, misquotations, answers to leading questions, or selective editing of statements or conversation may place an officer in a difficult position.

SECURITY AND ORGANIZED LABOUR

Essential to the role of security officers is that they provide protection without any actual or perceived bias.

While it's possible that security officers may be union members, they are required to carry out their security function effectively and without bias to any group or individual. It is therefore a management expectation that labour **allegiances** will not interfere with the unbiased execution of an officer's duties as a member of its security team.

The officer's job embraces the responsibility for the safety and security of all parties, regardless of individual politics or affiliation. As such, in any labour dispute, it is crucial that the officer deal with everyone professionally, whether they are management or labour.

Again, in labour situations, regardless of personal opinions or feelings, security officers are bound by the media policy and should not communicate any information relating to a labour dispute to the public or the media.

SECURITY AND THE PUBLIC

Security officers frequently come into contact with members of the public. The nature of these interactions varies depending on the type of client or employer a security officer is working for; however, in general, duties with respect to the public can include the following:

- admittance/entry control;
- crowd control;

non-stakeholders
people who do not have an interest or concern in something

press releases
written statements given to the media for publication

public statements
comments made openly, not in private

documented research
written proof of some facts, inquiries, or investigations

allegiances
faithfulness or loyalty

- crime prevention and deterrence; including conducting searches, and making arrests;

- provision of information/directions;

- assistance to individuals with physically disabilities; and

- emergency medical assistance.

In all interactions with the public, security officers should be mindful of their role as representatives of the client or employer. The security officers' deportment, in the eyes of the public, should reflect favourably on the organizations for which they work.

INDIVIDUALS WITH SPECIAL NEEDS

Dealing with certain groups of individuals within the general population requires special sensitivity and unique skills. These special groups include youth, the elderly, physically challenged/mobility impaired individuals, and people with cognitive impairments. In some cases, a disproportionate amount of time and resources are required to deal with these individuals as compared with the general public. Nonetheless, the client service requirement extends equally to all groups. Provision of a lesser standard of service due to the particular characteristics of a person is unacceptable.

Youth have special needs, and they often tax the patience of security personnel with displays of "attitude" or defiance. A firm, professional, and courteous manner will go a long way toward avoiding problems.

In situations involving interaction with the elderly or physically challenged individuals, the best guideline is *common sense*. For example, security personnel should anticipate the need for extra space when a person is in a wheelchair or using a walker. Also, objects in the environment that pose no risk to others may be dangerous to a sight-impaired person or someone in a wheelchair.

Security personnel should not be afraid to ask if a person needs assistance. If the person is sight-impaired, verbal instruction is in order. For example, the security officer might say, "We are approaching the door to the security office, on your left. Here it is. Allow me to open it for you. There is a chair to your immediate right." If appropriate, the officer should make contact with a light but firm touch on the person's forearm. Whenever possible, another security officer or employee should be present to assist.

It's also important to remember that people with cognitive or physical disabilities may be at increased risk for victimization by others. For example, a thief may offer assistance to a person in a wheelchair and steal the person's purse or wallet in the process. It's important that security officers be alert to the possibility of such victimization, so that they can adequately protect clients.

Finally, adjustments may need to be made to emergency medical assistance for certain individuals, if providing such assistance is within the security officer's mandate. There are certain limitations, for instance, to the way CPR would be administered to an epileptic person or a person with a deformity affecting the torso.

As a representative of the client, it is the security officer's responsibility to ensure the safety and security of all persons while on site. Efforts to deal with situations fairly, professionally, and with compassion will be appreciated by all.

MULTICULTURALISM

In Canada's diverse society, security officers must be sensitive to cultural differences among people of different origins. For example, some cultures require head covering at all times; some require a person to carry a ceremonial dagger (kirpan), which should not be regarded as a concealed weapon.

In a situation involving a misunderstanding or miscommunication with a person from another culture, a security officer should consult someone from that culture for a better understanding of the circumstances. As mentioned above, common sense will help the security officer handle unfamiliar situations, as will a commitment to treating everyone with respect. Security officers should also:

- formally identify themselves and indicate their intentions clearly;

- refrain from touching someone unless absolutely necessary;

- avoid being alone with youths or people of the opposite gender;

- send for help immediately when they cannot communicate with a person;

- allow individuals to have their personal belongings within their sight, but not necessarily within reach, as the situation warrants; and

- refrain from taking any action that they would find personally offensive.

SUMMARY

Security services can be delivered through various arrangements, the most common of which are on a contract basis or in-house—as a proprietary function of the organization being served.

Private investigators require special licensing and carry out special investigative functions.

Emergency response is an emerging specialty in the security industry and will be discussed in greater detail in chapter 26.

In this chapter, we have discussed the security officer's role in dealing with:

- public emergency response forces (police, fire department, emergency medical assistance providers);

- the media;

- organized labour; and

- the public.

Security does not exist in a vacuum. Professional security providers must learn to interact with external groups as well as representatives of organized labour within the workplace. Failure to deal effectively with these groups severely limits the ability of security to provide the level of service the client deserves.

KEY TERMS

allegiances

arson

documented research

electronic countermeasures (ECM)

industrial espionage

non-stakeholders

press releases

public statements

PERFORMANCE APPLICATION

1. Explain the differences between contract security providers and in-house or proprietary security.

2. Decide whether you would prefer to work for a contract security provider or an in-house security service and explain why.

3. List four typical functions of a private investigator.

4. Private investigators often organize their businesses differently. Look in the local yellow pages to determine what proportion of private investigators work in large agencies and what proportion are in private (individual) practice.

5. Why is it important for security officers to cooperate with public emergency response workers?

6. Name four ways that a security officer might assist a public police investigation at the security officer's work locale.

7. Why is it essential that security officers avoid discussing security-related incidents with the media?

8. List four ways that a company usually presents information to the media.

9. What do security officers need to know about working in a locale during a labour dispute?

10. Write a 300-word essay on the importance of professional interaction with the public by a security officer.

3 Professionalism and Deportment

INTRODUCTION

Security officers are the most visible representatives of a security company. It is therefore essential that all officers present themselves as professional, effective, and approachable.

COMPLIANCE WITH LAWS AND STANDARDS AS A GUARANTEE OF SERVICE QUALITY

Quality security providers embrace a commitment to provide their clients with competent and professional service. One way that providers and their employees can honour this commitment is to demonstrate compliance with the wide variety of professional standards, laws, and regulations that apply to the security industry. Security companies must also communicate to their employees the importance of honesty and integrity in performance of all job duties.

Codes of professional conduct may be developed and published by individual employers (that is, contract security companies or corporate employers of in-house security departments) and/or by organizations that regulate the profession, for example, CSIS (introduced in chapter 1) or its American equivalent, the American Society for Industrial Security (ASIS).

Security officers have a responsibility to comply both with the standards of professional conduct embraced by the company that hires them and those of any association to which they belong.

In addition to compliance with professional standards, security officers must also comply with applicable legislation and regulations, the criminal law, and all the other laws that apply at both the provincial and federal levels. Laws that apply specifically to security officers will be discussed in chapter 4.

Every security officer also has the responsibility to report any suspected crimes, business misconduct, fraud, or abuse of client or public assets. Such activities negatively affect client company operations and reputation, and could expose the company or its executives to significant **liability**.

Chapter Objectives

When you have completed this chapter, you will

- have an understanding of the standards of professionalism, dress, and deportment required by a company for all security officers on duty.

- have an understanding of the concepts of discipline, integrity, appropriate attitude, and self-improvement as applied to the job of a security officer or guard.

codes of professional conduct
policy documents prepared either by an employer, or by a body that regulates a profession that reflect the key values of either the employer or the profession and express standards of performance, integrity, and ethical behaviour for employees or association members

liability
legal responsibility for a wrongful action

professionalism
skills, integrity, ethical conduct, and competence that is expected from members of a profession

Management must fully support the officers' exercise of these responsibilities. This includes promoting throughout the workforce an awareness of compliance issues and providing a simple method of reporting any unprofessional or illegal conduct. **Professionalism** must be kept visible. Its impact on the perceptions of other company employees as well as members of the public can only benefit immediate security teams, and the security industry at large.

Flashpoint

Does Growth in the Security Sector Let Public Policing Off the Hook?

In chapter 1, we noted that security officers outnumber public police in Canada by more than two to one and that growth in the security industry is expected to far outstrip growth in public policing in the decades to come.

Budgetary restrictions have led police forces at all levels to express concern about insufficient human and equipment resources and to warn about threats to the public safety should service standards decline. Whether or not these concerns are well founded, the media and the public have been paying attention. Business and individuals with the means to do so have increased their use of security in an effort to protect assets and personal safety.

But does growth in the security market reduce pressure on the government to maintain adequate levels of public policing? Or do private and public security officers perform essentially separate functions, such that growth or cutbacks in one sector do not affect the other?

Assignment: Work in three groups, one group taking position A, one taking position B, and one acting as the jury. Members of the groups representing the positions should collaborate to make a list of points in support of their position. Each spokesperson for the group has five minutes to present the arguments of the group's position to the jury. The jury members have five minutes to come to a decision with respect to which position is more convincing. The jury's foreperson presents the decision.

Position A: Growth in the security industry reduces pressure on governments to fund public policing and is unfair to lower-income earners and small businesses.

Position B: Security functions complement, rather than overlap with, the work of the public police, and growth in the security sector supports, rather than threatens, the work of public law enforcement.

UNIFORM DRESS STANDARDS

When security officers are hired, they are provided with uniforms, which may consist of a shirt, tie, belt, pants, formal jacket, and safety footwear. Some uniforms include headwear, and/or seasonal items such as sweaters, parkas, and short-sleeved shirts. Companies often provide badges to be worn with a uniform. The uniform is to be worn with all buttons and fasteners fastened, and no modifications or substitutions.

Workplaces may also have rules for clothing items that are not part of the uniform, such as socks, T-shirts, footwear, and underwear. For example, some workplaces allow a T-shirt to be worn underneath the uniform shirt, provided it is white, or similar in colour to the uniform shirt. Sock colour is often specified (usually grey, black, or navy).

Wearing some items, such as clip-on ties in positions where the public is likely to be greeted, may be compulsory, while other items, such as seasonal headwear, may be at the employee's option. Uniform rules may vary depending on an officer's contact with the public.

At some workplaces, **personal protective equipment** will be required. In such cases, the employer supplies the equipment and its use is compulsory, either throughout the workplace or in designated areas according to risk.

NON-UNIFORM DRESS STANDARDS

Professionalism in appearance as well as behaviour encourages compliance and respect. As ambassadors of the security industry, the first impressions security officers create can dictate the type of cooperation and respect they receive from others. Thus, security officers wear the uniform provided by their contract company or client at all times while on duty. Only licensed private investigators are authorized to wear civilian clothes when working.

In certain cases, where a security guard is employed by a company and only performs security duties on property owned by that company, the guard is permitted to work in street clothes, usually a suit. Wearing business dress can help a security officer blend into the business environment of offices, hotels, or conference centres.

GROOMING STANDARDS

It is not enough to simply wear the prescribed uniform: security officers must also take care to maintain the uniform in good condition. This usually means keeping uniform components clean and neatly ironed and keeping footwear clean, polished, and in good repair.

Security officers are also expected to maintain high standards of personal grooming; for example, hair, beards, and moustaches should be neatly trimmed and, for safety reasons, long hair should be tied back.

Managers may restrict hair length or prohibit moustaches or beards for safety reasons, such as the possibility of having to wear a respirator.

There may be workplace rules in effect that prohibit the use of strong fragrances, such as scents found in some perfumes, aftershave lotions, deodorants, or hair sprays.

Anything that is worn as an accessory for personal adornment, such as jewellery, is generally classified as a **non-issue item**. Many employers have rules with respect to such items. Most such rules stem from safety concerns; for example, hoop earrings may be prohibited because of the risk of them being grabbed in a physical altercation; and necklaces and chains may be required to be worn inside collars for the same reason. Another reason for restrictions on the wearing of non-issue items relate to the employer's desire to project an image that is appropriate to the business environment in which the security officers are working.

personal protective equipment
equipment or clothing, such as bulletproof vests, hard hats, and respirators, designed to protect the wearer against job hazards

non-issue items
items of apparel, jewellery, hair accessories, etc., not supplied or authorized by the employer

SUMMARY

Security officers are often the first representatives of the company that the public encounters. Their attitude and appearance have the power to reflect either positively or negatively on the employer or client. Because of this, it is essential that security officers comply with the law and with codes of professional conduct that apply to them. It is also important that security guards wear and keep in good repair the uniform issued by their employer and that they maintain high standards of personal grooming.

KEY TERMS

codes of professional conduct

liability

non-issue item

personal protective equipment

professionalism

PERFORMANCE APPLICATION

1. Why must security guards be mindful of their image and appearance?

2. What is a code of professional conduct? How would you determine which code(s) applies to you?

3. Which laws are security officers required to obey?

4. List two essential qualities of security officers.

5. Why do security guards wear a uniform?

6. How might uniforms vary from worksite to worksite?

7. How should a uniform be maintained?

8. Describe any special rules that an employer might have with respect to:

   a. long hair

   b. beards

   c. necklaces

   d. aftershave or perfume

PART I EXERCISE

In chapter 3, reference was made to negative portrayals of security guards in entertainment and occasionally in the media. Most people are familiar with the negative stereotype of an out-of-shape, disheveled guard, who is either asleep on the job or treating the public with contempt.

Assigment: For the duration of this course, look for positive and negative portrayals of security officers in entertainment, the news media, or in real life. In a file folder, scrapbook, or notebook, make notes or collect clippings documenting each portrayal of a security officer that you notice. Note how the person is portrayed—both with respect to physical appearance and demeanour—how they interact with the public, and the impression that they make.

Include notes about any observations of security officers that you make in real life, for example, while visiting a museum, a concert, or an office building.

At the end of the course, review your material and answer the following questions:

1. How many portrayals have you recorded? Were you surprised with how often security guards are portrayed in entertainment? Were you surprised at the number of security officers you noticed when you were specifically looking for them?

2. How many portrayals did you describe as positive? How many as negative?

3. Were the negative portrayals equally distributed in real life, media, or entertainment, or were they more prevalent in one of these three contexts?

4. Do you think movies and TV depict security officers fairly? Why or why not?

5. Do you think newspapers and magazines depict security officers fairly? Why or why not?

6. What steps might an individual security officer take to enhance his or her profession's image in entertainment and the media?

7. What steps might the profession as a whole take, through its professional associations, to enhance security's image in entertainment and the news media?

PART II

Powers and Skills

Functions and Licensing

THE CORE FUNCTIONS OF SECURITY

The security service has traditionally incorporated the important core functions described below.

Building and Perimeter Protection

Security providers may be charged with the installation, maintenance, and monitoring of physical security devices that are used in the protection of a facility and the area surrounding it. These include fences, gates, lighting, and external alarm systems.

Intrusion and Access Control

Security providers install, maintain, and monitor equipment designed to control access and prevent unauthorized access to a facility. They also provide staff for monitoring purposes.

Alarm and Surveillance System Monitoring

Security providers install, maintain, and monitor intrusion detectors, alarm sensors and closed-circuit TV camera systems for surveillance applications.

Fire Prevention and Control

Security providers often offer first-response fire prevention and containment for the facilities in which they work. This function includes the maintenance of fire alarm systems, the employment of basic fire suppression procedures, and the supervision of evacuations.

Emergency and Disaster Planning and Response

Security providers typically develop and provide training with respect to specific **emergency and disaster response plans** for the workplaces they serve. Security

> ## Chapter Objectives
>
> When you have completed this chapter, you will
>
> - know the core functions of private security.
>
> - have a basic knowledge of the terminology, requirements, rules of conduct, and penalties in the *Private Investigators and Security Guards Act*.

emergency and disaster response plans
policies or plans to maximize safety and minimize losses in the event of an emergency or disaster

officers who work in a variety of settings need to be prepared for emergencies in every type of workplace. The ability of security personnel to carry out an appropriate response and to provide support to public emergency response personnel can enhance the safety and security of tenants, owners, shoppers, visitors, and security staff.

Theft, Robbery, and Burglary Prevention

The protection of property and assets and the prevention of theft are essential functions of the security officer. The prevention of theft, robbery, and burglary is generally accomplished through a combination of physical security devices (locks, access control systems, etc.) and monitoring by trained personnel.

Accident Prevention and Safety

Security officers are often the first on the scene of a workplace accident. Most security officers are trained and certified in cardiopulmonary resuscitation (CPR) and first aid procedures. Depending on the nature of an accident, security officers may be required to secure the accident scene, provide first aid, call for public emergency response, and investigate the circumstances leading to the accident. Security officers are also required to understand and enforce the rules and regulations prescribed in the *Occupational Health and Safety Act* (OHSA); for a full discussion of the occupational health and safety system, see part VII of this text.

Enforcement of Regulations

Security officers are responsible for the enforcement of public laws and corporate regulations on the work premises. Supporting compliance with the law may include: advising individuals of the application of the law and the penalties for non-compliance, reporting breaches of the law, and, in some cases, making a citizen's arrest; for a discussion of arrest, see chapter 5. Examples of laws that security personnel may be required to enforce are the *Trespass to Property Act*, the *Hotel Fire Safety Act*, the *Occupational Health and Safety Act*, the *Liquor Licence Act*, municipal parking bylaws, and the *Criminal Code*.

Personnel Security

Protecting personnel presents one of the greatest challenges to the security profession. While buildings and physical assets can be protected with technology, such as alarms and barriers, protecting personnel requires knowledge of conflict management and interpersonal relations and often involves the delivery of safety training.

Information Security

Protecting information requires not only the protection of physical assets, such as filing cabinets, but also of trade secrets, such as recipes, blueprints, and formulas. Perhaps the most important aspect of information protection in modern society is the protection of information contained in information technologies, such as computer systems and databases. Protecting these systems is a highly sophisticated task that is typically assigned to IT security professionals with advanced computer training and credentials. This type of security is a specialized branch of security services.

PRIVATE INVESTIGATORS AND SECURITY GUARDS ACT (PISGA)

The *Private Investigators and Security Guards Act* (PISGA), a provincial statute, was originally enacted by the Ontario legislature in 1966. (Most provinces have very similar legislation; only the regime in British Columbia incorporates significant differences.) Though the Act has been amended from time to time since, the private security industry in Canada has greatly changed over the last 50 years.

There is currently an initiative in place to carry out a thorough redrafting of the legislation. This initiative has been inspired by a number of factors, including:

- new technological and strategic developments;

- a perceived need for improved emergency response planning since the terrorist attacks of September 11, 2001 in the United States; and

- changes in the relationship between public police forces and private security.

In the last 50 years, security providers have become increasingly visible. As noted in a June 2003 discussion paper by the Ontario Ministry of Public Safety and Security:

> You see private security personnel in shopping centres, nuclear facilities, commercial complexes, museums and condominiums. They patrol private property and public areas, guard bridges, and are engaged in highly sophisticated activities, such as intelligence gathering, **covert operations** and computer surveillance.

Today's security personnel are concerned with sophisticated strategic initiatives, such as **cybersecurity** and disaster management. A new version of the PISGA is needed to address these issues, and other challenges facing the industry.

AN OVERVIEW OF THE CURRENT LEGISLATION

Terminology

Section 1 of the PISGA defines certain key terms. For example:

> "private investigator" means a person who investigates and furnishes information for hire or reward, including a person who,
> (a) searches for and furnishes information as to the personal character or actions of a person, or the character or kind of business or occupation of a person,

---

FAST FACT

Hot Law Reform Issues

The Ontario Ministry of Public Safety and Security is currently conducting a review of PISGA to determine which issues should be covered by the new legislation. The ministry is focusing on three main areas of reform: training standards; licensing; and standards for uniforms, vehicles, and equipment.

There is no doubt that there will soon be mandatory basic training and licensing for all security officers and private investigators (including in-house employees); higher levels of education required for basic security courses; more standardized use of equipment such as bulletproof vests, batons, and guard dogs; more comprehensive background checks on security officers and private investigators prior to licensing; and more specialization for security professionals.

One glitch in licensing that the security industry hopes to see corrected in a revision of the PISGA is automatic licence expiration. Currently, each time security personnel change jobs, they have to be relicensed. This creates bottlenecks in security services for companies who have to wait for new employees' licences to be processed before they can put them to work. A system that would allow security course graduates to be licensed without employer sponsorship and that would allow for "portable" licences is welcomed by many in the industry.

---

covert operations
investigations or observations of a suspect or a place while remaining hidden or "undercover"

cybersecurity
protection of information that is vulnerable to theft, access, or corruption via the Internet or other computer networks

> (b) searches for offenders against the law, or
> (c) searches for missing persons or property;
>
> "security guard" means a person who, for hire or reward, guards or patrols for the purpose of protecting persons or property.

(The full text of the PISGA is available online at www.e-laws.gov.on.ca.)

Application of the Act

Like all legislation, the PISGA has specific application. That is, it applies to certain individuals who perform certain functions within certain contexts. The application of the PISGA is defined at section 2(1) by the use of exemptions, which describe to whom the Act does *not* apply.

Among those exempt from the PISGA are people who do credit checks (and not other kinds of background checks—that is, not private investigators); members of the Corps of Commissionaires; lawyers; police officers; insurance company employees "while acting in the usual and regular scope of their employment"; municipal workers; and employees of out-of-province security firms who are in Ontario in conjunction with a multijurisdictional investigation.

The most important exemption is with respect to in-house security officers:

> 2(1)(g) private investigators and security guards who are permanently employed by one employer in a business or undertaking other than the business of providing private investigators or security guards and whose work is confined to the affairs of that employer.

Licensing

The Lieutenant Governor in Council appoints a Registrar of Private Investigators and Security Guards to administer the licensing and other requirements created under the Act. The Registrar determines who is eligible for licensing.

Licensing is a precondition for two things: (1) the provision of private investigators and/or security guards; and (2) acting as a contract (that is, non-proprietary) private investigator or security guard (section 4). A person is also prohibited from "holding out" (claiming or advertising to be) a security guard or private investigator without being licensed as such.

In deciding whether a person is eligible to be licensed, the Registrar is entitled to verify the applicant's character, competence, and financial situation; and an applicant may be required to pass an examination before the licence will be issued. Licences are issued with respect to specific employment and expire either at the termination of that employment or on March 31 of each year, at which time they must be renewed.

A licence can also be suspended or cancelled for misconduct, as follows:

> 14. The Registrar may, after giving the licensee an opportunity to be heard, suspend or cancel a licence where,
> (a) the licensee is convicted of an offence under the *Criminal Code* (Canada) or under this Act or the regulations;
> (b) the licensee is in breach of a term or condition of the licence; or
> (c) in the opinion of the Registrar, to do so is in the public interest.

Flashpoint

Are Background Checks for Security Officers Too Lax?

As with all professions, there is a need in the private security profession to balance the privacy and human rights of individual licence applicants with the public interest.

At present, there is some controversy in the industry over the issue of background and criminal record checks for private security and private investigator licence applicants. Under the current system in Ontario (according to the Ontario ministry's PISGA discussion paper for proposed legislative changes), screening of private security applicants is limited to

> federal convictions, outstanding criminal charges and warrants, and as such, fails to identify provincial convictions and convictions for which pardons have been granted. ... Under the Act, applicants with a criminal record are entitled to a hearing to assess whether it is in the public interest to issue them licences.

There is concern in the industry that this screening situation leaves the public vulnerable by potentially allowing untrustworthy candidates to apply successfully for licensing. The system is currently under review, and there is a parallel review process going on in the United States, where the background check high-water mark is the Illinois model. If applied in Canada, that model would require that applicants

- be at least 21 years of age;

- be Canadian citizens or landed immigrants;

- have no history of criminal convictions for 10 years;

- be free of substance abuse;

- have upstanding moral values;

- be sound of mind and body;

- be insurable for liability up to $100,000 per individual; and

- (if they have served) be honourably discharged from the Canadian Armed Forces.

This model provides much stiffer screening than current legislation, and enforcing it might be a challenge from a human rights standpoint. For example, an individual who has served a sentence for a minor criminal conviction would be excluded from applying until the 10 years have expired. The model might also exclude people with disabilities and people who have struggled with issues such as alcoholism or gambling addiction.

The legislation also provides that no person under 18 years of age can act as a private investigator or security guard and that every security guard shall wear a uniform while carrying out his or her duties.

Private Investigators: Identification

The PISGA sets out rules with respect to how private investigators must represent themselves:

- private investigators are prohibited from describing themselves as "private detectives" (section 23); and

- private investigators are required to carry identification cards prescribed under the Act, and no other "identification cards" (or badges, shields, etc.) apart from a business card that does not make reference to licensing under the Act (sections 25(1) and (2)).

Also, security guards who are also licensed as private investigators cannot act as private investigators while in security guard uniform (section 25(3)).

Security Guards: Identification, and Holding Out

Security guards must work in uniform. They must also carry prescribed identification cards and produce them for inspection on demand (section 28). Security guards are prohibited from holding themselves out as police officers or as providing services connected with policing.

Finally, regulation 938 under the PISGA requires that security guards wear a patch on their chests bearing the word "security guard." The colour and size of the lettering are regulated. The purpose of the regulation is to prevent the security guard from being mistaken for a member of the public police force.

Penalties

The PISGA imposes penalties on those who contravene its provisions. Section 32 provides that a person who (1) furnishes false information (where the provision of information is required by the Act), (2) fails to comply with an order or other requirement imposed under the Act, or (3) "contravenes any provision" of the Act or the regulations is liable for a fine of up to $5,000, or imprisonment up to one year, or both. Fines are higher for corporate offenders: up to $50,000.

ASSIGNMENT

Divide into small groups. Split each group into three subgroups. One subgroup takes position A, one subgroup takes position B, and the third subgroup acts as the jury.

Position A: Security officer and private investigator applicants should be held to an exceptionally high standard of conduct (for example, the Illinois model—see above) for the protection of the public, even if it means that some individuals will feel that the process violates their human rights or their rights under the ***Canadian Charter of Rights and Freedoms***.

Canadian Charter of Rights and Freedoms part of the *Constitution Act, 1982* that sets out constitutionally protected rights and freedoms

Position B: The Illinois model is excessively rigid, violates human and privacy rights, and would exclude many good-quality applicants unnecessarily. A more flexible model that allows for case-by-case screening is preferable and can adequately protect the public interest.

Each side should collaborate to make a list of points in support of their position. They will then choose a spokesperson, and the jury will choose a foreperson. Each spokesperson has five minutes to present arguments for the position, and then the jury has five minutes to come to a decision with respect to which position is more convincing. The foreperson then presents the jury's decision to the whole group.

SUMMARY

This chapter introduced the core functions of security officers:

- building and perimeter protection;
- intrusion and access control;
- alarm and surveillance system monitoring;
- fire prevention and control;
- emergency and disaster planning and response;
- theft, robbery, and burglary prevention;
- accident prevention and safety;
- enforcement of regulations; and
- personnel and information security.

The chapter also provided a basic overview of the *Private Investigators and Security Guards Act*. It described who is covered by the Act and who is exempt from its application. The basic licensing requirements were discussed, as were the rules with respect to carrying identification, and rules against holding oneself out as a private detective or police officer. Finally, there was a discussion of penalties for contravention of the legislation.

The need for change in the legislative regime was introduced in the context of technological changes and changes in security needs. The issue of sufficiency of background checks was raised in a discussion feature at the end of the chapter.

KEY TERMS

Canadian Charter of Rights and Freedoms

covert operations

cybersecurity

emergency and disaster response plans

PERFORMANCE APPLICATION

1. What are the core functions of private security?

2. Why is the PISGA in need of reform?

3. Which issues are the focus in drafting new legislation?

4. Is the PISGA provincial or federal legislation?

5. List five classes of individuals who are exempt from the application of the PISGA.

6. Why do you think a private investigator is not permitted to carry out private investigation duties in a security officer's uniform? Why must security officers work in uniform?

7. List the features of the Illinois model for private security screening.

8. Why might a very strict screening model be subject to challenge on the basis of human rights?

5 Powers of Arrest

INTRODUCTION

The most common reason for employing security guards at any facility is for the protection of assets. This often includes controlling access to the facility from trespassers. After the *Criminal Code*, the *Trespass to Property Act* (TPA) is the most important statute for security officers, because this Act (along with the doctrine of citizen's arrest) defines the role of security personnel to make arrests.

The TPA sets out security officers' rights to search, to arrest on private property, and to exclude intruders. It provides a mechanism for working out disagreements, clashes, or conflicts of interest on private property. Most provincial trespass legislation is similar to the Ontario laws studied here, but students outside Ontario will need to refer to the laws of their province to complete their study of this chapter.

TRESPASS TO PROPERTY ACT: KEY DEFINITIONS

The TPA provides some definitions that must be understood for the proper application of the Act. In particular, the terms "occupier," "premises," and "trespass."

Section 1(1) of the Act describes an occupier as:

    (a) a person who is in physical possession of premises, or

    (b) a person who has responsibility for and control over the condition of premises or the activities there carried on, or control over persons allowed to enter the premises, even if there is more than one occupier of the same premises.

The same section defines premises as:

lands and structures, or either of them, and includes,

    (a) water,

    (b) ships and vessels,

    (c) trailers and portable structures designed or used for residence, business or shelter,

    (d) trains, railway cars, vehicles and aircraft, except while in operation.

Chapter Objectives

When you have completed this chapter, you will

■ have a basic knowledge and understanding of the *Trespass to Property Act* of Ontario.

■ have a basic knowledge and understanding of the legal authority of a security officer to restrict access, to protect property, and to arrest and detain persons.

trespass
unlawful interference with the person, property, or rights of another

Trespass is defined in section 2, which makes activity falling within a particular description an offence. According to section 2, a person is trespassing when he or she without legal right or authority and without the permission of the occupier enters or engages in activity on property where entry is prohibited by the Act

(a) without the express permission of the occupier, the proof of which rests on the defendant,

(i) enters on premises when entry is prohibited under this Act, or

(ii) engages in activity on premises when the activity is prohibited under this Act; or

(b) does not leave the premises immediately after he or she is directed to do so by the occupier of the premises or a person authorized by the occupier,

colour of right
circumstances that lead to an understandable but mistaken belief that one has the right to do something

A person charged with trespassing can argue the defence of **colour of right**. This defence provides that a person is not guilty of trespassing if he or she reasonably believes he or she has an ownership interest in the premises.

Step Aside

Colour of Right Defence

A simple example of a fact situation supporting a colour of right defence is that of a pathway beside a house that runs from one street to another. Because the pathway is well worn, a person might assume it is a public access route and use it as a shortcut to another street without the homeowner's permission. The person does not mean to trespass, and if the owner of the property (the plaintiff) brings legal action against the trespasser (the defendant), the defendant might offer this explanation as a defence.

Where an alleged trespasser claims that he or she had permission to make the entry complained of, it is up to the trespasser, not the occupier, to prove this.

tort
harm caused to a person or property for which the law requires a civil remedy

Trespassing is a **tort** (a harm caused by one person to another or against another person's property). As such, trespassing is a **civil wrong** rather than a **criminal offence** and cannot result in a jail term or a criminal record. However, trespassers can be liable to a fine of up to $2,000.

civil wrong
non-criminal wrong that can form the basis of a civil lawsuit—either a tort or a breach of contract

TRESPASS TO PROPERTY ACT: PROHIBITING ENTRY

No Notice Required

criminal offence
act that contravenes a provision of criminal law

In order for trespassing to occur, intruders must know that they are not welcome. In some cases, intruders are expected to understand this without specific notice. For example, people are expected to understand that they are not allowed to enter a private residence uninvited. Other areas that need not have special notices posted include: gardens, fields, vineyards, agricultural woodlots, tended orchards, and enclosed outdoor areas such as livestock pastures (section 3).

Limited Permission Areas

Some locations may restrict entrance to certain individuals. For example, entry on a construction site may be restricted to construction workers. In other cases, the general public may be allowed entry, but certain activities may be prohibited. For example, the public may be allowed to enter a park that has a pond, but people may be prohibited from swimming.

Methods of Giving Notice

When an occupier wants to limit entry to a premises, he or she must give notice of the intended restrictions. Notice can be given orally or in writing. Most commonly, notice is given by posting signs.

There are often regulations, which may be found under a wide range of legislation and bylaws, with respect to how certain signs need to look. Some signs need to be of a particular size or colour or need to incorporate recognized symbols.

Types of Signs

To give notice that an activity is permitted, a sign should describe the activity or provide a graphic representation (picture) of it (section 6(1)). To prohibit the activity, the same wording or graphic representation should have an oblique line (usually red or black) crossed through it (section 6(2)).

Other sections of the legislation describe specific signage conventions. For example, red markings generally are used to prohibit entry, while yellow markings are used to restrict entry or activities permitted on a premise (section 7). Section 7 gives additional information about the size and placement of warning signs.

TRESPASS TO PROPERTY ACT: ARREST RULES

Section 9 of the TPA gives security officers the authority to make an **arrest**. The section applies to police officers, occupiers, and "a person authorized by the occupier" (that is, a security officer).

To be able to arrest a trespasser, a security officer must have "reasonable and probable grounds" that the person is in contravention of section 2. As discussed above, section 2 defines trespassing and makes it an offence.

Section 9 further provides that "[w]here the person who makes an arrest ... is not a police officer, he or she shall promptly call for the assistance of a police officer and give the person arrested into the custody of the police officer." At that point, the police officer will arrest the person as provided in the *Provincial Offences Act.*

arrest
legally deprive a person of liberty by touching that person to indicate that he or she is in custody

Reasonable and Probable Grounds

An important aspect of arrests under section 9 is the need for reasonable and probable grounds. "Reasonable and probable grounds" is a legal requirement that has application to many issues, both under provincial law and under the (federal) criminal law. There is a lot of **jurisprudence** (judge-made law) in place to describe what constitutes reasonable and probable grounds in various contexts. However,

jurisprudence
judge-made law

> ## Step Aside
>
> ### Provincial Offences Act (POA)
>
> The *Provincial Offences Act* (POA), which is discussed in greater detail in chapter 6, is a general piece of legislation that has two main functions: (1) it creates certain offences; and (2) it provides guidance with respect to the administration of other pieces of provincial legislation that contain offences.
>
> In general, where a provincial statute creates an offence and does not provide detailed guidelines with respect to certain administrative issues (penalties, enforcement, procedure, etc.), the general rules set out in the POA govern these issues. Where the provincial statute provides its own administrative rules, those specific rules override the POA.

the basic requirement is fairly simple to understand: a security guard's reasons for making an arrest must be both reasonable—based on reason, logic, and common sense—and probable. The validity of the assumptions and conclusions that the security officer is making with respect to what the suspect has done, is doing, and may go on to do (if not arrested) must be probable—that is, more than just hypothetically possible.

Summary of Requirements

To review the requirements for a legally valid arrest:

1. The security officer must be authorized to make arrests on behalf of the occupier.

2. The security officer must have reasonable and probable grounds to believe that the suspect either:

   a. has made a prohibited entry, or

   b. is carrying out a prohibited activity.

3. A prohibited entry or activity is one that violates the TPA.

4. The TPA allows occupiers to prohibit entry or activities by giving notice, either orally, in writing, or by posting signs.

5. The security officer must typically direct the person to leave and should not generally make an arrest until the person fails to do so.

6. Once the suspect has been arrested, the security officer must turn him or her over to the police as soon as possible.

Requests To Vacate Premises: Practical Issues

detain
legally deprive a person of liberty for the purpose of asking questions

When a suspected trespasser has been asked to immediately leave by a certain entrance and fails to respond within a reasonable time, the security officer has the right to **detain** the suspect and to turn him or her over to a peace officer. While this seems straightforward, in practice, commands to leave are a significant source of guard–public conflict. When a problem arises, it is often because the security officer either overzealously made the request and thus precipitates a further confrontation, or did not understand how to make the request properly—that is, did not give the person clear directions. In making a request to leave, the security officer must be courteous and clear.

A related problem arises when security officers fail to identify themselves properly prior to issuing a command. In these cases, the person to whom the command is made is often unsure of the officer's authority. Where the officer fails to sufficiently identify his or her position and/or authority, the trespasser may take advantage of the situation by relying on any uncertainty as a reason to prolong a confrontation. In a later defence, the person who refused to follow the security officer's direction can claim: "I was not sure he was who he said he was, so I was not going anywhere."

ARREST WITHOUT WARRANT FOR A CRIMINAL OFFENCE

Where the issue is not an unauthorized entry but the commission of a criminal act, or a case where the TPA does not apply, security officers can make arrests under the doctrine of "citizen's arrest," which is described in section 494 of the *Criminal Code*.

Under section 494(1), anyone may arrest without warrant:

    (a) a person whom he finds committing an indictable offence

    (b) a person who, on reasonable grounds, he believes

        (i) has committed a criminal offence, and

        (ii) is escaping from and freshly pursued by persons who have lawful authority to arrest that person.

(An indictable offence is a serious criminal offence that carries a severe penalty. The *Criminal Code* of Canada indicates whether or not an offence is indictable.)

Section 494(2)(b) includes a person whom the security officer finds committing a criminal offence on or in relation to the property.

As was the case under the TPA, a security officer who arrests a person without warrant must immediately deliver the person to a peace officer.

STEPS TO A CITIZEN'S ARREST

In making an arrest under either the TPA or the *Criminal Code*, a security officer should take the following steps:

1. Identify himself or herself and announce directly and simply that the person is under arrest.

2. At the same time, lightly grasp the person's elbow to indicate control of the situation.

3. Give the person a reason for making the arrest as required under the *Charter of Rights and Freedoms*.

4. Advise the person of his or her right to counsel under the Charter.

5. Caution the person to remain silent.

6. Turn the person over to a police officer as soon as possible.

Immediately following the arrest and turning the accused over to the police, the security officer should make detailed notes about what happened and why the arrest was made.

CANADIAN CHARTER OF RIGHTS AND FREEDOMS

All security officers making an arrest must protect the rights of the suspect under the *Charter of Rights and Freedoms*. The Charter requires that a person be provided with a reason for the arrest, advised of the right to counsel, and advised of the right to avoid self-incrimination. This is done by cautioning the suspect. A caution is a statement made to the suspect at the time of arrest for the purpose of advising him or her of his or her rights. There is no set wording for the caution; that is, there are no "magic words" that will guarantee that an arrest meets the Charter requirements. Whether or not the actual caution given will meet the requirements of the Charter depends on the circumstances of the particular case. For example, if a person speaks very limited English or appears to have a cognitive disability, a standard caution may be too complex.

As a starting point, however, it is useful to learn the following typical caution, which is consistent with current Charter jurisprudence (existing law) with respect to how the rights can best be protected.

Notice Upon Arrest

"I am arresting you for_____." (Describe briefly reasons for arrest.)

Right to Counsel

"It is my duty to inform you that you have the right to retain and instruct counsel without delay. You have the right to telephone any lawyer you wish. You also have the right to free advice from a legal aid lawyer. If you are charged with an offence, you may apply to the Ontario Legal Aid Plan for assistance. You can call this toll free number, 1-800-265-0451, and it will put you in contact with a Legal Aid Duty Counsel Lawyer for free legal advice right now. Do you understand? Do you wish to call a lawyer right now?"

Caution

"You may be charged with _____. Do you wish to say anything in answer to the charge? You are not obliged to say anything unless you wish to do so, but whatever you say may be given in evidence. Do you understand?"

SEARCH AUTHORITY

common law
rules that are formulated in judgments in case law

Following or in connection with an arrest, a security officer's rights to search a suspect are narrowly limited. There are, however, some **common law** rules (that is, rules based on **case law** rather than on **statute law**) that give limited rights to search a person, or his or her belongings or property.

case law
body of law based on decisions of similar cases

statute law
laws passed by the government

Search With Consent

A security officer can search a person or his or her property with that person's consent. In some cases, a person's contract of employment allows an employer's security staff to search employees or their property, such as purses, shopping bags, and lockers on the job site. But, according to Robert Gerden in *Private Security: A Canadian Perspective*, "a forced search against employees, especially if it is a requirement before leaving the property, may very well be considered a criminal assault; at the least, it will involve civil liabilities" against the company, and possibly the security officer as well. Under these circumstances, such an "assault" violates an individual's rights under section 24(2) of the *Charter of Rights and Freedoms* and the evidence secured may be excluded in court.

Search Without Consent

If a security officer reasonably believes the person just arrested has a weapon that he or she is in "harm's way," the security officer can search this individual without permission.

PROTECTION OF PERSONS ACTING UNDER AUTHORITY

When a security officer makes a citizen's arrest, the security officer is protected under section 25 of the *Criminal Code*. That section provides:

> 25(1) Every one who is required or authorized by law to do anything in the administration or enforcement of the law
> > (a) as a private person,
> > (b) as a peace officer or public officer,
> > (c) in aid of a peace officer or public officer, or
> > (d) by virtue of his office,
> is, if he acts on reasonable grounds, justified in doing what he is required or authorized to do and in using as much force as is necessary for that purpose.

This section requires that security officers base their actions on reason, and that their actions be controlled and measured, and not out of proportion to the needs of the situation. If security officers act in a firm, controlled, and rational manner, they can generally count on the protection of section 25.

Excessive Force

There are times when people use more force than they really need to control a situation. Section 26 of the *Criminal Code* states:

> Everyone who is authorized by law to use force is criminally responsible for any excess thereof according to the nature and quality of the act that constitutes the excess.

This means that if a security officer goes beyond firm, controlled, and rational behaviour in handling an accused and uses excessive force, he or she has committed a criminal act and can be charged. In some cases, however, the security officer may be able to defend against using greater-than-usual force to defuse a situation. Note the following two provisions under the *Criminal Code.*

Self-Defence Against Unprovoked Assault

Section 34 provides that a person is justified in using force to repel force when that person is assaulted as long as that person did not provoke the assault or use more force than was necessary to defend himself or herself.

Use of Force in Preventing an Assault

Section 37 provides that a person is justified in using force to prevent an assault upon himself or herself or any one under his or her protection from assault.

CIVIL ACTION AND THE SECURITY OFFICER

Security personnel and their employers may be vulnerable to civil lawsuits for such charges as: **assault** (often, verbally threatening someone to obey your demands), **battery** (often, using excessive force in an arrest), **false imprisonment** and/or **malicious prosecution** (often, by making false accusations or arresting someone without proper grounds), **conversion** (the civil version of theft), **negligence** (failure to perform to a certain standard, and thereby causing harm), and **defamation** (injuring someone's reputation either through **slander** or **libel**). A successful civil action involves reimbursing the plaintiff (injured party) for the damage caused.

The best way security officers can avoid being personally sued in civil court (or doing something that will get their employer sued) is to perform their duties using good judgment and restraint, while complying with the law and any professional standards, codes of practice, or company policies that apply to them.

PUBLIC RELATIONS CONSIDERATIONS

A final consideration when thinking about the issue of arrest is public relations. When the police make arrests, it is usually because they have been called to attend to a situation, on either public or private property, that has escalated to the point where it is considered by all onlookers to be a crime requiring prosecution.

For security officers, the situation may be different. Often, security officers are required to consider a response to events that may fall short of an indictable crime, particularly in the case of TPA violations. In dealing with any situation, security personnel must be mindful of their role as representatives of their employer. An overzealous response to a trespass, including the use of force and/or the making of an arrest, may reflect badly on the company or, worse, attract a civil action.

In deciding how to handle a situation, security officers must be mindful of the public relations aspects of their actions. In most cases, a discreet, minimally forceful, and collaborative response is far preferable to a confrontation and/or arrest.

---

assault
threat of imminent harm in the mind of the intended victim

battery
any unwelcome physical contact

false imprisonment
detention of a person without consent and without legal authority

malicious prosecution
wrongful prosecution of a person without reasonable or probable cause

conversion
unauthorized interference with another's property that deprives the owner of its use

negligence
careless conduct that causes foreseeable harm to another person

defamation
injury to a person's reputation by slander or libel

slander
oral statement that damages a person's reputation

libel
written or recorded statement that damages a person's reputation

What Would You Do?

Assessing Security Personnel Responses

Scenario One: April is a security employee working for a department store in a large shopping mall. She observes two teenage girls leaving the sunglasses aisle. As they approach the main aisle, the girls nervously pick up their pace and rush toward the exit. April follows at a run, leaving the department store and moving into the mall common area. One girl disappears into the food court crowd, but April catches up with the second girl. She grabs the girl's shoulder. Both women fall to the floor. April restrains the girl's arms behind her back and informs her that she is being taken back into the department store. The girl asks "Why?" and April answers "You'll know soon enough."

Scenario Two: Ben is a contract security guard who has been hired to provide security for the final game in a city-wide high school football playoff series. Ben is in charge of entry control and has been instructed to perform consensual searches of entrants to the stadium. There is no alcohol permitted at the event. Several boys who appear to be under the legal drinking age approach the entry door. Ben notices a bulge under one boy's jacket and requests that the boy open his jacket. The boy opens his jacket, revealing an open bottle of rye. Ben grasps the boy lightly by the elbow, explains that he is a security employee, and places the boy under arrest for underage possession of alcohol. The boy's friends attempt to intervene. They become argumentative and jostle Ben, who is attempting to explain the boy's Charter rights using appropriate wording. The situation breaks down and one of the boy's friends punches Ben, who attempts to place him in a submission hold, but fails when another friend grabs Ben from behind. Ben is overpowered and all the boys flee the scene.

Scenario Three: Cameron works as a security guard for a major department store. While patrolling the back of the store, he notices a female shopper moving quickly toward an employee-only area. She opens and walks through a door signed "Employees Only." Cameron catches up with the woman inside the employee area and advises her that she is not authorized to be there. The woman replies firmly "I need the bathroom." Cameron advises the woman that the washroom is for employees only and steps between the woman, who is now in tears, and the washroom door. The woman turns around and runs back into the public area of the store. Later that day, Cameron is called into the supervisor's office to discuss a complaint from a customer. The customer, who suffers from Crohn's disease, will be making a complaint to head office about the way she was treated by security at Cameron's location.

Scenario Four: Dharma and Eddie work as night clerks at a large furniture warehouse store. The store is closed during their late-night shift. One of their duties is to monitor the parking lot, which bears prominent signs prohibiting parking between the hours of 11 p.m. and 6 a.m. At 1:30 a.m., Eddie observes a car pull into the parking lot, stopping in a location near the parking lot entrance and far from the building. The car stops but no one gets out. Eddie suggests that he and Dharma immediately approach the car. Dharma prefers to wait a couple of minutes, while monitoring the car through a security camera. Five minutes later, no one has left the vehicle, which has begun rocking slightly. Dharma laughs and points this out to Eddie. The two of them walk out into the parking lot. Eddie stays back a couple of metres, and Dharma approaches the car. Dharma gives three firm knocks on the driver's side window, and says in a very loud voice: "No parking. Move along please." The two guards return to the store, where they record the licence plate number. The car does not pull away immediately. Eddie suggests that they go back out, but Dharma says "They're harmless. Let's give them five minutes." He checks the clock. Two minutes later, at 1:46 a.m., the car pulls out of the lot and drives away.

Assignment

Answer the following questions for each of the above scenarios.

1. Did the officer have the authority to intervene the way he or she did in the situation? Why or why not?

2. Was the officer's response appropriate in the situation? Why or why not? Be specific.

3. Describe an appropriate response to the situation.

SUMMARY

This chapter provided an introduction to the Ontario TPA. The definition of trespass was discussed, and the requirements for making an arrest under the TPA were reviewed.

Also covered was the doctrine of citizen's arrest, as codified by the *Criminal Code* of Canada. The requirements for making a citizen's arrest were explained. In particular, the wording required for the protection of a suspect's rights under the *Charter of Rights and Freedoms* was described, and the implications of using excessive force were introduced.

Security guards also have limited arrest powers under the common law. The rules with respect to these were discussed.

The chapter included an introduction to the tort doctrines under which a security guard might be sued in a case of, for example, overreaction. Strategies for minimizing tort liability were introduced.

Finally, there was a discussion of public relations issues that should be taken into consideration by any security guard who may be required to address an incident involving the public.

KEY TERMS

arrest	detain
assault	false imprisonment
battery	jurisprudence
case law	libel
civil wrong	malicious prosecution
colour of right	negligence
common law	slander
conversion	statute law
criminal law	tort
defamation	trespass

PERFORMANCE APPLICATION

1. Is the TPA a provincial or a federal statute? What kinds of offences does it create?

2. What is required before a security guard can make an arrest under the TPA?

3. List three ways that a person can be given notice that entry onto a premises is forbidden.

4. Review section 494 of the *Criminal Code* and describe at least two instances in which any person may arrest another person without a warrant.

5. What are the rights of a suspect upon arrest? How is a suspect advised of his or her rights?

6. How much force may a security guard use when arresting a person?

7. Which section of the *Criminal Code* protects those who may be required to make arrests in connection with their job responsibilities? What does the section say?

8. What is a tort, and why do security officers need to know?

9. How can security officers minimize their exposure to tort liability?

10. Why must a security officer consider the public relations implications of his or her actions?

6 Legislation of Interest to Security Personnel

INTRODUCTION

As mentioned in chapter 4, the enforcement of rules, legislation, and bylaws is one of the core functions of private security. There are hundreds of statutes in force in the province of Ontario alone. While it is impossible to be conversant in all of these, there is a short list of statutes that security officers are most likely to have to enforce. The *Trespass to Property Act* (TPA) was discussed in the previous chapter; and the *Occupational Health and Safety Act* (OHSA) will be discussed in part VII. This chapter will introduce other statutes of particular relevance.

> ## Chapter Objectives
>
> When you have completed this chapter, you will
>
> ■ have a basic understanding of the general purpose of the various provincial and federal statutes that are relevant to the work of many security employees.

PROVINCIAL OFFENCES ACT

The *Provincial Offences Act* (POA) of Ontario is a largely administrative/procedural statute. It governs the procedure in one division of the provincial courts, and it assists in the enforcement and administration of other provincial statutes.

A provincial offence is different from a criminal offence. For one thing, it is created not under the federal *Criminal Code*, but under provincial law—either the POA or another of the hundreds of provincial laws. Provincial offences tend to be less serious than federal offences and are often committed by people in the course of their everyday lives—good examples are offences like speeding under the *Highway Traffic Act*, or trespassing under the TPA, discussed in the previous chapter.

The procedure for prosecuting provincial offences is set out in the POA and is simpler and faster than criminal procedure. In many cases, defendants represent themselves. The fines and sentences are limited and, in most cases, are lower than the penalties under the criminal law.

In general, a person charged with a provincial offence is not kept in jail pending trial. The POA creates no search or arrest powers. In some cases it may be appropriate to search and/or arrest a person who is suspected of committing a provincial offence, but in those cases, the search/arrest authority must either exist at common law (as discussed in the previous chapter) or be provided under the individual provincial statute (for example, section 9 of the TPA, discussed in the previous chapter).

In many cases, charging a person with a provincial offence is done through a ticketing process. (Most people are familiar with *Highway Traffic Act* tickets—other provincial offences can be charged in the same way.) Security officers cannot charge or ticket a suspect. If charging or ticketing is appropriate, the security officer must turn the suspect over to police as soon as possible.

Security officers need to know what the POA is. Many provincial statutes, for simplicity of administration, are designed to work with the POA. Matters of procedure, sentencing, and so on that are not specifically dealt with in the individual statute are governed by the terms of the POA. Where the POA is *not* intended to govern the application of a provincial statute, the provincial statute must set out its own procedure in detail or specifically exclude the operation of the POA.

PUBLIC WORKS PROTECTION ACT

The *Public Works Protection Act* (PWPA) governs the status and duties of security officers who work for public works, such as nuclear power stations, waterworks, or transmission facilities. With respect to certain functions and while at work, security officers in these facilities have the same authority as a peace officer. This means that security personnel have the right to refuse entry, on reasonable and probable grounds, to anyone to public works property if that person refuses to be searched. The legislation is currently being reviewed for the purpose of amendment.

Definitions

In section 1 of the PWPA:

> "guard" means a guard appointed under this Act;
> "highway" means a common or public highway or a part thereof, and includes any street, bridge and any other structure incidental thereto and any part thereof;
> "public work" includes,
> (a) any railway, canal, highway, bridge, power works including all property used for the generation, transformation, transmission, distribution or supply of hydraulic or electrical power, gas works, water works, public utility or other work, owned, operated or carried on by the Government of Ontario or by any board or commission thereof, or by any municipal corporation, public utility commission or by private enterprises,
> (b) any provincial and any municipal public building, and
> (c) any other building, place or work designated a public work by the Lieutenant Governor in Council.

Appointment, Powers, and Duties of Guards

Section 2 of the PWPA provides as follows:

> For the purpose of protecting a public work, guards may be appointed by,
> (a) the Solicitor General;
> (b) the Commissioner of the Ontario Provincial Police Force;
> (c) any inspector of the Ontario Provincial Police Force;

(d) the head or deputy head of the municipal council or the chief of police of the municipality in which the public work is located, or the person acting in the place or stead of the head or deputy head;

(e) the chair or other person who is the head of a board, commission or other body owning or having charge of the public work, or the person acting in the place or stead of the chair or other person.

Every person appointed as a guard under the PWPA has, for the purposes of the Act, the powers of a peace officer. According to section 2(3), PWPA guards are responsible as follows:

Subject to the regulations and to any special direction of the Solicitor General or the Commissioner of the Ontario Provincial Police Force, every guard shall obey all directions of the person appointing him or her, any inspector of the Ontario Provincial Police Force, the chief of police of the municipality in which is located the public work that he or she is protecting, and the person who is in charge of the protecting of the public work.

Breach of Duty by Guard

Under section 2(4) of the PWPA, guards who breach their duties by

- neglecting or refusing to obey directions;

- failing to carry out their duties;

- leaving the location to which they are assigned or without leave; or

- "otherwise conduct[ing] himself or herself in a manner not consistent with his or her duties as guard"

are guilty of an offence. The penalty is a fine of up to $500 and/or imprisonment for up to two months.

Powers of a Guard or Peace Officer

The powers of a PWPA guard are set out in section 3:

A guard or peace officer,

(a) may require any person entering or attempting to enter any public work or any approach thereto to furnish his or her name and address, to identify himself or herself and to state the purpose for which he or she desires to enter the public work, in writing or otherwise;

(b) may search, without warrant, any person entering or attempting to enter a public work or a vehicle in the charge or under the control of any such person or which has recently been or is suspected of having been in the charge or under the control of any such person or in which any such person is a passenger; and

(c) may refuse permission to any person to enter a public work and use such force as is necessary to prevent any such person from so entering.

Refusal to obey a PWPA guard or peace officer can result in a fine of $500 and/or imprisonment for up to two months. A PWPA guard can arrest without warrant any person who is found entering or attempting to enter a public work without authority, or who refuses to obey an order.

PERSONAL INFORMATION PROTECTION AND ELECTRONIC DOCUMENTS ACT

In April 2000, Parliament passed the *Personal Information Protection and Electronic Documents Act* (PIPED Act). This federal Act is intended to assist in ensuring safety when conducting e-business and in recognizing electronic documents to be as reliable as their paper counterparts. The PIPED Act:

- criminalizes the wrongful disclosure of encryption keys;

- deters the use of encryption in the commission of a crime;

- deters the use of cryptography to conceal a crime;

- extends existing search and seizure laws to cryptographic situations;

- acknowledges the authenticity of electronic evidence in the Supreme Court of Canada; and

- provides acceptable electronic alternatives for communicating and recording information to the federal government.

The PIPED Act came into force in January 2004. It reflects the federal government's recognition of its need to continually review and improve policies for the protection of personal information and privacy in the electronic world.

Liability of Internet Service Providers

An area of current concern is how to determine the potential liability of Internet service providers (ISPs). The ability of ISPs to regulate content such as child pornography, defamation, and fraud is limited. What the government wants to do is make it easier to prosecute offenders who either spam (send out on a mass unsolicited basis) illegal material or present it on their own websites.

Compulsory Background Checks

One important change as a result of the PIPED Act is that all applicants for any job position are subject to a background check. If a company does not comply with this requirement, the company may be liable if an employee turns out to be, for example, a terrorist working undercover and causes harm or injury to other people or property.

Protection of Personal Information

Canada already has federal and provincial legislation (except in Prince Edward Island) to protect personal information collected and used by governments. Quebec is the only province to date that has enacted privacy legislation that applies to the private sector.

The PIPED Act requires that organizations obtain an individual's consent when they collect, use, or disclose the individual's personal information. The general rule is that no one else will be able to make use of a person's personal information without that person's permission. An individual will have the right to access his or her personal records held by an organization and to correct them, if need be. Personal information can only be used for the purposes for which it was collected, and if an organization is going to use it for any other reason, it must get the individual's consent again. While it sounds pretty scary to have this kind of "Big Brother" control, there are safeguards against misusing or abusing personal information. The Act assures individuals that their records will be kept safe in locked cabinets or protected with computer passwords and/or by encryption.

Personal information is defined as "information about an identifiable individual" and includes things such as race; ethnic origin; colour; age; marital status; religion; education; medical, criminal, employment, and financial history; address and telephone number; numerical identifiers such as the Social Insurance Number, fingerprints, blood type, tissue, and biological sample; and views or personal opinions. Protection of this information is achieved by requiring organizations to comply with the obligations in **CSA International's Model Privacy Code**. The Code is incorporated into the law as schedule 1 to the Act.

The Act will apply to every organization that collects, uses, or discloses personal information in the course of a commercial activity. "Commercial activity" is any transaction that is of a buy-and-sell nature, or for an exchange in trade, or a bartering of services. An organization includes a company, an association, a partnership, a person, or a trade union. The Act does not apply when an organization uses personal information solely for journalistic, artistic, or literary purposes, and it does not apply to personal information used solely for personal or domestic purposes, such as Christmas card lists.

All industry sectors and companies of all sizes across the country are subject to general principles outlined in schedule 1 of the Act. These principles are:

CSA International's Model Privacy Code
privacy obligations incorporated as schedule 1 of the *Personal Information Protection and Electronic Documents Act*

- Accountability: The organization is responsible for the protection of any personal information.

- Identifying purposes: The organization *must* define what the information will be used for before it is collected.

- Consent: Consent *must* be obtained from the individual regarding collection, use and disclosure of the information.

- Limiting collection: Only necessary information will be collected.

- Limiting use, disclosure, and retention: The organization may not change the purpose of the information after it was collected.

- Accuracy: The information *must* be accurate, complete, and up to date.

- Safeguards: The information *must* be adequately protected due to the sensitivity of the information.

- Openness: Policies regarding the management of personal information *must* be readily available.

- Individual access: An individual shall be allowed access to and challenge the accuracy of their own information.

- Challenging compliance: An individual may challenge the organization regarding the degree of compliance to any or all of the above principles.

The only exceptions to compliance are where obtaining an individual's approval would taint the information's accuracy; where information is required for a legal examination or aid in an emergency where lives and safety are at stake; or where releasing private papers publicly would assist the preservation of historically important records.

The drafters of this legislation tried to strike a balance with respect to the privacy of information that is fair to both organizations and individuals. The privacy commissioner acts as an **ombudsman** responsible for settling private differences without provoking retaliatory exchanges between organizations and their clients. Anyone or any organization that hinders the commissioner's investigation, destroys records prematurely, or dismisses or punishes a plaintiff is guilty of an offence and is liable to a maximum fine of $100,000.

ombudsman
public official who investigates complaints by citizens against public authorities or officials

LIQUOR LICENCE ACT

The *Liquor Licence Act* (LLA) is enforced by security officers on a fairly regular basis, largely because many of the rules with respect to liquor possession and consumption relate to specific locations, and security officers often work to regulate access into a premises or movement of patrons within a premises. For example, there are rules that prevent bringing liquor into a hotel lounge; but it is generally permissible to possess or consume liquor in a hotel room. A security guard working in the hotel may be required to explain and/or enforce this rule to guests of the hotel. A guard needs to know the limit of the law in each situation involving liquor and his or her workplace.

The LLA is an exceptionally long Act that deals with licensing, permits, individual compliance, and offences. Only those provisions that commonly affect security officers are discussed here.

Definitions

Section 1 of the LLA defines several terms, including the following of interest to security officers:

> "alcohol" means a product of fermentation or distillation of grains, fruits or other agricultural products, and includes synthetic ethyl alcohol;
>
> "beer" means any beverage containing alcohol in excess of the prescribed amount obtained by the fermentation of an infusion or decoction of barley, malt and hops or of any similar products in drinkable water;
>
> "government store" means a government store established under the *Liquor Control Act*;
>
> "licence" means a licence issued under this Act;
>
> "liquor" means spirits, wine and beer or any combination thereof and includes any alcohol in a form appropriate for human consumption as a beverage, alone or in combination with any other matter;
>
> "sell" means to supply for remuneration, directly or indirectly, in any manner by which the cost is recovered from the person supplied, alone or in combination with others, and "sale" has a corresponding meaning;
>
> "spirits" means any beverage containing alcohol obtained by distillation;
>
> "wine" means any beverage containing alcohol in excess of the prescribed amount obtained by the fermentation of the natural sugar contents of fruits,

---

Not Safe for Drinking!

These substances contain alcohol, but are not safe or legal to drink!

- rubbing alcohol

- mouthwash

- aftershave and perfume

- flavouring extracts (vanilla extract, almond extract, etc.)

- some disinfectants

- cough syrups and other alcohol-based medicines

- photocopier toner

---

including grapes, apples and other agricultural products containing sugar, and including honey and milk.

(The full text of the *Liquor Licence Act* is available online at www.e-laws.gov.on.ca.)

Compliance by Consumers

The LLA imposes rules on individual consumers of alcohol:

- Consumers can buy liquor only from a government store or from a person with a sale licence (for example, the bartender at a properly licensed bar). Special regulations govern gifts of liquor from manufacturers or their representatives.

- No person can buy, obtain, possess or consume liquor while under the age of 19 years (there are some exceptions).

- Underage individuals are prohibited from using fake identification to obtain or consume liquor.

- Opened liquor can be possessed or consumed only in certain places (discussed further below).

- There are rules against public intoxication (discussed further below).

- Opened liquor cannot be transported in a vehicle (including a boat or snowmobile) unless it is stored in a separate locked compartment or in baggage that is not readily accessible by the occupants.

- It is illegal to drink, or to supply to another person for drinking, alcohol that is not designed as a drink (for example, rubbing alcohol, aftershave, or mouthwash).

Compliance by Providers

Rules governing providers (government stores, licensed providers such as bars, and private providers such as party hosts) include the following:

- It is illegal to provide or sell liquor to a person who is, or appears to be, intoxicated.

- It is illegal to sell or provide liquor to a person who is or appears to be under the age of 19, or to "knowingly" allow him or her to consume it on licensed premises.

- It is illegal to sell or provide alcohol that is not intended for drinking to a person whom you believe will use it for that purpose.

Enforcing the Rules

Security officers are often called upon to enforce the provisions of the LLA by their employers, whether or not the employer has a liquor licence.

Controlling Entry

One of the common ways security officers enforce the LLA is by controlling entry. As noted above, there are rules prohibiting possession and consumption in certain areas. Security officers may restrict entry to a premises when a patron is attempting to bring in liquor for consumption in contravention of the law (because the patron is underage, the premises is not licensed, the licence does not allow patrons to bring in their own liquor, or the patron is violating rules with respect to motor vehicles).

Where the patron is suspected of being underage, the security guard will typically ask to see identification. If the identification is unsatisfactory, the patron can be excluded. Where the patron is suspected of attempting to smuggle liquor in, the security guard can ask the patron to volunteer to be searched (to open his or her coat or bags, or to allow him or her to be "patted down"—a same-sex guard should be available for this). Where the guard suspects improper transportation in a vehicle, the patron may be asked to submit to a voluntary vehicle search.

Patrons who refuse a search can legally be excluded. Section 34(5) of the LLA states:

> A patron who is or appears to be intoxicated may also be denied entry because of the rules against selling to intoxicated persons.

Removal of Offenders

In some cases, security officers will be required to assist in the removal from premises of a person who is or is suspected of being in contravention of the LLA.

Section 34 of the LLA deals with removal from the premises. It provides:

> 34(1) The holder of a licence or permit issued in respect of premises shall ensure that a person does not remain on the premises if the holder has reasonable grounds to believe that the person,
>   (a) is unlawfully on the premises;
>   (b) is on the premises for an unlawful purpose; or
>   (c) is contravening the law on the premises.
>   (2) The holder of a licence or permit may request a person referred to in subsection (1) to leave the premises immediately and if the request is not forth-

with complied with may remove the person or cause the person to be removed by the use of no more force than is necessary.

(3) If there are reasonable grounds to believe that a disturbance or breach of the peace sufficient to constitute a threat to the public safety is being caused on premises for which a licence or permit is issued, a police officer may require that all persons vacate the premises.

(4) The holder of the licence or permit for premises that are required to be vacated under subsection (3) shall take all reasonable steps to ensure that the premises are vacated.

(5) A licensee or employee of a licensee who has reason to believe that the presence of a person on the licensee's licensed premises is undesirable may,

(a) request the person to leave; or

(b) forbid the person to enter the licensed premises.

(6) No person shall,

(a) remain on licensed premises after he or she is requested to leave by the licensee or an employee of the licensee; or

(b) re-enter the licensed premises on the same day he or she is requested to leave.

You should read this section carefully, noting in particular:

- the need for reasonable grounds before a person can be removed or excluded;

- the prohibition against excessive use of force;

- the option of police support for a "mass removal" order; and

- the requirement of the licence holder to take all reasonable steps to support compliance on the premises.

Section 34.1 discusses removal/exclusion by police. This is normally used when a situation has gotten out of security's control, where a confrontation has arisen, or in an under-control situation where the licence holder or another party wants charges laid.

Unlicensed Premises

A security guard working in unlicensed premises should know that it is illegal to consume liquor or to carry open liquor anywhere except a residence, a licensed premises, or a "private place" as defined in the regulations, for example, a hotel room.

Public Intoxication

It is illegal to be drunk in a public place or in the common area of a residence of a multidwelling residence (for example, an apartment lobby or hallway). The police (at the request of security, in many cases) can arrest without a warrant any person who is intoxicated in a public place and who is a threat to the safety of others.

Civil Liability

Where a security officer's employer contravenes the LLA, the employer may be charged under the legislation and may be at risk of losing the liquor licence. By

FAST FACT

Where a person to whom liquor is oversold in contravention of the law commits suicide, the family of the person can bring an action against the provider of the liquor under the *Family Law Act* of Ontario.

enforcing the LLA, security officers protect their employers from such charges. But it is also important to know that there is also the potential for civil liability on the part of a person or corporation who fails to enforce the LLA where the failure to comply with the rules results in harm to people or property. The most common way that this happens is through over-serving—that is, providing or selling liquor to intoxicated guests, who then go on to cause harm to themselves or others, for example, by driving drunk.

This liability is outside (beyond) the LLA and in addition to any charges under it, and can be very significant. To avoid civil suits, security guards must be vigilant in preventing overconsumption of liquor on their employers' premises.

LEGISLATION APPLICABLE TO HOTELS/MOTELS

Some security officers work in hotels or motels. For these officers, it is important to be aware of two pieces of legislation: the *Hotel Registration of Guests Act* and the *Innkeepers Act*.

Hotel Registration of Guests Act

The *Hotel Registration of Guests Act* requires a hotel owner (hotels are defined in the Act) to have guests register under their legal names and to preserve this information, along with information about the length of the guests' stay. It is an offence on the part of the guest to register under a false name and an offence on the part of the hotelier (or his or her representative, such as a security officer) to allow the guest to do so.

Hotel owners must also publish and post rates for the room in the room. Failure to do so is a provincial offence.

Innkeepers Act

The *Innkeepers Act* provides that an innkeeper ("inn" is defined in the Act) "has a lien on" (that is, has a limited right in) the goods of patrons in the premises. This means that if the patrons do certain things, for example, damage the premises and fail to pay for the damage, the innkeeper has recourse against the goods of the guest. If the rules are followed, the innkeeper can keep and sell the baggage to recover losses.

The legislation explains how this is done, and security officers who work in hotels should be aware of the rules for doing this.

(The full text of the *Innkeepers Act* is available online at www.e-laws.gov.on.ca.)

AERONAUTICS ACT

The September 11, 2001 terrorist attacks on the United States motivated an initiative in Canada to update the *Aeronautics Act* (AA). The amended AA will introduce rules on the use of electronic and technological advances such as optical retina scanners, baggage x-ray machines, computer training programs for passenger security screeners and baggage handlers, and pilots in automated flight simulators. Proposed changes will also include government decisions on the placement of air marshals on board flights and whether they and pilots are to carry guns.

The current AA deals primarily with rules for air traffic; radio protocol; aircraft registration; pilot training, qualifications, and licensing; ownership of aircraft; maintenance of aircraft, parts, and equipment; commercial air services such as cargo charters; airport employees and airline personnel, including air mechanics, baggage operators, air attendants, and ground service or air ticket agents; and air passengers.

One of the most important things to know about aeronautics law is that if someone on a Canadian aircraft, such as a pilot, mechanic, air crew, or passenger, violates the provisions of this Act while outside Canadian airspace, that person will be treated as if the violation occurred on Canadian soil and will be prosecuted according to Canadian law. Conversely, where Canadian aviators, aircraft companies, and all those associated with them or with airlines working on foreign soil are afforded the privileges of that foreign state, they are subject to its laws and must comply.

Airport security is a separate field and requires specialized training beyond the scope of this text.

TENANT PROTECTION ACT

The *Tenant Protection Act* (TPA) governs the rights of landlords and tenants in Ontario. Its predecessor, the *Landlord and Tenant Act*, was drafted in an effort to codify the terms of the rental relationship and to create a balance of bargaining power between landlords and tenants.

Issues covered in the legislation that are of particular interest to security personnel include tenant privacy; rules with respect to eviction; lockout rules; and rules with respect to unacceptable tenant behaviour—for example, excessive noise.

Security officers employed in residential complexes need to understand these basic rules to be able to carry out any direction from a landlord or property manager that relates to or affects tenants in the performance of their duty.

Privacy Issues

The TPA protects the privacy rights of tenants by making it illegal, in most cases, to enter a rental unit without consent, or without giving appropriate advance notice to the tenant.

In general, where a landlord has a good, non-emergency reason (usually either to make repairs, carry out maintenance, or to show the unit to prospective purchasers) to enter the unit, the landlord must give the tenant 24 hours' notice of his or her intention to enter. The landlord is entitled to enter between the hours of 8 a.m. and 8 p.m. for this purpose. Section 20(3) allows the landlord, in cases where either the landlord or the tenant has given notice of termination, to enter without prior written notice to show the unit to potential renters (not purchasers). In this case, the landlord is required to enter only between 8 a.m. and 8 p.m. and to inform (or to make a reasonable attempt to inform) the tenant of the landlord's intention to show the unit.

The landlord is allowed to enter without notice and without consent only in the case of an emergency. There is an exception for units that offer housekeeping services. For those units, a tenancy agreement generally governs the landlord's access for cleaning.

In the above situations, the term "landlord" includes a representative, such as a security officer who has been authorized by the landlord to act as such.

Canvassers

A landlord or his or her representative is not allowed to unreasonably exclude the entry of political candidates or their canvassers.

Eviction

A landlord can evict a tenant from a rental unit for one of several reasons:

- non-payment of rent;

- the commission of an illegal act or carrying on an illegal trade or business—for example, drug dealing—in the unit;

- misrepresentation of income;

- willful or negligent causing of "undue damage" to the unit (in this case, the damage must be significant and well beyond normal wear and tear);

- where the tenant's behaviour "substantially interferes with the reasonable enjoyment of the residential complex for all usual purposes by the landlord or another tenant or substantially interferes with another lawful right, privilege, or interest of the landlord or another tenant" (this section is the one normally relied on in situations involving excessive noise, etc.);

- where the tenant does something that impairs the safety of others;

- where the number of persons living in the unit "results in a contravention of health, safety or housing standards required by law"; or

- where there is a second incident or reason for termination within six months of the tenant's avoidance of eviction by complying with the previous notice.

Each of these situations is governed by specific rules with respect to notice that must be given to tenants, and the nature of the behaviour that falls within the definition of the statute has been the subject of case law. Discussing each situation in detail is beyond the scope of the book, but security officers working in a residential complex should read the legislation carefully so that they are able to comply with all notice requirements on behalf of the landlord.

Distress Abolished

The TPA has abolished the exercise of "distress." Distress was the word used to describe a landlord's right to seize and sell a tenant's property for non-payment of rent without a court order. Landlords no longer have this right. Rules for the disposition of abandoned tenant property are set out in the act, as are rules for changing the locks.

SUMMARY

One of the important functions of security officers is to enforce the law. Law is contained not only in the *Criminal Code* of Canada, but also in a wide range of other statutes, regulations, and bylaws at the federal, provincial, and municipal levels. This chapter provided a review of some of the legislation most commonly encountered by security personnel.

Depending on the location in which a security officer works, there may be other legislation that is particularly relevant to the officer's day-to-day duties. Security officers must review and understand any legislation that they may be called upon to enforce.

KEY TERMS

CSA International's Model Privacy Code

ombudsman

PERFORMANCE APPLICATION

1. How does the *Provincial Offences Act* work in relation with other provincial legislation?

2. Name three powers of a guard under the *Public Works Protection Act* (PWPA).

3. To whom does a PWPA guard report?

4. Why should security officers know about the *Personal Information Protection and Electronic Documents Act*?

5. What are the rules with respect to the transportation of liquor in a motor vehicle?

6. Why should security officers know about the *Innkeepers Act*?

7. Name one offence under the *Hotel Registration of Guests Act*.

8. When can a landlord enter a tenant's unit without notice?

PART II   EXERCISE

The law shapes many aspects of our day-to-day lives. Part II introduced the legal framework within which private investigators and security officers work.

Security personnel are often called upon to enforce the law, but they are also themselves bound by it. Chapter 4 introduced the *Private Investigators and Security Guards Act* (PISGA), which is currently under review.

However, government legislation is only one way that a profession can be regulated. Many professions, including medicine, law, and accounting, choose self-regulation, which means that membership in the profession is conditional upon a member's compliance with rules that the profession, through a regulatory body, such as a College of Physicians and Surgeons, imposes upon itself.

At present, while there are some associations that provide guidelines for private investigators and security guards, there is no strong regulatory body chosen by members of the profession to create and enforce professional standards.

1. Should security personnel move toward self-regulation? Why or why not?

2. Imagine that you are the chair of a newly constituted committee or body charged with regulating security professionals. Draft a list of at least six rules or standards that you would include in a professional code of conduct for your profession.

PART III

Operational Procedures

7 Patrol Procedures

INTRODUCTION

In recent years, there has been an increasing demand for security guards in the private sector. This has happened partly because companies and people feel safer with a show of uniformed officers over the less visible but very sophisticated technology also in place, and partly because their role is seen to help people, especially the aging population, more than it is to regulate them. Security guards may provide information and give directions, or in some cases, escort visitors to specific areas within a complex, act as a building receptionist, or supervise safety measures. Hospitals and healthcare facilities, for instance, now provide their own security services, and often security guards are called upon to track down patients who have wandered from their rooms or to help restrain patients who have become uncontrollable and violent. Mainly, however, guards watch over entrances and exits, patrol premises, work to prevent major crimes, report to the police crimes that have occurred, and enforce private regulations on behalf of their employer for the protection of their company's property, goods, and employees or tenants. They may perform their guard duty on foot, on bicycles, or in patrol cars.

Although some may imagine that the daily patrol function of security officers is routine, once they understand this function, they will come to see that patrol duty is far from dull. Humans have five senses, some may even argue for a sixth. These senses make up one of the most sophisticated alarm and early warning systems on the planet. Security professionals use all these senses at any one time when they are on patrol.

For a company to provide a complete security service, it must have an effective and dynamic patrol program. This can be achieved only if officers understand how a patrol program works.

Chapter Objectives

When you have completed this chapter, you will

- have a basic understanding of how patrol theory, objectives, and practical techniques are applied to improve the effectiveness of security patrols and site security.

PATROL OBJECTIVES

A patrol program has five essential objectives:

- To gain an intimate knowledge of the site.

- To establish a visible presence to deter potential offenders within the complex.

- To build confidence in security on the part of employees, management, residents, and/or tenants.

- To detect crimes, safety hazards, and emergencies.

- To detect, investigate, and report on any and all situations that affect the normal routine of the site.

There are two types of patrols—foot patrols and mobile patrols. The benefits and disadvantages of each type are described below.

FOOT PATROLS

Unless responding to a specific incident, foot patrols are always preferable to mobile patrols. Officers on foot can interact more easily with their environment and the people on the site more freely. By being more accessible, security officers gather more information about the property and the people they are responsible for protecting. Foot patrols are the normal method of patrolling within most sites, unless the security supervisor takes over a specific mobile patrol.

Building patrols are designed to act as a deterrent against any form of security incident, breach, or problem. By conducting routine building patrols, security staff present a highly visible security presence in the workplace. Routine building patrols achieve four main objectives:

- To deter employees who feel inclined to conduct criminal acts.

- To prevent incidents from occurring by early monitoring of deteriorating situations in the workplace.

- To promote the service aspect of security, fostering a sense of safety in the workplace or facility.

- To develop a rapport between security and employees, giving employees confidence to report items that are out of place or situations that cause concern.

A disadvantage of foot patrols is that they take longer to complete, and response time to an incident is increased if security personnel are distant from the incident site (often an indication that there are too few security officers for the site).

MOBILE PATROLS

When a security vehicle is available, mobile patrols allow security staff to cover more ground in a short time. However, there is a price to pay for faster coverage—patrol officers lose the benefit of using all their senses. This can be mitigated to some extent by getting guards to an area quickly, and then having them conduct an area inspection.

An advantage of mobile patrols is that patrol vehicles are usually equipped with personal protective equipment, emergency gear, and full voice communication capability, including cellular.

In some cases, security guards may use equipment such as bicycles or golf carts in order to facilitate more comprehensive security coverage over a large area. A good use of this would be patrols in a multilevel parking garage operation, where the ability of a properly equipped officer to respond to a remote section of the facility quickly may be essential.

PATROL PLANNING

Patrols must be organized in a logical fashion to maximize coverage and limit gaps in surveillance. Buildings or outdoor areas should be systematically patrolled floor-by-floor and area-by-area. Outside zones should be divided into "blocks" and covered individually.

It is important for officers to pause often, ideally, once every two minutes for a minimum of 15 seconds. These pauses allow the officer to switch from walking mode into observing mode, so that he or she can better focus on the surroundings.

Building Patrol Functions

During a building patrol, an officer inspects, records, and reports on the following:

- Improperly secured doors, windows, gates, offices, equipment, computers, files, personal items, materials, or documents.

- Signs of fire, flooding, spills, leaks, structural failure, or other safety hazards.

- Signs of theft or break-in.

- Signs of a threat from properties adjacent to the site.

- Presence of employees or other personnel within the complex who have not signed in at security.

- Any situation of an unusual nature.

Building Patrol Routes

During normal business hours, a useful formula for patrols involves having each officer complete four separate patrol routes at least twice during his or her shift. During **silent hours**, officers should increase patrols to at least three times each during the shift. While on **high-risk patrol** in dangerous areas, coverage should be increased further.

To confuse anyone who may be monitoring security routines, officers must be careful to randomly select the order of their patrol routes so that anyone monitoring is never sure where an officer will be at any given time. If there is an increased threat against one of the buildings or if there is any cause for suspicion, the security supervisor will include this building in the silent hours patrol route.

silent hours
time outside of normal business hours

high-risk patrol
patrol that takes place in an area known for dangerous activity or in an area that may be dangerous due to a particular situation, such as a labour dispute

SITE COORDINATION OF PATROLS

The normal chain of command is that security officers report to and are directed by the security supervisor. The control room is usually the command centre for security response on a site. All security systems can be monitored and activated from the control room, and the various modes of communication are also provided from there.

In most cases, the operational chain of command from the top down is as follows:

Site Security Manager
↓
Security Supervisor
↓
Control Room Operator or "Control"
↓
Patrol Officer

In situations where the security supervisor is responding to an incident at a different site or is disabled as part of the incident, the routine chain of command remains. However, the patrol officer is now directed by the control room operator, who also fulfills the role of the security supervisor until a suitably qualified relief can be found.

PATROL COMMUNICATIONS

It is critical that patrolling officers *always* maintain regular, high-quality communications with the control room. This includes the use of proper voice procedure and reporting schedules. During patrol, communications checks are conducted at regular intervals by radio.

There may be areas of the site where radios do not function reliably. Microwave interference, iron ore content in building materials, or many other factors can limit the effectiveness of radio devices. It is essential to identify these areas in advance of an emergency and to establish alternate communication systems (telephones, intercoms) in these areas.

"Missed communication" drills should be conducted regularly. An appropriate procedure would be to conduct a radio check every 15 minutes between the control room and the patrol officer. If one check is missed, the officer should immediately contact control via other means or return to the control room. In the event of two missed checks, an emergency should be declared and a response plan initiated.

SITUATIONAL AWARENESS

situational awareness
well-developed sense of the specific patrol function being performed

Situational awareness describes a state of mind that every patrol officer must develop with respect to the specific patrol function being performed. A well-developed sense of situational awareness keeps the patrol function dynamic and provides a high level of safety. Training in situational awareness helps security personnel detect even the subtlest change in both the physical and human environments.

The Physical Environment

If security officers focus on their surroundings, over the course of several patrols, they will develop a mental picture of a particular location. Then, on subsequent patrols, they will notice any changes that affect that mental picture of the **physical environment**. Sometimes simple changes will trigger an alert—a truck that has been moved or a garbage bin that's been emptied. Trained security officers will notice the change, consider it, and then mentally file it away for later reference. They are able to train their minds to do this automatically. It's useful, in understanding this skill, to compare an officer's mind to that of an airline pilot.

physical environment
surroundings or particular locations at the worksite

When a plane is on autopilot, a pilot doesn't have to think; but the tradeoff is that he or she loses the ability to react immediately. When the pilot takes the controls off autopilot and takes over the aircraft manually, he or she is in greater control. It's as if the controls become extensions of the pilot's hands, feet, and mind. The pilot and the plane function as one to become an integrated machine performing at its peak. So, the more aware security officers become of what they notice, consider, and mentally file away on patrol, the more they are aware or in control of their surroundings and any changes that may affect security.

The Human Environment

Worksites are often large facilities with many departments and functions. There may be hundreds of employees with different backgrounds, interests, and concerns. While patrolling, security officers should include this **human environment** in their mental picture of each location. By talking to employees and observing their routines, security staff can become fully aware of what a "normal" day is, making it easier to spot differences.

human environment
personnel at the worksite

Survival Mental State

Unlike a police officer who has been told what to expect when called to an alarm, a security officer usually has no idea what to expect. Police can rely on a firearm, baton, and back-up from other police; security officers cannot carry a gun in self-defence, may not be wearing a bullet-proof vest, and may not have a partner in a squad car. All they can rely on when they arrive at the site of the alarm is themselves, and their situational awareness skills. Before getting out of the patrol car, they should be anticipating all the possibilities that may confront them and they should have a plan of action to handle them. This level of preparedness is sometimes described as a "survival" mental state.

QUICK QUESTIONS

What To Look For

In observing the human environment, consider these questions:

- Is an employee distraught or acting peculiar?

- Is an entire department nervous, angry, or distressed?

- Is an employee in an area where he/she should not be?

- Is an employee missing from his/her post?

Heightened Recall

There is another advantage to adopting a state of situational awareness. Not only do officers train themselves to detect early warnings of impending events, in subsequent investigations they can also access sharper recall from their mental "files" to report more accurate details about locations and people. They will likely find themselves able to recite licence plate numbers and describe faces with remarkable clarity after only a glimpse. Answers to questions such as, "Was a valve open or shut?" or "Was that door open or closed?" will come like a flash and they will be accurate.

Switching On and Off

No human being can be in a state of alert all of the time. Neither can they sustain situational awareness forever. The demand on the conscious and unconscious mind is simply too great. As a result, security officers must get into the habit of mentally "turning on" when setting out on a patrol and, during the course of the patrol, maintaining that level of concentration even when chatting casually with employees. On returning to the control room, however, they need to "turn off" and rest. Let the security system's automated surveillance pick up the slack. This does not mean that they can become oblivious to their duties, but their level of concentration can be substantially reduced. Security officers should practise moving quickly from a state of increased awareness to a normal state, and back.

RECORD KEEPING

While on patrol, any important change must be written in a notebook. Remember, while an accurate verbal description of events is a valuable aid in an investigation, the combination of accurate recollections supported with accurate notes is the best record of events.

All patrols must be logged in and out of the control room and records of radio checks and communications must be maintained. Report writing is discussed in chapter 14.

USE OF GUARD DOGS

Canine units have become vital security assets on patrols. Though the Royal Canadian Mounted Police first used sled dogs to guard property in the Northwest Territories, dog patrols grew in popularity during World War II with the military. In 1942, the Coast Guard introduced dog patrols along the Atlantic coast to warn of offshore enemy activity.

Today, the Canadian Police Canine Association holds field trials for their dogs to show off their special skills. In Canada, the dogs that participate are already certified, whereas in the United States, the National Canine Association conducts training classes to certify police dogs for duty as well as for competitions.

"Dogs are used to increase the safety of other security officers because of their speed, power and intimidation tactics," says Alain Martineau, site security manager for Paladin Security in Calgary, Alberta. He uses a guard dog to accompany him on his patrol of the Southern Alberta Institute of Technology (SAIT) Campus. Most handlers prefer males, but he has trained Raven, a rare black German Shepherd female, since she was eight weeks old. According to Martineau,

> Our canine friends have better night vision, a more sensitive sense of smell, and superior hearing, which make them generally more alert than their human counterparts. She makes a difference just by being with me.

That difference is respect. People know guard dogs are highly trained animals that are fiercely loyal to their masters, so having a guard dog on patrol is a psychological deterrent to criminals.

Canine units are also great for public relations. They perform at the snap of their handler's fingers or whispered command. They make everyone feel safer as they walk patrols, ride in security vehicles, search and track missing persons, sniff for drugs or explosives, and disperse disorderly crowds. In security, guard dogs perform many tasks.

Step Aside

Requirements for Guard Dogs

To be certified for a security canine unit, dogs must be able to demonstrate competence in obedience, agility, article search, suspect search, tracking, criminal apprehension, and handler protection.

Requirements for Dog Handlers

Dog handlers must:

- pass all company requirements for employment as a security officer.

- own a canine that meets the canine criteria.

- have reliable transportation with working air conditioning.

- pass an oral examination with the canine unit.

- complete a 120-day probationary period.

- be healthy and able to undergo physical stress for the purpose of training.

- do field trial exercises and be able to handle their canine.

SUMMARY

Patrolling a complex is the most effective method of providing security on site. As yet, no technology is the equal of the human brain and five senses for detecting changes and threats in the environment, except for the keener nose, eyes, and ears of a trained canine companion. Used effectively, a uniformed patrol program in concert with automated and technology-based surveillance, early warning equipment, and in some cases, guard dogs, makes for a formidable, proactive security system.

KEY TERMS

high-risk patrol

human environment

physical environment

silent hours

situational awareness

PERFORMANCE APPLICATION

1. What are the five objectives of a patrol program?

2. List two advantages and one disadvantage of foot patrols.

3. List two advantages and one disadvantage of mobile patrols.

4. What is the function of the control room?

5. Why is it important to select the order of patrol routes at random?

6. What is situational awareness?

7. What is the human environment?

8. Explain five ways that guard dogs augment the safety of security officers on patrol.

Traffic Control

INTRODUCTION

Facilities patrolled by security officers are often private property. This means that provincial traffic legislation is not enforceable on these sites. However, security guards acting according to the instructions of their employer or client are entitled to set limits on the use of the employer or client's property and that includes controlling traffic and parking.

AUTHORITY OVER VEHICULAR TRAFFIC

Drivers are typically admitted to private roadways by the property owner's authorization. This authorization can either be express or implied. An example of **express authorization** is when entry is allowed after swiping a card at an entry gate. **Implied authorization** occurs where, for example, there is a sign denoting the boundaries of private property, but no barrier restricting the flow of traffic from a public roadway onto a private one.

Authorized users of a private roadway (for example, employees, contractors, and suppliers) are often invited to do so on condition that they comply with all parking and traffic rules in force on the site. Since provincial traffic legislation is not in force on private property, property owners do not have at their disposal the range of penalties (under both provincial legislation and the criminal law) that are normally available to support the enforcement of traffic rules. However, the owner of the property typically reserves the right to suspend a user's driving privileges for failure to comply with the rules of the road.

RULES OF THE ROAD FOR PRIVATE PROPERTY

In general, the easiest way to manage traffic on private property is to adopt the same rules of the road that apply to public property, because these rules are familiar to drivers. It also makes sense for private property owners to adopt and use, where necessary, traffic signs, road configurations, and road markings consistent with those in public use.

Chapter Objectives

When you have completed this chapter, you will

- have a basic understanding of the duties of a security officer with respect to traffic control and parking management.

express authorization
admission to private roadways by invitation of the property owner

implied authorization
admission to private roadways is not prohibited by the property owner

ACTIVE TRAFFIC MANAGEMENT AND HAND SIGNALS

In some cases, where there is heavy traffic due, for example, to a special event or to work being carried out by construction or transportation vehicles, security personnel may be called on to actively direct traffic.

Apparel, Equipment, and Safety

When directing traffic, security personnel should wear appropriate clothing and carry appropriate equipment. In daylight and/or clear weather, this means wearing or carrying:

- fluorescent-coloured clothing or a fluorescent vest that fits over the regular uniform;
- steel-toed footwear;
- a hardhat; and
- a whistle.

In addition to the above-noted clothing and equipment, in darkness or foul weather, security officers should wear or carry:

- clothing or a vest with large reflective (able to reflect light from headlights) stripes or markings;
- where appropriate, reflective wristbands and/or ankle cuffs; and
- a flashlight.

Equipment that may be used in support of traffic control includes:

- hand-held signs (for example, "SLOW") designed according to provincially legislated standards;
- flags to increase the visibility of hand signals;
- flashlights and/or signalling wands for increasing the visibility of hand signals at night;
- barricades with fluorescent and/or lighted reflective markings; and
- radio equipment for communication with other traffic control personnel.

Equipment designed to control traffic without a human operator—for example, traffic lights—may be used in very high-traffic areas. Where employed, this equipment should meet similar standards as used in public roadway applications. Ontario standards for traffic control equipment and the meanings of signals are described in RRO 1990, Reg. 626, "Traffic Control Systems" made under the *Highway Traffic Act*. Similar standards exist under other provincial traffic control regimes.

Many traffic control garments are designed to incorporate both fluorescent colours and reflective materials. There are government standards with respect to some items of traffic control apparel—for example, fluorescent/reflective vests. Apparel purchased for wear by security personnel should meet or exceed these standards for visibility.

Also, where the employer or client anticipates that nighttime traffic direction will be needed, roadways and intersections should be equipped with good-quality lighting.

Security personnel directing traffic should be instructed to stand only where they can be clearly seen from all directions and where they have a safe escape route. Ideally, a person directing traffic should stand not in the roadway, but on a median or raised platform that is clearly not part of the right-of-way. Where it is necessary to stand in the roadway, security personnel normally position themselves in the middle of an intersection, so that their position is not blocked from view by traffic from any direction.

Finally, where security personnel will be required to work near, or to direct the movements of, construction equipment or vehicles, they should receive training with respect to safe work practices for work near the relevant equipment or vehicles.

Traffic-Management Signals

Where an employee is required to direct the flow of traffic, he or she should use standard traffic-management hand signals shown in figure 8.1 when stationed on the driver's (left) side of the traffic lane. The alternative signals shown in figure 8.1 must only be used when the employee is stationed on the passenger's (right) side of the traffic lane. The paddle must not be used to wave traffic on and must never be displayed to traffic in other than a static manner.

Effective and safe traffic control depends on good communication. Signals, whether hand signals or audible signals (whistle), must be precise and unambiguous. When directing traffic, security personnel should be conscious at all times of the degree to which they are visible from the direction or traffic, avoiding, where possible, having their back to traffic. They should not make any unnecessary movements that could be mistaken for hand signals, and when making traffic signals, they should strive for precision and authority in their body language. Making eye contact with both motorists and pedestrians when giving signals is essential.

PARKING

Where necessary, a private facility may need to develop and enforce rules for parking. In so doing, these rules are usually communicated to drivers either by signs or pavement markings.

Signs

Parking signs should be clear, simple in content, placed for good visibility, and to the extent possible, similar to public parking signs. Parking signs at a private facility may be used to indicate reserved parking spaces, handicapped parking spaces, no-parking zones, and seasonal no-parking zones (for example, snow removal zones).

Pavement Markings

Pavement markings are typically used to delineate parking spaces (including reserved and handicapped spaces). Properly marked parking areas ensure that vehicles will park in such a way as to permit safe entry and exit from the parking area.

FIGURE 8.1 Hand Signals for Traffic Control

Normal

1. To STOP Traffic

(A) By Day

- Face traffic.
- Display static "STOP" paddle in left hand.
- When approaching vehicle has almost stopped, use right arm to indicate stopping point.

*Alternative
Reverse of normal signal

Normal

(B) By Night

- Face traffic.
- Display static reflectorized "STOP" paddle in left hand and flashlight, with red signalling baton attached, in right hand.
- Move right arm from 3 to 6 o'clock.
- When approaching vehicle has almost stopped, use flashlight/baton to indicate stopping point.

*Alternative
Reverse of normal signal

Normal

2. To SLOW Traffic

(A) By Day

- Face traffic.
- Display static "SLOW" paddle in left hand.
- If traffic slows below desired speed, give appropriate "Move Traffic" signal.

*Alternative
Reverse of normal signal

Normal

(B) By Night

- Face traffic.
- Display static reflectorized "SLOW" paddle in left hand and flashlight, with red signalling baton attached, in right hand.
- Move right arm from 3 to 6 o'clock.
- If traffic slows below desired speed, give appropriate "Move Traffic" signal.

*Alternative
Reverse of normal signal

EMERGENCY VEHICLES

Emergency vehicles are typically exempt, at least while on emergency duty, from normal traffic signals and parking prohibitions. In an emergency, security officers may be called upon to direct traffic in support of access by emergency vehicles. In general, to allow entry for emergency vehicles, other traffic is directed to pull over as quickly as safety permits to the far right-hand side of the roadway.

ENFORCING TRAFFIC AND PARKING RULES

As mentioned in the introduction, private facilities are exempt from the application of the *Highway Traffic Act*, which means that the penalties under that legislation are not enforceable on private property. However, private property owners have a right to control entry onto and activities on their property by drivers.

In general, private facility owners enforce parking by issuing verbal or written warnings to people who violate traffic and parking rules. Repeat offenders may have their entry and/or driving privileges suspended. In some cases, employers may use other sanctions against employees who violate traffic rules—for example, serious offenders may lose certain employment privileges or be subject to disciplinary procedures and notices. In support of these sanctions, some private facilities issue traffic or parking tags or tickets, similar in design to public tickets. Where there is a ticketing policy in place, all security officers should receive training about how to fill out a ticket and how the system is administered.

In cases of serious violations—for example, where a driver's actions threaten the safety of others or damage private property—facility owners may seek to have the offender charged under the *Trespass to Property Act* or the *Criminal Code*.

ACCIDENTS

When a traffic accident occurs, security personnel should adopt the same priorities as with any security incident, working first to assist victims, before moving on to other concerns, such as preserving the crime scene.

When there are injured parties or damage to property is in excess of $1,000, the police should be called.

Regardless of whether police are involved in investigation of the accident, security personnel should quickly identify witnesses who might be useful in documenting the occurrence. When possible, witnesses should be interviewed at the scene of the accident, before their memory of the details has had a chance to erode. Security officers should also, as soon as possible, prepare a sketch or sketches describing the accident (see figure 8.2), because in many cases, vehicles will need to be moved to restore traffic flow. For a full discussion of reporting procedures for traffic accidents, see chapter 14.

SUMMARY

Security personnel may be called upon to manage traffic and parking on an employer's or client's property. While provincial traffic legislation is not enforceable

FIGURE 8.2 Sketch of an Intersection for an Accident Report

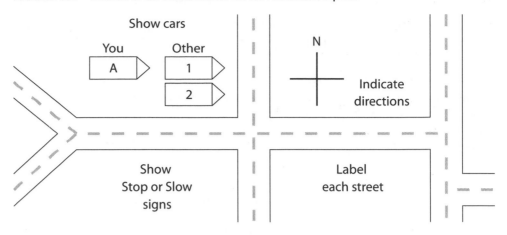

on private property, for the sake of consistency it is useful to adopt the same rules and standards for traffic management on private property.

In the interest of safety, security personnel must wear appropriate apparel to direct traffic, and they must receive training on how to position themselves for the task.

The key to traffic management is clear and authoritative communication with drivers. This includes knowing the appropriate traffic-management hand signals, using them with precision, and maintaining authoritative eye contact.

Finally, accidents occurring on private property should be responded to in the same way as any other security incident. Even where police are involved, security personnel should gather the information needed to conduct their own investigation and submit an accurate and detailed report.

KEY TERMS

express authorization

implied authorization

PERFORMANCE APPLICATION

1. Why are security personnel responsible for the management of traffic on private sites?

2. In choosing signs, road configurations, and road markings for a private site, what should the security department keep in mind?

3. How does a private property holder enforce rules with respect to traffic on his or her property—that is, what are the consequences of traffic violations?

4. What type of clothing should a security officer wear for directing traffic?

5. List four different kinds of equipment that a security officer might use in support of his or her traffic-management duties.

6. What should a security officer consider in deciding where to stand to direct traffic?

7. How can a security officer ensure that his or her signals are clear and unambiguous?

8. What is the first priority in the event of a traffic accident on private property?

9. Why should security personnel sketch a diagram of the accident?

9 Radio Procedures and the Phonetic Alphabet

INTRODUCTION

In the 21st century, keeping up to date on developments with respect to communications is more vital in the security industry than in any other commercial field. Communications are key to managing emergency response systems. For example, the events in the United States on September 11, 2001 may not have been as tragic were it not for certain failures in communications. The radio networks of the New York fire departments and the police were on separate systems. They could not hear one another, so vital information that could have saved more lives was lost.

Professional security companies realize how important it is to have radios that work so they can pass critical information from point to point in their operations. Consequently, radios and radio systems used in the security industry are chosen carefully for their reliable performance under all circumstances.

> ## Chapter Objectives
>
> When you have completed this chapter, you will
>
> - have a basic knowledge and understanding of the use of hand-held radios.
>
> - have a basic knowledge and understanding of the phonetic alphabet.

PARTS OF A HAND-HELD RADIO

A hand-held radio has several parts. These parts and their use are as follows:

- **Antenna:** usually helical or whip style with a threaded base, the antenna is necessary for receiving transmissions.

- **External antenna jack:** connects an optional 50 ohms external antenna to the radio; also used for test procedures. The jack is fitted with a threaded protective cap, which should be left in place when the jack is not being used.

- **Universal accessory jack:** connects the optional external speaker-microphone or surveillance accessory to the radio. When an external speaker-microphone is connected, the internal speaker and microphone audio is muted and the transmitter can be keyed via the radio PTT switch or the remote PTT switch.

antenna
part of a hand-held radio for receiving transmissions

external antenna jack
part that connects an optional 50 ohms external antenna to a hand-held radio

universal accessory jack
part that connects the optional external speaker-microphone or surveillance accessory to a hand-held radio

Focus on Technology

Motorola MTX 8000 Hand-Held Radio

While there are many excellent hand-held radio systems available on the market, including digital and hybrid systems, an example of a radio system that is used by many security companies today is the Motorola MTX 8000 model.

This radio represents the most advanced and common hand-held radio technology used in the security industry today. One of the series' most important features is its noise-reduction microphone, which allows the user to hear every message clearly and without distortion, even in noisy environments. Powered by a 3-watt battery, it can remain operational up to eight consecutive hours. Another key feature is that officers can have private conversations with other members of the radio fleet or, if they need to talk to someone outside the radio fleet, they can make telephone calls via the radio's telephone interconnect capability. This radio model also has *Call Alert*, a pager service, and all three models in the series have *TalkGroup Scan*. With this feature, officers can monitor any combination of trunked systems, subfleets, or conventional channels in the same scan list.

	800	**900**
Frequency	851-870 MHz	935-941 MHz
Systems/Talkgroups	$^4/_4$ or $^{15}/_{10}$	$^4/_4$ or $^{15}/_{10}$
Size	6.3" x 2.34" x 1.54"	6.3" x 2.34" x 1.54"
Weight	19.4 oz.	19.4 oz.
Battery Life (@ 5-5-90)	8 hrs. (high cap)	8 hrs. (high cap)
Power Output	3W	3W
Channel Spacing	25 kHz	12.5 kHz
Sensitivity (12dB SINAD)	.28µV	.35µV
Selectivity (EIA SINAD)	−72 dB	−60 dB
Audio Output	500mW	500mW

frequency select switch
switch on a hand-held radio used to select the operating channel

on/off volume control
part on a hand-held radio that turns the radio on and off and adjusts the audio output level

monitor/reset switch
switch on a hand-held radio that monitors the channel for voice communication when depressed and held

PTT (push to talk) switch
switch on a hand-held radio that puts the radio in the transmit mode when depressed and held and in the receiving mode when released

■ **Frequency select switch:** selects the operating channel.

■ **On/off volume control:** turns the radio on and off and adjusts the audio output level.

■ **Monitor/reset switch:** when the switch is depressed and held, the channel is monitored for voice communication.

■ **PTT (push-to-talk) switch:** when the switch is depressed and held, the radio is in the transmit mode. When released, the radio operates in the receive mode.

Battery Installation or Replacement

Different radios have different installation set-ups. The following is an overview of general instructions for replacing a battery:

1. Turn off the radio and hold it in the left hand with the front of the radio facing up.

2. Disengage the battery latch from the battery by pushing and holding the latch toward the top of the radio.

3. With the battery latch disengaged, slide the battery from left to right to remove it from the base plate on the bottom of the radio housing.

4. To install the new battery, mate the notched end on the battery with the grooved base plate and slide the battery, from right to left, onto the base plate until engaged by the battery latch.

RADIO STORAGE

Usually, the radios kept on site for security officers are stored in a specific location within the main security office or operations centre. Strict control over who has access to the communication equipment is usually enforced. Upon opening the radio cabinet, the following procedure is usually followed:

Taking Out Radio

- Check to see if any batteries are on green. If they are, move them to the top shelf.
- Uplift carrying case and microphone.
- Lock up and return the key to Control.

Replacing Radio

- Turn radio off.
- Check to see if any batteries are on green.
- Take recharged battery and place in radio.
- Put used battery into charger.
- Store carrying case and belt attachment in the cabinet.
- Place radio in numbered slot in cabinet.
- Place microphone on top of radio.
- Lock up and return the key to Control.

SAFE USE OF HAND-HELD RADIOS

Follow these rules to avoid accidents:

- Do *not* hold the radio such that the antenna is very close to, or touching, exposed parts of the body, especially the face or eyes, while transmitting. The radio will perform best if the microphone is held two to three inches away from the mouth and the radio is vertical.

- Do *not* hold the transmit switch on when not actually making a transmission.

- Do *not* allow children to play with any radio equipment containing a transmitter.

- Do *not* operate a portable transmitter near unshielded electrical blasting caps or in an explosive atmosphere (for example, gas leak, bomb threat) unless it is a type specially designed for such use.

RADIO PROCEDURES AND ETIQUETTE

When using the radio, be aware that there may be "eavesdroppers," including members of the public, who have access to the network. Because officers never know who may be listening, good radio procedures can greatly enhance their professional image. Conversely, inappropriate radio procedures or etiquette can also be overheard and must be avoided. Officers should adopt a courteous code of behaviour at all times.

To enforce proper radio etiquette, most employers deal severely with all instances of improper or illegal use of the radio, profanity, or the use of the radio to play games, pranks, or practical jokes.

Besides general etiquette principles and the protocols developed by employers and clients, there are regulations in place with respect to the use of radio frequencies. In Canada, radio broadcasts are regulated by the Canadian Radio-television and Telecommunications Commission (CRTC), and by the minister of industry.

Step Aside

CRTC

Established in 1968 as the Canadian Radio-Television Commission, the CRTC reports to Parliament through the Canadian Heritage Ministry. The commission was established by the *Broadcasting Act* to set rules for the broadcast industry that ensure Canadians control the public airwaves. In 1976, Parliament gave the CRTC control over telecommunications companies and the name was changed to the Canadian Radio-television and Telecommunications Commission.

Minister of Industry

The minister of industry administers the *Radiocommunication Act*. The *Radiocommunication Act* and the regulations made under it establish rules for the use of radio equipment, and radio frequencies. Under section 5 of the *Radiocommunication Act*, the minister can issue licences for radio operators. Security service providers who use hand-held radios may be subject to such licences and the terms included in them. The *Radiocommunication Act* creates offences that can be charged in the event of misuse of a radio, or unlawful interference with radio frequencies (see section 9 of the Act). Good corporate radio-use protocol should incorporate rules for employees that promote compliance with the *Radiocommunication Act.*

SECURITY RADIO PROTOCOL

The following are general rules of protocol for operating hand-held radios:

- Do *not* cut into other people's transmissions.

- Do *not* use the paging encoder when others are transmitting.

- If someone else cuts into a transmission, do not retaliate with derogatory comments, as most interruptions are unintentional.

- Avoid unnecessary transmissions such as excessive numbers of radio checks or time checks.

- Do *not* use the radio for lengthy, non-urgent, and/or personal conversations.

- Speak at a normal voice level.

- Enunciate clearly.

- Think before you speak to avoid stuttering and repetitiveness.

- Be brief and to the point.

- Do *not* use slang, and this includes CB jargon. Professional security officers do not imitate a CB (citizens band) operation. Do not use, for example, "Roger … Over and Out," or "That's a Big 10–4."

- Use the standard 10 code, where possible, but also remember that clarity is the most important concern. Briefly clarify your message using plain English if required. Remember that 10–4 means "Message Understood/End of Transmission," *not* "Yes." Use "Affirmative" and "Negative" for "Yes" and "No."

- Do *not* use proper names on the radio. Always use assigned unit designations where possible. Some non-security personnel (for example, a maintenance worker) may be assigned "W" or workplace codes. They should be recognized and used at all times. For other people who have not been designated security "W" codes, or private codes, refer to them by title. Example: "Please call the scheduling coordinator" or "Please see the superintendent."

- Switch radios off and store them in the proper battery charger units when not in use.

- Report all damaged or malfunctioning radios immediately to the security supervisor and submit a full report. Radios needing repair should be sent out with a covering report listing specific details of the problem. The person who picks up a radio for repair usually signs for it at the control room.

CODE RED (FIRE)

When an alarm sounds, Control will come on the air and announce a Code Red in location X. Upon receipt of this, units should maintain a listening watch on their radios and refrain from transmitting anything to allow Control to proceed with emergency measures without any interruptions. Shortly after the Code Red transmission, security officers should receive a call advising them of the intended entry point of the fire service. At this stage, Control radios the various security officers on duty with directions as to who goes where and for what purpose.

Upon arrival of the fire department, the security officer who meets the trucks and the security officer who subsequently escorts them to the location of the fire keep in close contact with Control to report each step of the operation.

STANDARD RADIO 10 CODES

While not a complete list of the standard radio 10 codes, the list below represents the codes most used within the security industry:

10–0	Radio check
10–1	Negative copy
10–2	Positive copy
10–3	Stop transmitting
10–4	Message understood
10–5	Relay message
10–6	On standby unless urgent
10–7	Out of service—off the air
10–8	In service—on the air
10–9	Repeat
10–10	Go to
10–12	Mobile transport
10–19	Return to
10–20	Your/my location
10–21	Telephone
10–28	Vehicle licence check
10–30	Illegal use of radio
10–35	Cash escort
10–36	Time check
10–56	Coffee break/meal break
10–60	Suspect has no record
10–61	Undesirable personnel in area
10–76	En route to
10–77	ETA (estimated time of arrival)

Emergency 10 Codes

10–32	Officer down … requires assistance immediately
10–33	Emergency status (state nature)
10–50	Motor vehicle accident at
	Nature is (F) fatality
	(PD) property damage
	(P) personal injury
10–52	Request ambulance at
10–99	Bomb threat
10–100	Request police at

DEAD ZONES

Security officers may experience poor reception in some areas of a site and should move to another area to call for assistance if required. Security officers who are accustomed to a site will be able to identify communications problem zones, and these sites may require the use of TAC–2: a higher frequency range to allow confidential communications between two officers in the same general location. Be advised that TAC–2 is usually not monitored by Security Control and should only be used in emergencies where no other alternative is available.

RADIO LANGUAGE

The phonetic alphabet has been in use in maritime radio communications for almost a century. Developed to assist radio operators in sending and receiving clear messages over the airwaves, it became a standardized procedure for the military services during World War II. The use of standard phonics to clarify the sound of letters and vowels has been adopted in all parts of the world, including air traffic control. Some variations exist for specific groups of users and activities, such as truckers and CB users, but the phonetic alphabet used by the security industry is based on the standard military version.

Phonetic Alphabet Chart

ALFA—AL fah	**NOVEMBER**—no VEM ber
BRAVO—BRAH VOH	**OSCAR**—oss KAR
CHARLIE—CHAR lee	**PAPA**—Pah PAH
DELTA—DELL tah	**QUEBEC**—keb BECK
ECHO—ECK oh	**ROMEO**—ROW me oh
FOXTROT—FOKS trot	**SIERRA**—see AIR rah
GOLF—GOLF	**TANGO**—TANG go
HOTEL—hoh TELL	**UNIFORM**—YOU nee form
INDIA—IN dee ah	**VICTOR**—VIK tah
JULIET—JEW lee ET	**WHISKEY**—WISS key
KILO—KEY loh	**X-RAY**—ECKS RAY
LIMA—LEE mah	**YANKEE**—YANK key
MIKE—MIKE	**ZULU**—zoo loo

Note: The syllables printed in capital letters are to be stressed; for example, the two syllables in BRAH VOH are given equal emphasis, whereas the first syllable of AL fah is given emphasis.

Sample Sheet of Radio Transmissions

Radio Check

M8:	"Alpha 6 call M8 for a 10–0."
Alpha 6:	"M8 you are 10–2 Sir."
M8:	"10–2, 10–4 thank you, Sir."

Cash Escort

Alpha 6:	"M8 call Alpha 6."
M8:	"Go ahead Alpha 6."
Alpha 6:	"Sir, could you 10–10 the Yonge Info Booth for a 10–35?"
M8:	"10–4 Sir, be advised I'm 76 that 20, 77 2 minutes."
Alpha 6:	"10–4 Sir."

10/61

M5:	"M2 call M5."
M2:	"Go ahead M5."
M5:	"Sir, be advised there is a 10–61 approaching your 20. Blue shirt, white pants, bald headed, white male approx. 40 years old, carrying a bottle in a brown paper bag."
M2:	"Sir, be advised I have visual, will advise if back-up is needed."
M5:	"10-4 Sir, standing by."

Name Check

M3:	"Alpha 6 call M3 for a name check."
Alpha 6:	"Go ahead M3."
M3:	"Yonge Mall, level 3 west, opposite KSA Jewelers. Surname is Boyd. That is BRAVO, OSCAR, YANKEE, DELTA, G1 of Phillip, G2 of Andrew. Date of birth: 12th Nov. 1954."
Alpha 6:	"10–4 Sir, stand by."
Alpha 6:	"M3 call Alpha 6."
M3:	"Go ahead, Sir."
Alpha 6:	"Sir, be advised your suspect is 10–60, that is 10–6, 0."
M3:	"10–4 Sir, thank you."

Store Front Patrol

M7:	"Alpha 6 call M7."
Alpha 6:	"Go ahead Sir."
M7:	"Be advised M7, M8 commencing storefront checks, level 4."
Alpha 6:	"10–4 Sir."
M7:	"Alpha 6, be advised employees still in Pizzazz."
Alpha 6:	"10–4 Sir."
M7:	"Alpha 6, be advised M7, M8 completed storefronts, level 4, commencing storefront checks, level 3."
Alpha 6:	"10–4 Sir."

Stat 100

M8:	"Stat 100 Yonge Parkade, level 3 south."
M9:	"M9 responding – 77– 30 secs."
M10:	"M10 responding – 77– 1 min."
M11:	"M11 responding – 77– 2 mins."

Lost Property

Alpha 6:	"M5 call Alpha 6."
M5:	"Go ahead Sir."
Alpha 6:	"Could you 10–10 the Yonge Info Booth to take a lost property report?"
M5:	"10–4 Sir, 76, 77 approx 2 mins."

A Spill or Clean Up

M4:	"HB1 call M4."
HB1:	"Go ahead Sir."
M4:	"Sir, could you have one of your employees go to the bench in front of The Nag's Head, level 2 Yonge Mall, to clean up a spill of coke and ice-cream?"
HB1:	"10–4 Sir, I'll have someone there shortly."
M4:	"10–4 Sir, thank you."

Status Check (after midnight)

M1:	"M2 call Ml."
M2:	"Go ahead Sir."
M1:	"Status in Dundas Mall Sir?"
M2:	"Very quiet, no incidents to report Sir."
M1:	"10–4 thank you Sir."

Note: The radio transmission protocol used in these examples is only a guide.

SUMMARY

This chapter introduced the use of the security radio for operational duties. Also introduced were the basic care, maintenance, security, and operating principles of a radio unit. By combining the operational functions of the radio with approved voice communication protocols, you can now use any security radio system with more confidence.

KEY TERMS

antenna

external antenna jack

frequency select switch

monitor/reset switch

on/off volume control

PTT (push to talk) switch

universal accessory jack

PERFORMANCE APPLICATION

1. What do each of these 10 codes stand for?

    (a) 10–35

    (b) 10–19

    (c) 10–100

    (d) 10–4

    (e) 10–61

    (f) 10–50

    (g) 10–3

2. Give the appropriate 10 code for each phrase listed below:

    (a) Time check

    (b) On standby unless urgent

    (c) Emergency status

    (d) Radio check

    (e) In service—on the air

    (f) Bomb threat

3. Why do security officers use 10 codes in their messages to each other?

4. Identify the following aircraft call signs in phonetic alphabet words:

    (a) TCF

    (b) BHP

    (c) AMZ

    (d) GRW

5. Spell your first and last name using the phonetic alphabet.

6. Explain why using the phonetic alphabet is so important to radio communications today.

7. What is a communications dead zone? How are communications handled in such an area?

10 Monitoring Security Systems

INTRODUCTION

As explained in chapter 7, there is no better security system than the human (or canine) senses. However, having every inch of a facility under continual human observation is unrealistic—the human resources costs would be much too high, and the presence of an excessive number of security personnel might make other employees and the public nervous, rather than provide a sense of security. For these reasons, most facilities complement their human security resources with security technologies, such as alarms, intrusion detectors, and surveillance systems. To do the job well, the technologies chosen must be appropriate for the site, and their operation and maintenance must be well understood by security staff.

TYPES OF SECURITY TECHNOLOGIES

The primary automated security technologies with which security officers work are alarms, intrusion detectors, and **closed-circuit television (CCTV) systems**. These technologies will be discussed in detail in chapter 18. This chapter is intended to introduce the security duty of monitoring security technologies.

Chapter Objectives

When you have completed this chapter, you will

- be able to explain how automated security technologies support and complement the work of security personnel.

- be able to describe the duties of security professionals with respect to the maintenance and monitoring of security technology.

closed-circuit television (CCTV)
surveillance technology that allows security personnel to observe or record activity from a remote location

Step Aside

Security Technology Needs Assessment

An important facet of security is planning. The director of security (or whoever is in charge of security at a site) must work with the organization to determine the site's security needs. It is important to match security staffing and technology to the site's needs. Too few staff or outdated technology can put a site at significant risk; unnecessary or excessively sophisticated technology may represent an unwarranted expense.

In determining a site's security needs, the security planner will consider the site's security history. It's useful to ask:

- have there been actual robberies or acts of vandalism?

- if so, how often?

- when—during the day or night?

- have there been other crimes where unauthorized entry was achieved? Where? How?

- have other facilities in the area experienced similar, fewer, or more intrusions?

- how do your facility's breaches compare with local, provincial, or national industry benchmarks compiled by either the Canadian Society for Industrial Security, the Royal Canadian Mounted Police, or Statistics Canada?

Once these questions have been answered, the security planner will go on to study the interaction between security personnel and the physical security provided, taking into consideration the limitations of any physical barriers. Are there sufficient employees to patrol the outer barriers frequently enough to apprehend intruders at any given point along the perimeter?

If the answer is "no," the security planner will consider appropriate security technologies, such as alarm systems. Installing these will free up officers to do higher priority tasks, while presenting them with sufficient time to respond to intrusions of either the outer or inner defence barriers.

Alarms and Intrusion Detection Systems

An alarm system comprises three components (see figure 10.1):

1. A sensor that registers a triggering event, such as an intrusion;

2. A system (usually electrical, but there are other types) for transmitting a signal between the sensor and the receiver/sounder; and

3. A receiver/sounder that, upon receipt of the signal, either:

    (a) alerts security personnel to the triggering event (often by means of a sound or light signal); or

    (b) triggers an automated response, such as the operation of a sprinkler system.

Alarm systems have a wide range of applications. They can be designed to detect:

- fire;

- smoke;

- chemicals (such as carbon monoxide, carbon dioxide, or natural gas);

- humidity/water/flooding;

- changes in temperature;

FIGURE 10.1 Components of a Basic Alarm System

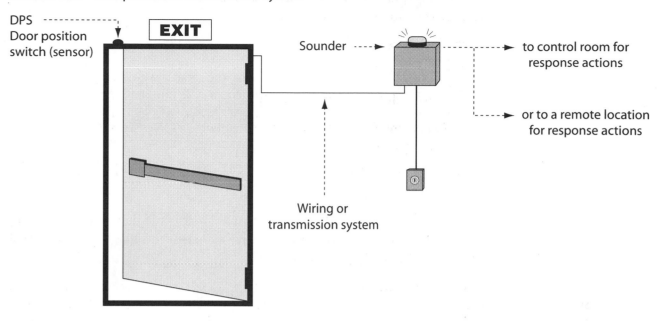

- machinery malfunction (for example, by detecting excessive vibrations from too-fast operation);

- disturbance/movement of objects; and

- intrusion.

A facility's choice of alarm systems will depend on the risks identified by the business. For example, a gallery where valuable artworks are stored may require sensors that detect an unacceptable increase in humidity. Any facility where flammable chemicals are stored may require sensors that detect high temperatures. Banks and many other businesses require intrusion detectors.

Closed-Circuit Television

Closed-circuit television is surveillance technology that allows security personnel to observe or record activity from a remote location. Where continual surveillance is desirable, and where it is impossible to patrol all parts of a facility at once, CCTV can be an invaluable early warning system, allowing for prompt security personnel response to an intrusion or other event.

CCTV also complements alarms and intrusion detectors by making it possible to "see" what has triggered an alarm. Knowing what to expect at an incident site greatly improves safety and helps personnel to prepare for problems, manage false alarms, and prioritize their responses.

Finally, the presence of CCTV acts as a deterrent to intrusion and other crimes.

ORIENTATION TO WORKSITE TECHNOLOGY

While this book and the course in which it is used provide an introduction to security technologies, it's important to realize that technology changes continually

What Would You Do?

Responding to an Intrusion Alarm

You are on midnight patrol and have been called to respond to an intrusion alarm in a mall. You have no information about what has triggered the alarm. Describe in detail the thoughts that should go through your mind as you drive into the parking lot and pull to a stop outside the mall entrance. Answer the following questions:

- What equipment might you need?

- What will you do first upon arriving on the scene?

- What will you do next?

- What will you do if you cannot identify the cause for the alarm?

- What will you do if you encounter an intruder whom you suspect may be armed?

- What will you do if you encounter a simple trespasser?

- What will you do if you determine the alarm was caused by an equipment malfunction?

- What will you do after the situation is under control?

---

and that many facilities have systems that are custom-designed to meet their security needs. In order to understand the technological environment in which they are working, security personnel must request and be offered a thorough orientation to, and training in, the technology in use at a particular facility.

In particular, security personnel should know:

- which types of technologies are in place in the workplace;

- how multiple technologies are integrated (see chapter 18);

- the basic principles of operation of the systems in use;

- what the relevant sensors/receivers look like, where they are located, and their best position for proper functioning;

- common causes of false alarms;

- the nature of any past problems the security department has had with the equipment;

- how to test the equipment to determine whether it is working properly;

- how to inspect, clean, and maintain the equipment, and what problems to look for.

For those with an interest in technology, there are many sources, both in print and on the Internet, for further study of how a particular technology works. Being knowledgeable about the technology that supports the job and its benefits, applications, and limitations will make the security officer an asset to the security team.

AUTOMATED SECURITY SYSTEMS MAINTENANCE

Primary responsibility for the maintenance of a security system may lie either with the security department, or with an outside contractor. Regardless of the arrangement, the security department should have a good, basic understanding of how to troubleshoot the system, how to identify worn out parts, and how to keep it in good working order.

Inspections of all pieces of the security equipment should take place on a regularly scheduled basis. In addition, patrol officers should be instructed to examine sensors, wiring, control panels, and other equipment as part of their patrol function. Any changes observed with the position or operation of the equipment should be reported promptly. Tampering with equipment in advance of an intrusion attempt (including triggering nuisance alarms) is a common intrusion tactic, and patrol officers should be alert to this possibility.

AUTOMATED SECURITY SYSTEMS MONITORING

Monitoring an automated security system means much more than simply sitting around waiting for an alarm to sound, or for something suspicious to appear on the CCTV system. It is easy to become too reliant on technology and to become less vigilant as a result. Security officers must be trained to think dynamically about the monitoring function. For example, where a system triggers numerous nuisance alarms, instead of reflexively resetting the system each time, security officers should actively work to eliminate or reduce the false alarm triggers. They should watch for patterns and the possibility that false alarms are being caused by new factors. Routine factors that personnel have become used to should never be dismissed.

In monitoring CCTV technology, security officers should use all of the active observation skills that they would normally use on patrol (see chapter 7), because when the only sense being used is the visual (looking at a TV monitor), it's more difficult to pick up on potential problems.

SUMMARY

While no replacement for human senses and human judgment, modern alarm and surveillance technologies support the security function. They can assist in improving security coverage both in terms of area and time. While patrolling security officers cannot be everywhere at once, technology can, providing an early-warning system for security response.

Nevertheless, technology is useful only when it has been chosen for the needs of the site, when it is monitored intelligently by well-trained personnel, and when it is maintained in reliable working order.

This chapter introduced the duties of security personnel with respect to security technologies; chapter 18 will provide more technical detail about the technologies themselves.

KEY TERM

closed-circuit television (CCTV)

PERFORMANCE APPLICATION

1. List three kinds of security technologies.

2. Who decides whether security technologies are warranted in a facility? What kinds of factors dictate the choice of technologies?

3. What is an alarm? What are the three main components of an alarm system?

4. What is closed circuit television? What is it used for?

5. When monitoring alarms and CCTV technology, what skills must security personnel employ?

6. Draft a simple four- to six-point protocol for responding to what is suspected to be a false alarm.

11 Taking Notes

INTRODUCTION

People who think of security is as an action-based job are often surprised by the amount of paperwork required. Working in security means documenting a wide range of occurrences, both routine and non-routine. Because of this, security officers must either have or develop strong communication skills, both verbal and written. They must be able to speak clearly with enough detail for their instructions to be understood completely. They must be able to jot down notes and write reports that not only contain all information necessary to support informed decision making but are also neat and easy to read.

SECURITY REPORTS

In recording security-related incidents, security officers rely on three standard types of reports:

1. officers' notebooks/memo books;

2. the logbook;

3. incident/occurrence reports.

This chapter will introduce note taking and the use of the notebook or memo book. Report writing will be covered in chapter 14.

PURPOSE FOR MEMO OR NOTEBOOK

A notebook is intended to serve as a chronological record of a security officer's activities while on duty. It represents his or her findings, observations made, and actions taken during each duty period. The evidential integrity of the notebook requires that all matters—whether trivial or important—are recorded with the same level of accuracy and detail. A notebook is a security officer's lifeline. It serves the following purposes.

Chapter Objectives

When you have completed this chapter, you will

- know why a security officer must keep notes.

- know how to use a memo book properly.

- know how to make appropriate and useful notes.

Aide-Memoire

Because the significance of details may not become apparent until after an occurrence, appropriate notebook entries provide an essential written reference for later consultation—for example, when preparing for a court appearance months or even years after the fact.

Background for Other Officers

Accurate and complete notebook entries allow other security personnel and/or police to pick up the investigation where the security officer left off without reinterviewing witnesses and after the crime scene has been disturbed.

Grounds for Action

Notebook entries can serve as support for a security officer's decisions. For example, certain actions, such as searches, require that the officer had reasonable grounds to believe that an offence had been committed before the action was taken. Because actions, such as searches and arrests, will be scrutinized later, accurate notes help establish the appropriate grounds for an officer's actions. They can also establish that actions were taken to preserve the Charter rights of suspects.

Official Document

A security officer's notebook often becomes an exhibit—an official document—in any court case arising out of a security incident, and as such, may be examined by lawyers, judges, and the jury.

Legal Research Reference

Crown attorneys and defence lawyers may request access to your notebook for the preparation of their cases.

Performance Measurement and Employment Record

An officer's notes are a measurement of his or her work performance, competency, efficiency, and character. The way notes are kept and written can lead to recommendations for promotion and specialized duties.

Notes also become a record of the officer's days off, sick days, overtime, and special duties to verify his or her salary and vacation time.

SPECIFICATIONS AND SAFEKEEPING

Notebooks are generally issued by the security department. The typical notebook is hardbound, pocket-sized, with lined pages. Notebook pages are numbered to ensure continuity. Under no circumstances should pages be removed; doing so jeopardizes the integrity of the entire notebook.

Notebooks are considered the property of the organization, not the user. Notebooks are returned to storage at the end of a shift, and filled notebooks are placed in long-term storage for a minimum of seven years. Security officers are responsible for protecting their notebooks during a shift, which means keeping them in their possession for the entire shift. An officer should have only one notebook in use at a time. Requests to review another officer's notebook are generally processed through the supervisor.

At the end of a shift, the supervisor reviews all the notebooks. Any comments are made in red ink. Requests for corrections and additions are communicated promptly to the notebook's user, and the notebook is signed by the supervisor after his or her review.

RULES FOR TAKING NOTES

There are several general rules for taking notes. From a formatting standpoint, notes should be:

- in chronological order, with date and time recorded using the 24-hour clock;

- made as soon as possible after the event is observed;

- in the officer's own handwriting;

- in the same colour and type of ink (no pencil);

- corrected by crossing out the whole word(s) with a single line, *never* with whiteout or correction tape;

- handwritten or printed neatly and legibly;

- written on all lines and both sides of each page; and

- signed on each page with any corrections initialled.

From a content standpoint, the information should be:

- concise—use as few words as possible;

- detailed—while the notes should be concise, they should be complete in the sense that they contain all the necessary detail to support an officer's recollection of events;

- attributed to its source;

- neutral, objective, and free of personal bias;

- specific with respect to time (enter, for example, the time of gate checks while on patrol); and

- recorded using point form or abbreviations in common usage (see figure 11.1 on page 106) or abbreviations should be listed in the notebook.

Accurate notes are *correct*, *precise*, and *complete*. Not only, for example, must an officer be correct in noting that a broken window pane is on the west side of a door and not the east, but he or she must also be precise in noting the type of break (crack, shattered glass, hole), the time it was observed, and any other relevant information the officer observed that might be connected with the occurrence (for example, hearing a crash, or finding a projectile (a rock) on the inside near the broken pane).

WHAT TO REPORT

Security officers must report both routine and non-routine incidents. Routine incidents reported may include:

- patrol observations (including all clear/all's well observations);

- observations with respect to the state/condition of objects/equipment;

- observations with respect to things to watch, for example, potential hazards that may be developing (ice on walkways, etc.);

- observations with respect to human activities/normal traffic;

- false alarms and how they were handled; and

- anything else the officers have been instructed to observe.

Non-routine incidents may include:

- fires;

- bomb incidents;

- violence/assaults;

- thefts and intrusions;

- floods, lightning strikes, and other weather events;

- equipment malfunction;

- trespass incidents;

- medical emergencies and workplace accidents;

- vandalism;

- protests/demonstrations/labour relations incidents; and

- information technology (IT) incidents.

WHAT'S IMPORTANT?

In recording the details of an incident, it's important to learn how to prioritize information and express it in a complete and organized way. Determining what information is most relevant is a skill that can be learned, just like any other. A tool that may help officers develop this skill is self-questioning—asking questions of themselves and answering them with their notes.

For example, if an object needs to be described, officers can determine what information is required by using the acronym "wanted":

W   What are you describing?

A   Appearance (colour, size, material)

N   Number (how many articles, pieces, serial number)

T   Type (make and model)

E   Extraordinary (Are there any additional features that make it identifiable?)

D   Dollars (apparent value or worth)

Another common strategy for organizing information is to ask the "five W" questions: Who, What, Where, When, and Why, as well as How.

Who?

When describing a victim, suspect, or witness, and depending on the nature of the incident, an officer might note:

- gender;
- age (ask for a birth date; consider whether the age given seems plausible based on observation);
- height;
- weight;
- build;
- hair colour, texture, and style;
- facial hair;
- skin colour (be specific—is the person's skin fair, light, brown, black, olive?) Are there scars or marks? Birthmarks? Tattoos?
- eye colour and whether glasses are worn;
- teeth (protruding, false, irregular, decayed);
- speech (refined, vulgar, foreign, lisp, rapid);
- physical deformities;
- mannerisms/peculiarities;
- a full description of clothing;
- a full description of articles carried (purse, briefcase, cell phone, packages, etc.).

Upon interviewing the person, an officer should make note of some or all of the following, depending on the circumstances:

- complete and correct name, including full name, other names, initials, maiden names for married women, aliases, and nicknames; ensure spelling is accurate;
- address and phone numbers for home and business;
- occupation, employer, address, and phone number for work.

What?

Record details of injuries or damage observed. Describe vehicles involved, if any. Make notes about any physical evidence secured, where and how it was marked, where it will be stored, and in whose possession it was placed.

Where?

In describing locations, provide a complete street address. Then, describe the specific location of the incident by reference to non-movable landmarks—for example, 4 metres to the west of the main entrance gate. Be very specific. Note also the location of any evidence collected—for example, from the passenger-side floor of the silver Honda Accord, plate number ASKW 305.

When?

The time of an incident should be as accurate as possible. If unknown, it may be estimated—for example, between 1330 and 1430 hours. Use the 24-hour clock to ensure the time of day is never ambiguous.

The date recorded should include day, month, and year, and the day of the week. Note the weather conditions as well. Information such as light conditions, visibility, the position of the sun and the presence of moonlight may be useful in screening witness testimony for investigations or may be useful in court later.

Step Aside

Describing Vehicles

When describing a vehicle, the following information should be recorded:

1. licence plate number, colour, province/state, year, and validation number;

2. year of manufacture and make;

3. body type and colour;

4. numbers: vehicle identification number (VIN) and engine number;

5. accessories: radio, CD, cell phone, leather or fabric interior, etc.;

6. contents of car (trunk and passenger areas);

7. type of transmission, number of cylinders, size of engine;

8. odometer reading;

9. unusual details: damage, rust, dirt, stains, noise, smoke, dragging/dangling parts, stickers, and decorations; and

10. other basic information: owner's name, address, phone number, driver's licence number.

Why?

Include information regarding any actions or omissions that contributed to the incident. For example, were possessions left unattended or were keys left in a vehicle? Did a suspect use break-in tools? How do you know?

How?

When describing what has occurred, explain the events in chronological order. Note which information came from your own observations, and which information came from another person's description of the events.

RECORDING STATEMENTS IN THE MEMO BOOK

During a shift, it may be necessary for the security officer to take statements from witnesses at an accident or make one to an accused at the time an arrest is made. The information may be recorded in a memo book and transferred later to a statement form.

In both the memo book and on the statement form, quotation marks must be placed around everything the person was quoted as saying directly. Any paraphrasing of the person's comments must be made clear.

After recording the statement, the security officer should read back what has been written to the person being quoted. Then that person should initial the statement to confirm that it is correct. Any mistakes should be crossed out with a single line and initialled by both the security officer and the witness or the accused.

ABBREVIATIONS

Because security officers are expected to record notes as they occur throughout their shifts, using abbreviations familiar to all security personnel not only becomes part of the professional language but also a more efficient way to write notes. Contract security companies may provide their own list of abbreviations; if so, officers should comply with the employer's list. Some of the most common acronyms used in the security industry are shown in figure 11.1.

A SAMPLE DAY'S ENTRIES

Figure 11.2 is typical of entries security officers may make in their notebooks. As you can see, notebook entries (even in shorthand) must be accurate, readable, understandable, and meaningful; otherwise, they are of little value to the officer, to the supervisor, to fellow officers, or to lawyers presenting the notes in court. For accuracy, the time in the left margin is noted according to the 24-hour clock.

FINAL VERSION OF NOTES

Notes are prepared in several stages. Sometimes errors have to be corrected, facts corroborated, witness statements taken, and information checked and verified before the final version is produced.

FIGURE 11.1 Common Acronyms in the Security Industry

Acronym	Meaning
AC	Access control
AAO	All appears to be in order
A/D	Account director
CPIC	Canadian Police Information Centre
DOB	Date of birth
FL X FL	Floor-by-floor patrol
ID	Identity
MP	Mall patrol
M/S	Mobile supervisor
NFA	No fixed address
NFC	No found cause (of alarm)
OC	Operations centre
O/S	Operation supervisor
PLS	Please
PO	Police or peace officer
PP	Perimeter patrol
R & PG	Reasonable and probable grounds
SAG	Special assignment group
S/O	Security officer
SOR	Special occurrence report
S/S	Shift (or site) supervisor
TPA	Trespass arrest
TPI	Trespass notice issued
U/K	Unknown

When preparing the final version of your notes, check the following:

- If something has to be altered, say so.

- Make alterations by drawing a line through the entry, add the correction, then initial and date it.

- If it is discovered that material has been omitted, add it by putting the word "Addendum" at the end of the notes and adding the date.

USE OF NOTES IN COURT

When security officers are asked to give testimony in court, they should bring their notebook(s). All confidential information that does not relate to the incident that is the subject of the court case should be secured by binding the pages containing unrelated notes both before and after the pages required for use in court with rubber bands.

If it will help in giving testimony, officers should ask the judge for permission to refer to their notes. Officers should be prepared for defence counsel to challenge the accuracy and the integrity of their notebooks.

In court, security officers should candidly admit if they have prepared their notes in conjunction with another person, omitted or altered anything, or made a mistake.

FIGURE 11.2   Entries in a Security Officer's Notebook

	Wednesday, September 10, 2003	**1**
0700	Start shift. Walk around. Weather clear, cool.	
0730	Good visibility, roads dry. Call to attend warehouse B; motion detector triggered.	
0736	Arrive scene & observe minor disarray, trashcan upturned, spillage of discarded coffee cups, paw prints, apparently raccoon tracks on linoleum. Scuffling sounds heard behind styrofoam sheets against east wall.	
0743	Raccoon located behind styrofoam sheet and chased out of warehouse. Inspection of premises revealed no other animals or humans present. Garbage cleared.	
0752	Return to control room, alarm reset.	
0756	False alarm report completed.	

SUMMARY

This chapter described the purpose and procedures for using memo books, the basic rules of taking notes, and the kinds of details that should be included in notebooks.

The importance of taking proper notes and writing reports cannot be overemphasized. The preparation of notes and report writing are tasks that are performed daily. An officer who is capable of producing accurate and concise reports on a consistent basis will prove to be an asset to any organization.

PERFORMANCE APPLICATION

1. Whose property is the memo book?

2. Why are notebook pages numbered, and why must pages not be removed?

3. List three things a security officer should *not* do in a memo or notebook.

4. List three purposes of keeping a memo or notebook.

5. How can a notebook protect a security officer?

6. List 10 details a security officer should record when describing a person.

7. Explain how information collected from others is incorporated into the notebook.

8. Describe the potential role of an officer's notebook in a court case.

PART III   EXERCISE

On a memo book lined page, make complete entries to note the incident described below:

It is Wednesday, September 10, 2003. Your shift starts at 1000 and ends at 1730. You are on duty in plain clothes at the Dundas and Yonge Street Eaton Centre in Toronto in the "Cool Fashions" boutique. The boutique is owned and operated by Janet Pickering, 118 St. Clair Avenue East, Toronto, Ontario. Phone 416-928-0001. At 1030 you observe a woman wearing an oversized trench coat walk into the store. It's 25 degrees Centigrade outside and sunny with clear skies. The air conditioning in the store is working, and you are comfortable wearing short sleeves. She slowly ambles up and down the aisles, touching the countertops and fingering the displays. Suddenly, she whisks a silk scarf into her right front hip pocket. Next she tries on a cloche hat and looks at herself in the mirror. She sees you in the reflection of the convex mirror behind her and puts the hat down. She picks up a white wool tam. As you pass her, you can see her slip it off her head in the reflection of the storefront window at the end of the aisle and stuff it inside her left-front hip pocket. You see her eye the jewelry tray, and she moves out of her line of sight of you, while you keep her in yours through the window's reflection. She fingers a gold chain and gold-loop earrings. She appears to hold them up to her face to see how she looks in them and as she removes the earrings, slips them into her left-front breast pocket and then gathers up the chain and pockets it in her right front hip pocket. You watch her walk past the cashier and exit the boutique's private property onto the public property of the mall floor.

You step forward and identify yourself as the boutique's security officer and invite her back into the store. She refuses. You tell her: "I saw you take a silk scarf, a white wool tam, a gold chain, and gold earrings and stuff them into your coat pockets without paying the cashier for these items. This is a prohibited activity. I am arresting you for stealing these items. It is my duty to inform you that you have the right to retain and instruct counsel without delay. Do you understand?" She looks stunned but nods in agreement. You further tell her, "I am calling the police to meet us here." You call the police and report the theft, while standing beside her and holding her right arm at the elbow. She looks ready to bolt but changes her mind.

At 1045, two officers arrive from 55 Division—Constable Michael O'Shea, 11 Manor Road, Willowdale, Ontario, and Sergeant Cathy Madison, 119 Forke Road, Leaside, Ontario. You report that the shoplifter refused to step back into the store and did not comply with a voluntary search. Sgt. Madison takes her by the elbow and tells her to step back into the store and directs her to stand in front of an empty cash counter. She tells the woman suspect to empty her pockets on the countertop. The suspect pulls out the scarf with a $59.98 tag, the tam tagged $34.95, and the gold chain tagged $69.85. She doesn't reach into her left-front breast pocket to remove the earrings. You tell the police officers that there are still earrings to retrieve from her left-front breast pocket. The suspect tries to deny it. You tell her, "I saw you put them there." Sgt. Madison tells her to remove the earrings or be subject to a body search. The suspect finally pulls out the earrings and lays them on the counter. They are tagged at $128.35. The sergeant informs the suspect that they are arresting her for stealing items from the boutique for a total value of $293.13. They take down the shoplifter's name, date of birth, address, and phone number and call in a criminal records check to the Canadian Police Information Centre (CPIC).

At 1055, the sergeant is called back and learns the thief has not been convicted of shoplifting at this time but has a history of being apprehended for this crime. Sgt. Madison informs her they will be taking her back to the station and asks you if you will deliver your notes on the incident to them after you finish writing them up. You agree. At 1100, the police officers escort the shoplifter from the store.

PART IV

Operational Practices

12 Interviewing

INTRODUCTION

When something out of the ordinary has occurred, particularly an incident that may lead to a criminal charge or civil court proceedings, it's essential to identify witnesses at an early stage.

From a practical perspective, passersby and other "chance" witnesses may be difficult or impossible to locate at a later time.

From a strategic perspective, having plenty of reliable witness evidence makes a successful investigation and/or prosecution much easier than a case in which it is necessary to draw inferences from things like physical evidence.

Witnesses who are particularly useful will often be those who:

- were at the scene of the occurrence;

- live near the scene or might have heard something;

- maintain records that are useful;

- had a reason or opportunity to observe what happened;

- had possessions found at the scene;

- know personally the party or parties involved.

To obtain evidence from witnesses that will stand up in court, security officers need to develop effective interviewing techniques. The success of the interview often hinges on the relationship the officer forms with subjects at the outset of the interview.

So, prior to requesting information, it is important for security officers to make it known that they have the authority to question witnesses in an ongoing investigation. Since people tend to be more impressed by what they believe than by what they see, they need to be given a definite reason to believe that their being interviewed is necessary and that their information will help the overall investigation.

Chapter Objectives

When you have completed this chapter, you will

- have a basic understanding of the cognitive interviewing process.

- understand successful interviewing techniques.

BEFORE THE INTERVIEW

Background and Planning

If time permits, it's useful to gather background information on a person before beginning an interview. The more information officers have about the person, the more details they will have to form questions. Some sources of relevant information are CPIC checks, other records, and information from previous cases.

In planning an interview, security officers will need to consider what information needs to be covered that is not yet covered by other witnesses, and then decide on the order of the witnesses for questioning.

In general, it's best to first interview people who have volunteered to make statements. Not only does it boost an officer's confidence, but the interview may also provide information that will help open up more reluctant or even hostile witnesses in later interviews.

The interview schedule should allow enough time for extensive questioning.

Interview Location

It is usually desirable to conduct the interview in a location that is unfamiliar to the subject, although cooperative witnesses may be interviewed in their home or office.

It's best to conduct the interviews at a time that is convenient for the witnesses so that they don't feel rushed or irritated.

Make sure there are no distractions while the interview is being conducted. For example, if the interview is being conducted in a patrol car, the vehicle should be positioned so that the subject is not continually looking at the scene. The best setting for an interview is a private room that has no view from the windows, no telephones, and no possibilities of interruption. Sometimes, it may be necessary to take the witness back to the incident scene.

Another reason why private interviews are best is to avoid witness conformity. When there are multiple witnesses at the crime scene, it is not uncommon for one or more witness to conform to the group's opinion, even if it's based on inaccurate information.

Consider Motive and Capacity

A witness's motive for speaking may be a clue to his or her reliability. Some individuals who seem excessively eager to discuss the incident may have an agenda of their own that is not consistent with an officer's investigation. Be alert to this possibility, and, if necessary, question a witness about his or her motives.

Other witnesses may simply be attention-seekers looking for an audience. While they may have useful information to share, they may have an increased tendency to exaggerate or to overemphasize their role in the events under examination.

Besides motive, it is essential to assess a witness's capacity to give a reliable statement. Factors that may affect capacity or the reliability of a witness's evidence may include:

- cognitive impairment or handicap;

- the influence of alcohol or drugs;

- problems with eyesight, hearing, or other senses;

- mental illness;

- memory problems, whether due to injury or aging; and

- language barriers.

Suspicion of any of these factors should be noted in the officer's notebook.

PROMOTING WITNESS COOPERATION

Resistant Witnesses

In many cases, particularly when a witness is a suspect, he or she may be hesitant to speak, because the witness does not believe he or she is duty-bound to answer to a stranger.

Encouraging a hesitant witness to speak openly requires a considerable degree of interpersonal sensitivity. In the first few seconds of the conversation, try to determine the reason for a witness's reluctance. Perhaps the witness is simply unsure of the officer's role. Security officers should introduce themselves and explain their authority as the person charged with investigating the incident. Maybe the witness is shy or intimidated by the officer's position? Without excessive informality (which might undermine authority), the officer should put the witness at ease. A good way to do this is to begin with easy, neutral questions, such as name and address. One useful technique may be to have a friend or relative encourage the witness to help out.

If the witness appears to want to challenge an officer's authority, the task is more difficult. Often the best approach is to explain politely that the witness's information is important and useful to the investigation. Speaking now may save the witness from being summoned by police later (though security officers can't guarantee this). Encourage the witness to see the interview as a way to assist the victim, rather than as a favour to the security officer. Finally, while it is never acceptable to threaten a suspect–witness, some people respond to the suggestion that an interview is an opportunity to "clear the air" or to "get something off your chest."

Developing an attitude that is both authoritative and approachable is a true art, and well worth practising.

Encouraging Disclosure

Even if a witness is willing to speak, it is important to create an atmosphere in which the witness is comfortable enough to speak freely and in detail.

Security officers may have to overcome a natural tendency to be reserved with people they don't know. Witnesses are not likely to cooperate or give the required information, if they detect doubt, coolness, or even hostility in an officer's tone. Most witnesses and suspects are nervous about giving information, so officers need to show a friendly interest in them to encourage their disclosure.

What is even more important is that officers need to be sensitive listeners, the kind who can mirror the feelings of others with empathy. It goes back to the old saying, "You can catch more flies with honey than you can with vinegar."

In general, it is best to begin the interview by listening, and to move only at a later stage into a more questioning approach.

THE INTERVIEW PROCESS

While security officers should develop an interview technique that is comfortable and effective for them, there are some proven strategies that may assist in getting the most out of witnesses.

To put the interview subject at ease, first establish their cooperation. Start with easy questions that they can readily answer and avoid those that intimidate or cause a contrary reaction. Show them there is no doubt about their willingness to cooperate. If a witness does begin to talk spontaneously, listen actively without interruption to encourage the maximum possible disclosure.

Security officers should control their reactions to the information a witness gives. Very positive feedback may encourage a witness to embellish, and negative feedback may encourage a witness to change the story in an attempt to please the officer. A witness may feel uncomfortable or embarrassed by some of the details. Failure to react to these details helps the witness "save face," builds trust, and promotes disclosure.

Specific and Open-Ended Questions

direct question
question that requests a specific piece of information

While **direct questions**—ones that request a specific piece of information—can help clarify ambiguous issues, or address needed points, they should be used sparingly. Witnesses can find these questions intimidating, and there is a danger that a suggestion will later be made that the officer "led" the witness to a particular conclusion.

open-ended question
question that requires an expanded answer

Open-ended questions, by contrast, encourage longer answers and are less likely to influence the content of the answer. An open-ended question is formed so that it cannot be answered with "yes" or "no." Instead, the question requires an expanded answer or in the case of a why/why not question, an opinion.

When using open-ended questions, consider the following:

- allow plenty of time for an answer, and do not interrupt;

- use the occasional direct question to get the interview back on track if the witness is wandering;

- ask for clarification about confusing points before having the witness continue;

- encourage the witness to add as much detail as possible. This can be accomplished by asking why/why not questions, by asking the witness *how* something happened, or by simply asking if the witness has anything more to add.

Learning to use direct questions judiciously is a skill. The following guidelines are helpful:

- Ask only one question at a time, and frame the question so that one answer is required.

- Do not use shrewd approaches or tricks on a witness. Be honest and straightforward. Give time for answers.

- Avoid suggesting answers in the question. For example, do not ask, "Did you see a blue Chevrolet"? This makes the witness think of this kind of car.

- Do not use direct questions as a means of sharing new evidence with a witness in an effort to influence the witness's own statement. For example, do not say, "We found a chisel at the scene. Did the man you saw have a chisel in his hand"?

- If a witness appears to be "drying up," change the subject for a while or switch to open-ended questions.

- Before making an assumption, be sure to understand a witness's answer. Ask further questions if necessary instead of making inappropriate inferences.

- If repeating a question fails to elicit a response, rephrase it. The witness may not have understood what is wanted.

QUICK QUESTIONS

Direct Questions and Open-Ended Questions

Examples of direct questions are:

- Was it a grey car or a silver car?

- Did the intruder have a gun?

- Did you hear the door slam shut?

- Were the kids spray painting the fence?

- Are you sure the man was clean shaven?

- Did she mean to force the gate?

Examples of open-ended questions are:

- Please describe the car you told me you saw.

- Do you believe the man you saw was armed? Why?

- What did you hear?

- Did you see the kids? What did you see?

- Can you describe the person you saw?

- What did she do when she reached the gate?

THE COGNITIVE INTERVIEW

The **cognitive interview** is another tool that security officers can incorporate in their interview routine. This technique was first developed by Ronald P. Fisher and Edward Geiselman and is now used extensively in law enforcement circles.

The basic premise of the cognitive interview is that information recall is best promoted by assisting the interview subject to revisit the context of the information. In conducting a cognitive interview, the interviewer seeks to recreate the environment, mood, setting, and experiences for a witness by asking him or her to mentally relive the events before, during, and after the incident.

This process consists of four steps—reinstating the context, changing sequence, changing perspective, and retrieving specific details.

cognitive interview
technique developed by Ronald P. Fisher and Edward Geiselman to promote information recall by assisting the interview subject to revisit the context of the information, using four steps—reinstating the context, changing sequence, changing perspective, and retrieving specific details

Reinstating the Context

To put the witness back in that space and time, an officer might say, "Let's see. It is about 9:00 in the morning and you have already put in a full day. How did your day start? What time did you get up? What did you have for breakfast? What did you and the children do? What did they wear? When did you leave to take them to school? What route did you take after you dropped them off? What route did you follow to work and is there anything else you want to share about what you did before you arrived at work?"

By the time the witness is asked to discuss the bomb threat that happened at 9:00, it has been placed into a framework where she is comfortable remembering what happened that day.

Changing Sequence

The natural way for a witness to recount events is in sequence starting at the beginning. To test the reliability of the information, you need to determine whether the witness's story changes if the sequence is disrupted. You start at the end of the event (that is, when you arrived) and work backward. This forces the witness to concentrate harder on each detail because telling a story backward feels unnatural. It is easier to tell a lie over and over in the same chronological order from the beginning than it is to recount a story haphazardly from the end.

Changing Perspective

Changing perspective reduces stress. This allows witnesses to detach themselves from their emotional involvement with the event and to seek their recall of the event from the point of view of another person. You might have the witness imagine himself as the victim, as another witness in another area of the incident scene, or as someone observing the scene through the lens of a camera.

By prompting witnesses to consider events from a different physical perspective, interviewers give them the opportunity to recall more of their experiences.

Retrieving Specific Details

After a witness has described an event in the order it occurred, in reverse order, and then from different points of view, help her remember more specific things by asking her to relate what she saw to something familiar.

"You said the suspect was very tall. How tall? Does he remind you of anyone you know or maybe a character you've seen in a movie?"

"Earlier, you said the suspect glared at you. Do you know why he did that? What were you doing when he glared at you? Could you describe his expression in more detail, please?"

When trying to get witnesses to remember a licence number or phone number, get them to focus on the first letter or digit. And then direct them to concentrate on the next letter or number like building blocks of memory.

This technique attempts to avoid the original sequence of the event and requires witnesses to recall specific parts of the event as instructed. It is especially useful in checking the accuracy of certain parts of the event such as times, arrival of specific persons to the scene, and the sequence of important details.

WITNESS STATEMENTS

witness statement
formal, written record of what a witness observed, knows, and perceives

A **witness statement** is a formal, written record of what a witness observed, knows, and perceives. It represents what a witness, if asked appropriate questions, will say in court.

A witness statement does not replace the witness's verbal version of the testimony in court, and a security or police officer cannot read it during court proceedings.

Rather, witnesses can use this statement to refresh their memory before a trial, providing:

- they read the statement at the time it was given to the security officer or police;

- they signed it; and

- they gave the statement shortly after they made their observations.

Witness statements (sometimes called "will-says") serve several purposes:

- They let the Crown know what the witness is going to testify about in court.

- They provide a record that can justify the security or investigative officer's authority to make an arrest, issue a subpoena to the witness, and/or get a search warrant.

- They help officers and witnesses refresh their memory about what happened.

A witness statement can also help a Crown or defence attorney to identify **hostile witnesses**—witnesses who, even though called by a party, may present evidence that does not support the party's position. A person declared a hostile witness can be cross-examined by his or her own "side" of the case.

Witness statements should:

- be written in the first person;

- be a reflection of the witness's own perception;

- contain no hearsay;

- be written on only one side of ruled paper;

- be recorded in sequential order;

- be specific with respect to detail;

- be structured in four parts:

  1. heading (name of person giving statement, date and time statement was made, location where statement was made, and name of security officer taking the statement);

  2. identification (person making the statement writes in first person and provides name, age, address, telephone number, and occupation);

  3. body (chronological narrative of what was experienced and seen in detail); and

  4. closing (witness and security officer sign each page of the statement at the bottom; the witness signs the statement at the end, declaring that the written text is true and indicates the total number of pages and the date).

Recording information provided by witnesses can be very difficult, especially hand-written, word-for-word accounts, because people tend to talk faster than most people can write. When remarks become too drawn out, officers may resort to paraphrasing what was said in favour of cutting down the wordiness in the report.

hostile witness
person who may present evidence that does not support the position of the side that called the witness

Focus on Technology

Recorded Interviews and Statements on Cassette Tape or Digital Recorder

In some instances, and if the technology is available, interviews or statements can be recorded on a portable tape recorder. There are many types available, and some models are designed specifically for this type of use. More sophisticated tape recorders offer features that allow officers to "mark" places on the tape for future reference or to play back a tape at a slower speed.

When an interview is very important to the investigation, it is essential that nothing be missed. The officer should ask the witness if he or she would mind the conversation being recorded. It is not appropriate to record a conversation without the witness's express consent.

When taping an interview:

■ Be sure there are fresh batteries and a cassette in the machine, and that there is sufficient room left on the cassette; for a digital recorder, ensure file space is available.

■ Have the witness repeat his or her consent to be taped while the tape is running.

■ If the witness seems uncomfortable about the taping despite having consented, it may be necessary to stop taping in order to get full and uninhibited disclosure.

■ Even when an interview is being taped, an officer should take backup notes in case there is a problem with the recording.

■ After the interview, the necessary quotations should be entered into the officer's notebook, and/or into the appropriate report; save the cassette for later reference.

■ Have the witness review the transcription and initial it to indicate accuracy.

---

beyond a reasonable doubt
standard of proof whereby a defendant's guilt must be proven to the extent that a reasonable person would have no choice but to conclude that the defendant committed the offence

actus reus
act referred to as a voluntary action, omission, or state of being forbidden by the *Criminal Code*

Condensing what someone says, however, leaves room for interpretation, and thus error. To avoid misrepresenting the witness, have the witness read the finished statement. If mistakes exist, the witness should draw a line through them, initial them, and add any corrections. The security officer must make sure the witness signs or initials the bottom of every page after the last word and initials all corrections, before he or she initials the witness's signature.

The security officer must also note the time the interview started, when it was completed, the location of the interview, and the presence of any other people during the interview. Always remember to thank witnesses for their time.

USE OF REPORTS AND STATEMENTS IN COURT

As a minimum requirement in a court of law, the Crown must establish the following in all offences: day, date, and time of the offence, where the offence took place, and the identity of the accused.

Before an accused can be found guilty of an offence, the Crown must prove **beyond a reasonable doubt** that the accused committed the *actus reus* (physical act) and had the **mens rea** (mental state or motivation) to commit the offence. Witness statements and written reports provided by security and law enforcement officers to court attorneys help determine whether the evidence presented in a case does qualify beyond a reasonable doubt the guilt or innocence of the accused.

mens rea
deliberate intent to commit a wrongful act, with disregard for the consequence

SUMMARY

Despite sophisticated forensic technology, solving crimes still depends on information supplied by witnesses, and the way a witness is interviewed may prove to be key to the outcome of the investigation. Most victims and witnesses are willing to cooperate, but trying to remember exactly what they saw, heard, smelled, tasted, or touched during a traumatic moment in their life may be limited by the brain's protective shroud over painful or frightening memories. Simply asking the same questions over and over again is not enough. The cognitive technique in interviewing has proven more successful in opening the closed doors of a person's memory.

Learning the skills required to be an effective interviewer takes time and energy. After each interview, officers can assess their own performance by checking the authenticity of the information they got from the witness.

KEY TERMS

actus reus

beyond a reasonable doubt

cognitive interview

direct questions

hostile witness

mens rea

open-ended questions

witness statement

PERFORMANCE APPLICATION

1. How can a security officer make a victim or witness feel comfortable before the interview?

2. List three reasons why a witness may resist being interviewed, and how an officer might overcome that resistance.

3. Describe the ideal setting for a witness interview, and explain why it is ideal.

4. Why should a witness be interviewed alone (without other people around)?

5. List five factors that can affect a witness's capacity to give credible evidence.

6. Give six examples of direct/specific questions. Explain why these are used.

7. Give six examples of open-ended questions. Explain why these are used.

8. Explain the basic theory behind the cognitive interviewing technique.

9. Describe two questioning methods that are part of a cognitive interview.

13 Investigations and Physical Evidence

INTRODUCTION

Security personnel involved in investigations or attending incident scenes may become involved in the securing, handling, and processing of evidence or exhibits. A wide range of types of physical evidence can come under the control of a security officer, and each type requires particular handling and processing precautions. In certain minor incident investigations, a security officer may be responsible for exhibits from the start of an investigation to its conclusion. In the wake of more serious occurrences, security guards will play a role in securing and protecting evidence until other investigating authorities are on site and able to take over control.

TYPES OF SECURITY INVESTIGATIONS

Security officers typically conduct internal investigations if an incident falls under one of three categories—illegal activities, reportable illegal activities, and security breaches.

An **illegal activity** is any security violation or any activity or action contrary to any federal or provincial statute, such as the *Criminal Code*, *Trespass to Property Act*, or *Public Works Protection Act*. This includes activities such as theft, fraud, mischief, assault, trespassing, and weapons offences.

Reportable illegal activities are illegal activities including those that are suspected or known to have taken place in the past, currently taking place, or likely to take place in the future, that are required by law to be reported.

A **security breach** is defined as any violation of a workplace policy, procedure, practice, or direction. This class includes all non-criminal security incidents.

Chapter Objectives

When you have completed this chapter, you will

- have a basic understanding of how a security officer investigates incidents that occur at his or her place of work.

- know how to collect and protect the evidence that supports that investigation.

- be familiar with procedures for specific incidents.

- know how and when to notify of the proper authorities.

- know how to collect, protect, and dispose of evidence and protect an incident scene.

illegal activity

any action that is contrary to any federal or provincial statute

reportable illegal activity

any illegal activity that is suspected or known to have taken place in the past, currently taking place, or is likely to take place in the future that is required by federal or provincial statute to be reported

security breach

any violation of a workplace policy, procedure, practice, or direction

CONDUCTING AN INVESTIGATION

Security officers have to respond to every incident, conduct initial assessments, and submit incident reports to the security supervisor. The security supervisor may direct the officer to conclude the incident report or, in consultation with the security manager, assign someone to assist the officer in the investigation.

If, during the course of an investigation, it becomes apparent that a criminal act has taken place, the security supervisor must be notified immediately. The security supervisor will then call the external policing agency with jurisdiction in the area and advise them of the circumstances.

The most common investigation a security officer is asked to conduct is an investigation of an accident on the employer's or client's property.

If the investigation is not conducted properly, the security company may be held responsible for any actual or perceived acts of omission or negligence found to have violated the rights of any suspects. It is therefore essential for the security officer to perform in a way that preserves the rights of suspects and supports the credibility of the client and the security company.

Vehicle Accident Investigation

Security officers are usually the first responding authority to vehicle accidents on site. The officer's responsibilities here depend on existing conditions at the time of the incident.

Minor accidents are incidents that fall under the following:

minor accidents

any incident that is non-reportable to the provincial authority and in which there are no injuries, no serious vehicle or criminal violations, and damages are under $1,000

- Damage to vehicles is less than $1,000.

- The accident is non-reportable to the provincial authority.

- There are no injuries.

- No serious vehicle or criminal violations are noted.

In accidents of this nature, a security officer assesses the scene and accident, controls traffic, offers assistance where possible, obtains vehicle and driver particulars for an incident report, clears the scene, and files an incident report.

Serious or injury accidents are incidents that fall under the following:

serious or injury accidents

any incident in which there are injuries, vehicle or criminal violations, and damages are over $1,000

- Damage over $1,000.

- Persons are injured.

- Criminal or motor vehicle violations are noted.

In accidents of this nature, a security officer assesses the scene and accident, notifies the security supervisor, contacts the required assistance agency (police/ambulance/fire/tow truck), calls for assistance (if required), tends to the injured, secures the accident scene, and awaits arrival of the external policing agency. The officer is also required to secure and protect any obvious evidence (liquor/drugs/weapons), control traffic and any crowds that may have gathered, and, as soon as practical, document his or her involvement and submit an incident report.

RULES OF EVIDENCE

Evidence is the means by which facts or points of dispute can be supported or established. In general terms, evidence is something that tends to prove or give grounds for belief, in accordance with legal principles, of various elements necessary to support or establish that a specific act was in fact committed by the subject or an accused individual.

Types of Evidence

A successful investigation has, as its primary goal, the collection of three kinds of evidence: witness (oral/verbal) evidence, physical (or "real") evidence, and documentary evidence.

Verbal Evidence

Witnesses give verbal evidence under oath where they describe exactly what they actually saw, heard, smelled, felt, and tasted. If they describe what they perceived with their own senses, it's called direct evidence. If they try to repeat what someone else told them about the evidence, the court will often refuse to admit this portion of testimony because it is considered hearsay or "indirect" evidence.

Physical Evidence

For physical or real evidence to be admitted into the court record as an exhibit, it must first be identified by a witness. This will often be the person who discovered or collected the evidence at the crime scene (for example, a security officer). The witness must also prove to the court's satisfaction that the evidence has been kept in continuously traceable possession (this may require the testimony of more than one person), and protected from any influences (water, other people's fingerprints, fibres, etc.) that could affect its original state at the time of collection.

Documentary Evidence

For the Crown to win a conviction, the evidence presented must prove beyond any reasonable doubt that the accused is guilty to the court and jurors. Thus, evidence is split into two categories. **Primary evidence** consists of the presentation of the actual objects, witnesses, and documents and is the only evidence admitted into court; however, **secondary evidence** or a representative copy of the real evidence may be admissible if the actual evidence cannot be brought into the court room, such as a bank's vault door. In this case, when a witness endorses a specific drawing or photograph as an accurate representation of the original object, it becomes acceptable secondary evidence.

primary evidence
actual objects, witnesses, and documents

secondary evidence
representative copy of the real evidence that is documented by a witness

To identify and confirm the legitimacy of any written document or secondary evidence (replica), a witness must:

- have seen the person writing it at the time it was written to recognize and identify the handwriting;

- have personal knowledge of the person's handwriting to recognize and identify it; or

- be an expert in handwriting analysis to identify the person's handwriting.

Another form of secondary evidence is an automated printing of an invoice, cheque, or computer hard copy where an expert can confirm its authenticity either through the issue number or production process.

Today, documentary evidence has gone beyond the traditional written or typed page to embrace computer data stored on diskettes, zip disks, CDs, and hard drives. Likewise, e-commerce and e-mail over the Internet produce the new phenomenon of virtual evidence, but this involves a science that is outside the realm of the security officer. What security officers need to be aware of is how traditional crimes can be committed using one or more computers as tools in the commission of a crime. Computer investigations rely upon evidence stored as data and the timeline of dates and times that files were created, modified, and/or last accessed by the computer user.

Circumstantial Evidence

Not all evidence has to be verbal or physical to convict an accused. While one unproven fact cannot convince jurors to find a defendant guilty, facts, when inferred from proven evidence already admitted and pieced together, can create circumstances that tend to suggest guilt.

Expert Testimony

Some evidence can be very complicated. In these cases, the court requires a specialist or expert with the knowledge, skill, experience, training, or education in the subject to help a judge and jury understand the significance of the evidence offered, before they feel confident enough to make decisions that will affect their verdict.

Step Aside

Private E-mail Can Be Intercepted for Computer Safety Purposes

Bill C-14, an amendment to the *Criminal Code*, was passed in April 2004. One of the changes made by this amendment was the addition of a new exemption under section 184 of the Code to the offence of interception of private communications. This new law allows, under appropriate circumstances, for private communications, such as e-mail, to be intercepted by a third party for the purposes of protecting or maintaining computer systems. Section 184(2) sets out the specific conditions under which a private communication can be intercepted.

Standards of Proof

In a criminal case, the Crown must prove beyond a reasonable doubt to the jury and judge that the defendant is guilty. In a civil lawsuit, the onus is on the claimant (plaintiff) to establish to the judge that the odds probably favour his or her version of events over the defendant's. This is known as a **balance of probabilities**.

balance of probabilities
the ratio of likelihood to unlikelihood that a particular fact or conclusion is true, based on available evidence

Admissibility of Evidence

Regardless of the quality of evidence, unless there are overwhelming reasons to override the general rule, evidence will only be admitted in court if it was obtained through means that respected the law and the rights of the accused.

The most common reasons for real evidence to be deemed inadmissible is that the evidence cannot be "placed" at the scene of the crime by a witness's testimony, or that it has been contaminated.

The most common reason for the exclusion of statement evidence is that the evidence was collected in the context of a violation of a suspect's rights under the *Charter of Rights and Freedoms* (see chapter 5 on Powers of Arrest).

COLLECTION AND PRESERVATION OF PHYSICAL EVIDENCE

When security officers first come across the incident scene, it is critical that they stop and scan the entire area, examining everything in view for possible evidence. At the same time, they need to fix the placement of every object in their minds. First impressions are important and security officers should use all their senses. A perfume's scent, the smell of cigarette or cigar smoke, or chemical fumes may become key clues later in the investigation toward identifying the suspect who has fled the scene.

It is just as important to note what's missing from the scene: a picture from a wall or a matching bookend on the mantle.

It takes discipline to resist the urge to rush in, help victims, and snatch up evidence. Such careless action, however, can lose the Crown's case in court. Why? Tiny shreds of evidence that may identify a suspect more precisely may be overlooked, disturbed, or damaged. Moreover, hasty actions may result in depositing evidence, such as careless fingerprints or hair, on the scene. Later, these are collected as part of the evidence and tie up **forensics** teams with misleading possibilities. This is called **contaminating the evidence**, and if the defendant's lawyer can prove the evidence has been contaminated, it is inadmissible in court.

Instead, a security officer should pause, take everything in, note where pieces of evidence are, and then cautiously move through the scene without disturbing anything.

forensics
application of science to police work

contaminating the evidence
destroying, altering, or depositing physical evidence at a crime scene

Evidence Control

When security officers control evidence in lesser incidents, they are expected to:

1. Photograph any evidence at the scene, whenever possible.

2. Mark all exhibits for identification including the time, date, and initials (on the item when possible or to an attached tag or seal). This includes photographs after processing.

3. Keep a list of exhibits secured as evidence.

4. Seal the exhibit in an exhibit bag, if possible, and keep it in personal possession or under lock and key.

5. Maintain a control ledger on any movement of the exhibit from the time it is secured.

6. Dispose of exhibits (as directed by the security manager) at conclusion of the investigation or at the end of appeal periods if it has been used in court as evidence.

7. Maintain entries in their notebooks, documenting all details of their involvement with any evidence coming into their possession.

Securing and Protecting Evidence

When a security officer is responsible for securing and protecting evidence involved in more serious incident scenes or criminal investigations, they must:

1. Keep visual contact with the scene at all times.

2. Not touch or move any exhibits.

3. Not permit unauthorized persons to move or touch any evidence.

4. Assist external investigators where possible.

5. Account for evidence coming into their possession or under their control.

6. Keep detailed notes about any role they played in securing or protecting an incident scene. If necessary, draw a diagram of the scene to show where original evidence was found. Officers may be required to give supportive evidence in court.

Protecting Evidence

Evidence can be contaminated in a variety of ways, depending on the type of evidence or weather conditions, for instance. Security officers need to follow only a few basic rules in controlling or securing evidence to make sure it is not contaminated and therefore inadmissible in court:

1. Do not handle or touch exhibits that may contain fingerprints—for example, paper, glass, or other solid items. If it is necessary to handle exhibits, wear disposable gloves.

2. Items like clothing and other soft material should be placed in plastic exhibit bags.

3. Any fluids, including blood or other body fluids, should be protected and left for the experts.

4. Any evidence exposed to weather should be covered where possible or moved to a protected area. If it becomes necessary to move or bag it, do so as carefully as possible.

5. Tire impressions, footwear impressions, etc., should be protected until all investigations involving them are completed.

6. Weapons or tools should be protected and left for the experts or moved with caution with a minimum of handling and all appropriate protection.

Control and Continuity of Evidence

In the course of an investigation, evidence may pass from one person to another. Such a transfer constitutes **discontinuity of possession**. A security officer has to show the chain of custody of the item from the time it was received until admitted as evidence in court. Once the evidence is handed over to another individual, accountability for that item passes to that person. When unexplainable breaks in the continuity of any evidence occur, it immediately suggests there was an opportunity to tamper with an exhibit, and based on that doubt, renders it inadmissible as evidence.

When it is a security officer's responsibility to ensure continuity, he or she must:

1. Tag all evidence showing his or her initials, time, and date. This begins continuity.

2. Secure any evidence that is to remain in his or her possession under lock and key. Keep control of the key until the evidence goes to court or it is turned over to another authority.

3. Document any movement of evidence on a control sheet to support total continuity. This control sheet must remain with the evidence.

4. Document the continuity of evidence in his or her notebook as well. This record may have to be used in court for reference, especially when evidence is turned over to another authority.

discontinuity of possession
transferring evidence from one person to another

Record Keeping

It is important to maintain accurate records relating to the handling of evidence. Again, record all proceedings that take place with respect to the protection of the evidence at the scene of an incident. The notebook should contain information about the incident scene and any evidence involving security. Any logs or other records about the evidence can then be cross-referenced with these notes.

Consequences

The main consequence of mishandling evidence is the possibility of failing to bring an investigation to a successful conclusion. There is nothing more disheartening than having a case dismissed in court because of poor procedures in the handling, protection, and continuity of evidence. Even worse, the court's dismissal of any case presented by the security company may result in a lawsuit against the company, its client, and any participating security officer.

SUMMARY

This chapter discussed the types of incidents that are most commonly investigated by security personnel. It also discussed the involvement of security personnel in more serious investigations requiring the assistance of public law enforcement agencies. The basic rules of evidence and methods on how to protect the admissibility of evidence were introduced.

The preservation and protection of incident scenes, and the collection and storage of physical evidence were described. Security officers must learn to use the utmost care and caution whenever they become involved with any items of evidence and make sure they apply the required procedures at all times.

KEY TERMS

balance of probabilities

contaminating the evidence

discontinuity of possession

forensics

illegal activity

minor accidents

primary evidence

reportable illegal activity

secondary evidence

security breach

serious or injury accidents

PERFORMANCE APPLICATION

1. What types of incidents do security officers usually investigate?

2. Distinguish between a minor and major vehicle accident? List the steps that should be followed to investigate each type of accident.

3. What is evidence? List three types.

4. Why might a security guard who collected a piece of evidence (say, a chisel left at the crime scene) be require to testify in court? What types of questions do you expect would be asked?

5. What is the first thing a security officer should do upon arriving at an incident scene (after ensuring his or her immediate safety, of course)?

6. If you were charged with collecting evidence at a crime scene, how would you collect or protect, for example: a dropped access control card; scrape marks on a parking garage pillar; drops of blood on a concrete floor; an abandoned car.

7. Why is continuity in the possession of evidence so important? How is continuity established in court?

8. What could happen if you mishandle an investigation?

14 Report Writing

INTRODUCTION

In dealing with security incidents, security officers must discover and report the facts about what has happened. Reports are useful not only to the employer/client in reviewing what has happened, but they may also be used in a criminal case for prosecuting offenders or in a civil lawsuit. In order to be useful, security reports must be clear and understandable to a wide range of different types of readers.

REPORTING BASICS

To create a successful report, a security officers must have:

1. complete knowledge of the facts surrounding every occurrence;

2. the intelligence to interpret the facts;

3. the discipline to identify facts from hearsay or outright falsehood for the reader;

4. the ability to express these facts in the report.

Thus, security officers must record all the information necessary to compile a good report in their notebooks. To make ensure they have all the information possible, they need to note every complaint they receive, regardless of its apparent importance. Trivial matters may later become significant details in a police investigation. Most security organizations have report forms that cover practically every aspect of any occurrence.

Distinguishing Facts, Inferences, and Opinions

While report writing often requires the security officer to make inferences from facts, excessive speculation and/or reliance on hearsay evidence may limit the usefulness of reports. Security officers must learn how to tell the difference between fact,

> ### Chapter Objectives
>
> When you have completed this chapter, you will
>
> - understand the basic principles of effective report writing.
>
> - be familiar with the various types of reports security officers are required to write in the day-to-day performance of their duty.

inference, and opinion. They must also learn how to indicate secondary material, by making it clear, when using information from other sources, that the security officer is reporting what the person said, not vouching for the truth of the statement.

Facts

Facts are things security officers know for certain and that they can substantiate. Proof may consist of physical evidence, or of direct observation evidence—either the officer's or that of reliable witnesses.

A purely factual description of a break-and-enter scene might read something like this:

> The rear door was open. The lock was broken. A crowbar lay on the floor, and there was a set of footprints with toes pointing toward the interior of the building. The victim reported that various items were missing from different rooms.

Facts answer six questions—Who? What? When? Where? Why? and How?

Inferences

Inferences are deductions or hypothesis of what probably happened based on the facts the officer gathered at the crime scene. Formulating a hypothesis is not the reader's function; it is the reporter's responsibility. And here, the reporter is the security officer, performing his or her duty.

To develop a hypothesis, officers must make statements about the unknown based upon what they do know: in other words, inferences based on the facts or physical evidence, interviews, and investigative results. They can be trained to observe and to think through each occurrence and, in doing so, write an impartial and logical account of what probably transpired.

Most of the time inferences will be correct. But, officers must also recognize that they may be wrong. This is why it is crucial that they recognize that they are making an inference and not recording a fact. To make the difference clear to the reader, an officer must "tag" each inference as an inference to prevent misleading the reader.

To make an inference clear to the reader or to "tag" it, an officer would write the following in the occurrence report, (but *not* in a memo or notebook, where facts only are recorded):

> Based on the evidence gathered at the scene of the crime, including the fingerprints on the gun and the matching bullets, it appears that the victim was attacked by the accused.

Note the tags: "based on the evidence" and "it appears." Presenting an inference allows an officer to re-examine new information that might come forward as the investigation continues.

Opinions and Judgments

In addition to the facts, which *must* be included, and inferences, which *may* be included, an officer has to know how to recognize opinions and judgments, which should *never* be included in written reports.

Opinions are personal beliefs or so-called gut-feeling reactions with no substantial basis of evidence. This lack of solid factual support distinguishes opinions from inferences.

Judgments also have no place in security or police work. By judgments, we mean expressions of approval or disapproval. These judgments may occur in a blatant statement or more covertly in the slanting of information. A reporting officer, for instance, aware that a witness's statement was false, may write: "Witness is a liar." Such a declaration involves two assumptions: first, the witness knew the truth, and second, the witness deliberately misstated it. Neither assumption may be correct. Consequently, officers must refrain from using such open expressions of approval or disapproval. After all, to call a witness a liar is to imply that the witness consistently and deliberately gives false information.

Officers must also guard against using influential words that indicate approval or disapproval and may, as a consequence, affect the reader's perception of the report. For instance, writing the opinion "the accused was personable and unlikely to commit such a horrible crime" would reflect unprofessional and inappropriate judgment.

Descriptors that have a negative connotation, for example, "squeegee kid" or "bag lady," are to be avoided, because they imply judgments.

Even apparently harmless adverbs may reflect a judgment. Suppose an officer wrote, "The complainant lamely stated, 'I thought I had locked the door.'" The adverb "lamely" implies the officer questions the validity of the statement or finds it inadequate. Either reflects disapproval. The officer unintentionally influenced the reader's perception of the incident.

TYPES OF FACTUAL REPORTS

There are four types of factual reports: general occurrence reports (initial reports), form reports, specialized reports, and supplemental reports. The type of report to be used is based upon the type of investigation to be carried out.

General Occurrence Reports (Initial Reports)

The **general occurrence report** covers the preliminary investigation of an incident and is prepared by the security officer who was the first to encounter it before handing over the suspect to the police. Examples include arrest reports and security reports. The general occurrence report contains all or most of the following information:

- Type of crime or incident (classified)

- Date, time, and location

- Names addresses, postal code, telephone numbers of all involved

- Details of conversations with persons involved (witnesses, suspects, complainants, and victims)

- Detailed descriptions of persons, vehicles, property, and locations

- Statements of all facts relevant to the case and inferences related to the facts (that is, the officer's hypothesis)

general occurrence report
report of the preliminary investigation prepared by the security officer who was first to encounter the incident

Advantages of the General Occurrence Report

The report is in a narrative format, is freeform, continuous, and does not follow a prescribed pattern or outline. The focus is on a written recount of the incident in chronological order.

Disadvantages of the General Occurrence Report

The report is often too long and confusing, difficult to read, and time consuming to write.

Form Reports

form report
standardized report consisting mainly of blank spaces or check-off boxes that cover the essential data relating to specific crimes or events

The **form report** is designed to cover essential data relating to specific crimes or events. It is used where standardization of essential information is necessary, and it consists mainly of blank spaces or check boxes. Traffic reports (see figure 14.1), missing-person reports, stolen bicycle or vehicle reports, and security violations are examples of the form report.

Advantages of the Form Report

Form reports are quick and easy to fill in. They also reduce the danger of overlooking essential data.

Disadvantages of the Form Report

The form is restrictive. No two cases are the same. As a result, variations in detail or complexity cannot be expressed fully.

Specialized Reports

specialized report
flexible report used for complex and detailed investigations

Specialized reports are used for complex and detailed investigations and other non-routine matters. The format is generally flexible and centres on the story. Examples of specialized reports include court (Crown) briefs, private investigation reports, and security surveys.

Advantages of Specialized Reports

A specialized report can fit any type of case. It is flexible and allows for a more detailed document with full and complete information.

Disadvantages of Specialized Reports

Like the general occurrence report, it can be too long and confusing for the reader to read. The narrative form also makes it difficult and time consuming to pull out statistics.

supplemental report
report that complements the general occurrence report and the specialized report

Supplemental Reports

Supplemental reports are a continuation or addition to the general occurrence report and the specialized report. A supplemental report may be submitted by:

FIGURE 14.1   Traffic Report

Insurer	Agent or Broker	Claim No.

POLICY HOLDER

Name of Insured	Policy Number

Residence Phone ( )	Business Phone ( )

Home address	Postal Code

Business address	Postal Code

VEHICLE

Registered owner	Address

Actual owner	Address

Make of vehicle	Year	Model	Serial No.	Plate No. & Province

Mileage	Describe damage	$ Estimate of damage

DRIVER

Name of driver	Age	State any physical disabilities	How long driving?

Home address	Business address

Residence phone ( )	Business phone ( )	Driver's licence no.

Previous accidents or convictions	Date of accident: day/mt/yr

Time ☐ A.M ☐ P.M.	Lighting conditions ☐ Daylight ☐ Dusk ☐ Dark	Location of accident

Purpose vehicle used for at time of accident	Weather conditions	Road conditions

Your speed	Direction	Other vehicle's speed	Direction

Police investigation by	Charges

Had you taken any alcohol or drugs prior to the accident	Who was responsible? (State reason)

FIGURE 14.1 (Continued)

DAMAGE TO PROPERTY OF OTHERS

Name	Phone No.	Name	Phone No.
Address		Address	
Year and make of vehicle	Licence No.	Year and make of vehicle	Licence No.
Name of insurer	Policy No.	Name of insurer	Policy No.
Description of damage		Description of damage	
Where vehicle can be inspected		Where vehicle can be inspected	
Name of driver	Phone No.	Name of driver	Phone No.
Address		Address	

DETAILS OF PERSONS INJURED

Name	Age	Address	Phone No.	Nature of injuries	Hospital

DETAILS OF WITNESSES

	Witness No. 1	Witness No. 2	Witness No. 3
Name			
Address			
In which Vehicle?	☐ In your car? ☐ Car No. 1 ☐ Car No. 2 ☐ Other	☐ In your car? ☐ Car No. 1 ☐ Car No. 2 ☐ Other	☐ In your car? ☐ Car No. 1 ☐ Car No. 2 ☐ Other

FIGURE 14.1 (Concluded)

DESCRIPTION OF ACCIDENT

Illustrate position of cars at time of collision. Show any skid marks. Show direction of traffic (one way, two way, etc.)

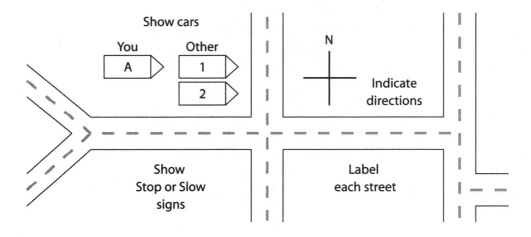

TO BE COMPLETED BY POLICYHOLDER

Who is the principal driver of your vehicle?	What is that driver's relationship to you?
Was the vehicle being used with your consent?	Vehicle leased from? Lien against vehicle by?
Signature of policyholder	Date: day/month/year

- the person originally assigned to the case;

- personnel assisting in the investigation;

- specialists, such as identification officers and youth bureau investigators.

Attachments to Reports

Attachments provide additional proof to regular reports. Examples of attachments that might be appended to reports are a driver's record check from the Ministry of Transportation, a criminal record, photos, and diagrams.

BASIC PRINCIPLES OF EFFECTIVE REPORT WRITING

A security report is any documentation recorded on a departmental form or other approved medium (for example, computer disks) and maintained as a permanent record. The goal of report writing is to recreate an occurrence or observation in its entirety and to eliminate confusion and loss of relevant information. Despite wide-ranging differences between the reports, the following general principles can be applied to write an effective report:

- Assume the reader has absolutely no knowledge of the occurrence, the people involved, or the location of the incident. Inform the reader of all details whether major or minor.

- Assume that there will be no opportunity to communicate verbally to the reader in order to clarify information. This will prevent vagueness and complacency in relating details.

- When describing an event or observation, avoid using general terms such as assault, theft, robbed, or damaged. Instead, describe the event fully so that the reader can recreate a mental image and conclude that an assault took place.

    Bill clenched his right fist and walked toward Helen. He raised his fist and struck Helen's chin.

- Avoid paraphrasing. Paraphrasing means condensing an observation to a minimal explanation. It lacks specific details and causes the reader to ask questions about the incident. An example of paraphrasing is, "Ralph saw Bill hit Helen." From this sort of statement, the reader would have several outstanding questions: Where was Ralph when he made the observations? Where was Bill? How exactly did Bill hit Helen? What were the relationships between these three people?

- All conversations, statements, and responses made by victims, suspects, or accused persons, and all witness statements (this includes the investigating officer, specialized officers, assisting officers, etc.) should be recorded verbatim.

- Physical evidence must be described in detail. Draw on the five senses and encourage witnesses to draw on theirs to recreate an image. Include the location in which the evidence was found and who had the chain of possession over the item.

- Use simple words to eliminate the need to explain further in explanatory phrases.

- Avoid grammatical and spelling errors.

- Avoid verbal diarrhea. Say it once in as few words as possible.

- Keep sentence length to no more than 15 to 18 words.

- Consider reader fatigue. Leave margins, use headings, and use a paragraph form, otherwise, readers will lose interest and will have trouble maintaining concentration.

- Before starting to write, collect the facts and assess and interpret their significance to the incident.

- Always use first person (the "I" voice) in the report.

- Note the condition and characteristics of the witnesses, suspects, and the accused. For example, are they intoxicated? Agitated? Do they have vision limitations? Write down everything that is relevant to the credibility of a witness.

- Include conclusions or inferences and recommendations in the report.

- Always reread the report for any mistakes in spelling or grammar and any omissions.

Step Aside

Remember the five Cs of good report writing: Clear, Concise, Complete, Correct, Chronological order.

SUMMARY

This chapter covered the basics of report writing, including the uses for security reports; distinguishing facts, inferences, and opinions; the different types of security reports; and tips for effective report writing.

Writing a good report is one of the most important communications skills security officers can develop, because they will do it every day of their professional life. It is, therefore, in their best interests to learn, practise, and perfect this skill to the best of their ability.

KEY TERMS

form report

general occurrence report

specialized report

supplemental report

PERFORMANCE APPLICATION

1. List at least two purposes for which a security report might be used.

2. What is an inference?

3. Why do security officers have to make inferences and how do they tag them in a formal report?

4. What important differences exist between the notes made in the security officer's notebook and the account of an incident in a general occurrence report?

5. Why is it important to avoid making judgments about individuals or situations in a report?

6. What is a supplemental report?

7. Give three examples of attachments that might accompany a report.

8. List at least four rules for effective report writing.

15 Courtroom Appearances

INTRODUCTION

A security officer's job is to protect assets, information, personnel, and facilities for either the employer or the employer's clients. Part of the routine, then, is dealing with people who have taken prohibited action or committed illegal acts. So, this means that some of the officers' time will be spent in court giving evidence as part of lawsuits against or criminal trials of these individuals.

For security officers, giving evidence in court means both stating the facts they've observed and reported for the plaintiff or prosecution, and answering cross-examination by the defence.

From the moment an investigation begins, the prosecution of a crime (or the pursuit of a damage settlement in civil court) also begins. The way security officers handle and record every detail directly affects the verdict in a criminal case, or the decision in a civil case.

Chapter Objectives

When you have completed this chapter, you will

- understand what is expected of a security officer who is called to testify as a witness in court.

- know how a security officer should conduct himself or herself in a professional manner.

BEFORE THE COURT DATE

The ability to provide useful evidence can depend significantly on the completeness and accuracy of the officer's memo book notes. Remember, in addition to testimony, the notebook and the general occurrence report can be presented as evidence and examined in court. Thus, written reports must also be a fair and honest account of what happened without any guesswork or suggestive hints to cloud the actual facts in the case.

Before security officers deliver any testimony in court, they need to study their notes to make sure they know the sequence of events, including times and dates, in the same chronological detail that they were recorded.

Accuracy is essential. If the defence establishes that a detail is lacking in even one area, it may be enough to cast doubt on all other aspects of an officer's testimony. Similarly, if an officer testifies on the witness stand to an important fact that is not reported in either the general occurrence report or the officer's notebook, the defence may suggest that the officer fabricated the fact because there is no recorded reference to it.

PROFESSIONAL APPEARANCE AND COURT APPAREL

Security officers can attain a high degree of credibility in the eyes of court officials and jurors simply by looking and acting professional at all times during the judicial proceedings. As an ambassador of both the client and the company, security officers are expected to remain professional at all times. In preparing for a court appearance, the following guidelines should be followed. A security officer should

- attend court in full security uniform, unless otherwise instructed; the uniform must be clean and neat in appearance—that is, clothes pressed, shoes shined, and so on;

- arrive early so that attendance can be noted by the lawyers prior to the beginning of the proceedings;

- act professionally outside the courtroom, both before and after the proceedings;

- avoid discussing the evidence with any person prior to court, except the prosecutor, the police officer in charge of the case, or a fellow security officer should it be required;

- commit the evidence to memory;

- stand erect, and speak slowly and distinctly while in the witness box;

- look in the general direction of the jury when speaking, unless responding directly to a question from the presiding court official.

USE OF NOTES IN COURT

If called to give testimony in court, after taking the stand, the officer should ask the judge for permission to refer to his or her notes. In particular, the officer may need to consult his or her memo book to provide such precise information as distances, measurements, or the exact words of a witness.

Security officers should be sufficiently familiar with their notes that they are prepared to quickly find the sections that apply to the case before the court. The fastest way to access their notes is to isolate the incident from other entries. Take one elastic band and wrap it from the first page of notes on what happened around all previous notebook entries to the front cover of the notebook. Similarly, separate the last page of the incident from all subsequent notebook entries and fasten those pages with another elastic band to the back cover of the memo book. This also prevents anyone from reading any confidential notes on other incidents not related to the case.

Security officers can expect the defence counsel to challenge their notebook by examining it, asking how, where, and when the notes were taken, and asking questions such as, "What was the weather like at the time?"

Officers should not be afraid to admit candidly in court that they have prepared their notes in conjunction with another person, especially with respect to confirmation of objective data, such as times and street names. They should also not be afraid to admit that they have omitted or altered something or that they have made a mistake.

What Would You Do?

An Error in Your Notes

You have been asked to testify in court about your fellow security officer's arrest of a teenage boy who was caught "keying" cars in your employer's underground parking garage.

At the time of the incident, you made only rather cursory notes, because you were busy with another security incident (a dog attack), and because you assumed that your co-worker would make detailed notes of his own. In particular, your notes about your own involvement in the early stages of the arrest—you were the first person to see the accused, and the first to approach him—are quite brief, and there is no thorough description of the accused.

By the time the trial comes around, however, your co-worker has been dismissed from his job, and cannot be located. As a result, you are being asked to testify. While you feel you remember the incident fairly well, you are worried about the sufficiency of your notes.

List at least six things you would do in this situation. Consider, for example:

- Would you add anything to your notes at this stage? Why or why not?

- What resources might you have at work to assist you in preparing for court (consider both people and things)?

- Is there anybody you should discuss your predicament with? Whom?

- How will you explain your incomplete notes in court?

- What approach will you take to answering cross-examination questions from the defence?

- How will you avoid this kind of problem in the future?

RULES FOR TESTIFYING

While providing evidence, security officers will most likely be asked open-ended questions. They should answer fully, but not volunteer more information than is requested. During cross-examination, officers should respond succinctly—if a simple "yes" or "no" will do and say nothing more. To volunteer anything further will only invite further questions.

If a judge rules that a particular question is not to be answered because the rules of evidence forbid it, officers should not show displeasure—to do so is disrespectful of the rules of court and is unprofessional.

Officers should *never* provide unsolicited information about a defendant's prior criminal record, convictions, or previous arrests. To do so could result in a mistrial, reversal of decision, or an appeal.

Never offer an opinion while delivering testimony before the court, unless requested to do so by the presiding court official, the Crown, or the defence counsel. Opinion evidence is usually provided only by expert witnesses.

Officers should avoid using police jargon or slang expressions. In many cases it will be a jury who has to understand the testimony. Officers should use words everyone can understand.

Step Aside

Roles of Courtroom Players in a Criminal Trial

The Judge

Criminal and civil trials are always presided over (directed) by a **judge**. In some cases, the judge is also the decision maker: he or she renders the verdict in the trial. In other cases, the **jury** renders the verdict, and the judge's role is to assist the jury in understanding, organizing, and considering the evidence. In all trials, the judge makes the decisions about whether to admit (let in to the court record) or exclude evidence. If evidence is presented but the judge feels, based on the rules of evidence, that it is not admissible, the jury (or the judge, if there is no jury) must not consider that evidence. The judge decides what happens in the course of a trial and answers all inquiries—from lawyers, witnesses, and the jury—about how the case will proceed.

The Jury

Many criminal trials and some civil cases are decided by a jury. The jury's role is mostly passive—jury members say nothing during the trial, they simply listen to the evidence. If they have questions, they address these to the judge. At the conclusion of the trial, after listening to the judge's instruction with respect to the evidence, the jury members go into a private room to discuss and agree on a verdict, which they then present to the court.

The Crown Attorney

The **Crown attorney** or prosecutor, sometimes also referred to simply as "the Crown," is the lawyer who presents the case on behalf of the government. The Crown needs to work closely with police and other key witnesses, including security professionals, to build a case on behalf of the government. The Crown may have assistants (usually other lawyers) who may contact security officers when they are asked to appear at trial. In order to win a criminal case, the Crown must prove beyond a reasonable doubt the necessary elements of the crime. Because of this, the Crown is said to have the **burden of proof**.

The Defence Counsel

The **defence counsel** is a lawyer either hired by the defendant privately, or, in the case of "duty counsel," provided by the court to work on behalf of the defendant. The defence's job is to refute (disprove) the Crown's case in an attempt to obtain an acquittal for the defendant. To do this, the defence needs to create, in the minds of the judge and/or the jury, a reasonable doubt as to whether the crime was committed by the accused. The defence may do this either by simply refuting the Crown's evidence, or by raising a **defence** (a denial or justification) on the defendant's part. If he or she chooses to raise a defence, the defence counsel has the burden of proof with respect to the elements of the defence.

The Witness

A **witness** is any person who is called to give verbal evidence in a court case. The accused can be a witness for the defence, though he or she is not required to testify. The victim can also be a witness, for the prosecution.

---

judge
court official appointed to try cases in a court of law

jury
group of 12 people (in criminal law) or 6 people (in civil law in most provinces) who decide the case based on the evidence presented

Crown attorney
lawyer who prosecutes the accused on behalf of the government

burden of proof
responsibility to provide evidence to support a particular conclusion

defence counsel
the lawyer who represents the accused

defence
denial of or justification for an act

witness
person who gives evidence while under oath

If either the prosecution/plaintiff's lawyer or the defence asks a question that the officer cannot answer, he or she should simply state, "I don't know." This will reflect poorly on the officer only if his or her investigation failed to uncover some important fact.

When responding to questions posed by the defence during cross-examination, officers should show the same respect for the defence counsel that they do for the Crown (or the plaintiff's attorney in a civil case).

Officers should listen very carefully and fully understand the defence's questions before attempting to answer during cross-examination. If a question is not understood, the officer should ask for it to be repeated or rephrased.

TIME OFF FOR COURT

Security officers are compensated by their employers at the regular rate of pay and/ or overtime rate, depending on the company's policies, for time spent off work to make court appearances.

Employers should be advised of the date of an officer's court appearance as soon as possible so that coverage for the work shift can be arranged.

SUMMARY

Security officers are expected to bring the same level of professionalism to their in-court duties that they bring to their everyday employment. The demeanour, appearance, and deportment of security officers reflects directly on the employer or client, so care should be taken to observe the guidelines described in this chapter.

A security officer's evidence can be of critical importance in a court case. As a result, it's essential for security officers to prepare carefully for court by reviewing their notes and to answer questions clearly, fully, and with complete honesty.

KEY TERMS

burden of proof

Crown attorney

defence

defence counsel

judge

jury

witness

PERFORMANCE APPLICATION

1. What should an officer wear to court? Why is grooming important?

2. List three tips for the effective use of notes in court.

3. Who will question an officer in court?

4. How does an officer's testimony for the prosecution differ from his or her testimony on cross-examination?

5. Why must an officer admit honestly to collaboration on notes, errors, and omissions?

6. How could an officer's testimony result in a mistrial, reversal of decision, or an appeal?

PART IV   EXERCISE

1. Write a missing-person report based on your interview of the victim's mother. Following the types of questions and interviewing techniques presented in this chapter, outline the questions you would ask the traumatized mother to get as much detail as you can about her missing daughter. Because this is a mock exercise, you will have to invent the details she would remember before you write up your missing-person report based on the following scenario:

   Shortly after your lunch break, you receive a call from the dispatcher telling you to go to apartment 603 in the Bellevue Condominium Building at 214 Moorehead Drive to take a missing-person report. You receive the call at 1255 hours and arrive at apartment 603 at 1305 hours. Mrs. Alma Williams answers the door and tells you that her five-year-old daughter, Mary Jane (DOB May 5, 1998), went to visit her friend, Susie Smith, who lives at number 26 in the block of townhouses next door to her condominium on Valley Crescent. This was at 1045 the same day. When Mary Jane didn't return for lunch, Mrs. Williams called Susie's mother, who told her that Susie had been home all morning but that Mary Jane had never arrived to play with Susie.

   Mrs. Williams says that Mary Jane has never been missing before and describes her as follows: white, short brown curly hair, brown eyes, height 40 inches, weight 45 pounds, regular build, no scars or birthmarks, rosy complexion, straight teeth. She has a cheerful disposition and enjoys talking to people. She was wearing blue jeans, a brown wool sweater, red rainboots, and a blue parka jacket. You contact the police by telephone from Mrs. Williams' apartment and report the child missing. You contact your dispatcher who takes the description and relays it by radio to the two patrol car teams and security guards patrolling on foot through the condominium grounds.

   At 1338 hours, you visit the home of Susie Smith at 26 Valley Crescent to talk to her mother, Joyce Smith (Ph. 416-384-3938). Mrs. Smith advises you that she has been home all morning and has not seen or heard from Mary Jane. At 1345 hours, you return to apartment 603 to interview Mary Jane's mother in more detail. After questioning Mrs. Williams, you leave her residence at 1410 hours. At 1415 you receive a call from dispatch telling you that Mary Jane has just returned home. Mrs. Williams explained to the dispatcher that her ex-husband had taken Mary Jane to lunch at MacDonald's.

2. Review the shoplifting scenario provided in the part III exercise and the memo book entries you created to report it. Use your notes about that incident to prepare verbal testimony for class, just as if you were to give it in court. Use a highlighter to mark the beginning and end of the selected period of time when this crime occurred in your notebook and use elastic bands as described.

   On the day of presentation, the class will be divided into teams of three members. One team member will play the role of the Crown. He or she will question another member of the team representing the security officer who arrested the defendant. The third member of the team will act as defence counsel and will cross-examine the security officer on his or her previous testimony. The roles will be rotated so that each team member will have a chance to play all three parts: the Crown, the security officer, and the defence. This exercise is to help you develop your public speaking skills, review your interviewing skills, and allow you to think like both the Crown and the defence when preparing to present testimony in court.

PART V

**Security Devices
and Systems**

16 Physical Defences

INTRODUCTION

Physical defences is a broad and general term used to describe any object, structure, or piece of equipment that is designed, at least in part, to enhance the security of a facility. The history of physical defences is ancient—the notion of protecting goods and people by discouraging access (or egress) dates to the earliest human societies. Many of today's modern physical defences can trace their roots to ancient gate and fortification technologies.

In this chapter, we will explore the concept of physical security in general, introducing the four lines of defence, and then moving on to cover the specific applications of fencing and gates; doors, windows, and glass; and security lighting.

PHYSICAL SECURITY: FOUR LINES OF DEFENCE

The most basic task in protecting premises is preventing intruders from getting inside. Comparing outer security defences to an onion may help you think in terms of layers. There is the outside barrier (or skin). If an intruder succeeds in breaking through this outside barrier, there are further layers to peel away before the intruder can reach the core. The key function of physical defences planning is to make each defensive layer of the physical protection of the facility as impassable as possible.

Besides unauthorized entry, some physical security features are designed to protect against other risks, such as vandalism, sabotage, fires, accidents, and natural disasters. The planning of physical defences requires a good understanding of the particular vulnerabilities of a type of facility. For example, a retail or wholesale facility that does a lot of shipping and receiving will need to consider enhanced security coverage for shipping bays and other access "weak points."

In planning physical defences, most security planners think in terms of **four lines of defence** (see figure 16.1): grounds perimeter

Chapter Objectives

When you have completed this chapter, you will

- have a basic understanding of the four lines of defence and how they are incorporated into outer security defences.

- understand the role of fence protection devices and the role they play in facility protection.

- understand how external storage areas are secured.

- understand the security applications for doors, windows, and glass in the security industry today.

- have a basic knowledge of the different forms of security lighting, understand how to recognize them, and know how to make informed choices and recommendations with respect to security lighting.

FIGURE 16.1   Four Lines of Defence

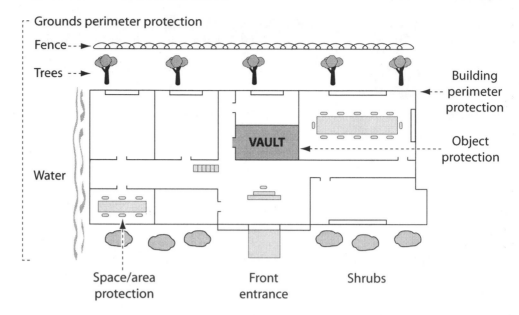

protection, building perimeter protection, space or area protection, and object protection.

Natural and structural barriers may be used to limit access to the perimeter of a site. **Natural barriers** are features of the natural landscape and may include rivers, canyons, swamplands, cliffs, and dense bush.

While not all of these features are impenetrable, they discourage access from the direction in which they are present and may reduce the need for structural barriers.

Structural barriers are created and installed for the protection of a facility. They may include fences, hedges, doors, walls, roadblocks, screens, bars, and grilles.

Examples of hybrid types of barriers—with both natural and structural aspects—include cleared perimeter lands; embankments; earthworks; and moats, canals, ponds, or other water features.

Consider, for example, waterfalls, rock walls, cliffs, and similar features used in zoos and amusement parks that serve both a decorative and a protective purpose.

Weak Points and Unauthorized Entry

Unauthorized entry to a facility can be made through areas that to the average person may seem impossible. However, to someone with criminal intent, they are as good as doors. Sewers and drainpipes, culverts, utility tunnels, exhaust conduits, air intake pipes, maintenance hole covers, coal chutes, and sidewalk elevators are examples of weak points.

When preventing entry is of paramount importance, any opening with a cross-section area about the size of a football (just large enough to get your head through), must be secured with bars, grilles, barbed wire, or locked doors. An opening blocked with a grille screen will deter most attempts at illegal entry and vandalism of most buildings. Where a greater degree of protection is desired, metal bars—ornamental or otherwise—should be considered.

physical defences
any object, structure, or piece of equipment that is designed, at least in part, to enhance the security of a facility

four lines of defence
grounds perimeter protection, building perimeter protection, space/area protection, and object protection

natural barriers
features of the natural landscape that discourage access to a facility

structural barriers
things that are created and installed for the protection of a facility

Fences as Perimeter Barriers

A **perimeter barrier** is a structure that defines the physical boundaries of a facility or area and restricts or impedes access. Properly located fencing can

- serve as a legal demarcation, which assists prosecutions under the *Trespass to Property Act* (TPA);

- act as a physical obstacle as well as a psychological barrier;

- delay an intruder's progress; and

- assist entry control measures.

The most common type of fencing used to protect premises is chain-link fencing. The Canadian security industry follows American standards for chain-link fencing. The industry standard calls for nine gauge or heavier wire at least 2 m high.

Certain types of high-security facilities use chain-link fencing with enhanced features. For example, around military compounds rows of coiled barbed wire are placed on the ground outside the high chain-link fence topped with **concertina wire**, a barbed wire extended in a spiral.

Corrections facilities (prisons, penitentiaries) also have special requirements with multiple rows of barriers. On the furthest outside perimeter, there is usually chain-link fencing topped with concertina wire angled outward. Between this fence and the concrete wall with guard towers at each corner is often 9 m of open, cleared land. And, between the concrete wall and another shorter chain-link fence bordering the prison compound is another dead zone of cleared land about 6 m deep. This makes it even more difficult for prisoners to escape, because they would have to scale three fence systems in open view of guards in the corner towers.

Railways, slipways, and docklands also commonly use a combination of chain-link fencing, concertina wire, and earthworks to guard against unauthorized entry

perimeter barrier
structure that defines the physical boundaries of a facility or area and restricts or impedes access

concertina wire
barbed wire extended in a spiral for use as a barrier

FIGURE 16.2   Common Chain-Link Fence Characteristics

Characteristic	Option
Gauge—size of wire	#9 (3.8 mm), #11 (3.0 mm)
Mesh—size of hole	40 mm (1.6 in.), 50 mm (2 in.), 60 mm (2.4 in.)
Coating	Galvanized or vinyl
Tension wires	Wire, rail, or cable attached at top or bottom
Support posts	Wood or metal (See Canadian Government Specifications RR-F-end RR-F-191/33)
Height	Varies from 1.5 m to 3 m (5 to 10 ft.)
Tie-downs	Buried, staked, or encased in concrete
Pole reinforcement	Buried or encased in concrete
Gate opening	Swing, slide, turnstile, or lift

Source: Adapted from Gary R. Cook, "The Facts on the Fence," *Security Management*, June 1990.

Temporary Fences

Temporary fences are placed around dangerous areas where on-site construction occurs. For example, a sign like "DANGER, OPEN HOLE" explains the danger and the need for temporary fencing.

Step Aside

Electronic Perimeter Surveillance

With today's technology, a security operator can digitally record an intrusion in progress by using active camera surveillance positioned at key areas around the perimeter. The officer can then report the intrusion to police and send them the video showing what is happening in real time.

FENCE PROTECTION DEVICES

Where intruders are highly motivated to get in, relying only on natural and structural barriers is not enough of a deterrent. Foot patrols provide an additional measure of protection, but security patrols cannot provide continual coverage for the entire perimeter. Consequently, it is often necessary to add electronic sensors that can detect movement at the perimeter, whether in cleared areas or adjacent to fencing.

Early outdoor sensors were imperfect; they were often plagued by frequent nuisance alarms caused by weather conditions or animals. Today's electronic sensors, however, are so sensitive that they are capable, in some contexts, of replacing fencing altogether. Sophisticated sensors are designed to identify suspicious activities (such as climbing, cutting, and lifting) while blocking other signals typically caused by wind, rain, snow, birds, lightning, storms, debris, and earthquake motion.

Yet, despite the sensitivity of these systems, most security professionals still prefer using sensors to supplement fences rather than relying on sensors alone. The most commonly used external intruder detection sensors are described below.

Electromagnetic Cable or Ported Coax Buried Line

electromagnetic cable detection sensor that releases electromagnetic energy through tiny punctures in close intervals throughout its outer shield, producing an electric field that surrounds the cable like an aura

Electromagnetic cable, which is mounted on the inside of a chain-link or mesh fencing, releases electromagnetic energy through tiny punctures in close intervals throughout its outer shield. These emissions produce an electric field that surrounds the cable like an aura.

Electromagnetic cable can also be buried in pairs of coaxial sensors about 1.5 m apart running 23 cm underground to create an electric field about a metre above ground. This electric field extends 3 m to 4 m over the area.

This type of protection device works by triggering an alarm whenever the electromagnetic field is disturbed.

False alarms with this type of technology often relate to the presence of metal (fence posts, ductwork) underground near the cable set-up. Excessive moisture and wind can also cause false alarms. Obviously, vehicles and larger animals in the area can trigger false alarms. A companion video system may be useful in screening out false alarms.

The most common way intruders bypass a detection zone protected with electromagnetic cable is to create a bridge over it.

Fibre Optic Cable

Fibre optic sensors use light rather than electricity for transmission and detection. Made of fine filaments of glass, a **fibre optic cable** reflects light waves from a light source at one end of the fibre to a sensor at the other end. This light is pulsed through the fibre in the same way as an electric signal is sent through wire; only it is more reliable. Neither electrical nor electrical magnetic interference (EMI) affects the light pulses to produce false alarms.

fibre optic cable
detection sensor made of fine filaments of glass that reflects light waves from a light source at one end of the fibre to a sensor at the other end

Fibre optic cable can be strung along a fence over great distances. Some manufacturers of high-security fences even fit fibre optic cable into hollowed-out tubes of their chain-link material, making it impossible for intruders to detect it. Like the electromagnetic cable, if the chain-link or mesh fence containing the fibre optic cable is cut or interfered with, the light pulses stop to signal an alarm.

Fibre optic sensors can also be used as an in-ground, pressure-sensitive, detection system. Encased in metal tubing to protect the fibre optics from rodent damage, the cable must be properly grounded. An electro optics unit transmits light using a light-emitting diode (LED) for the light source. The light then travels through the fibre optic and is picked up by the detector, which is very sensitive to slight alterations in the transmission caused by vibration or pressure resulting from walking, running, jumping, or crawling over the ground's surface. When an adequate alteration in the light pattern takes place, an alarm signal goes off.

Fibre optic cable can work in two ways:

1. A continuity-based system requires the fibre optic strand to be broken to trigger an intrusion alarm.

2. A micro-bending system detects alterations in the light pattern caused by movement of the fibre optic cable (for example, when someone leans on a fence).

Causes of false alarms with these systems include severe weather, unstable/wobbly fencing, and animal activity. As with electromagnetic systems, detection can be improved by adding a second system, such as infrared detectors, or cameras. In-ground systems can also be sensitive to excess moisture, rodents, or the movement of tree roots in severe storms.

Intruders attempting to defeat a fibre optic system will avoid disrupting the light pattern, either by building a bridge over the system, or by attempting to cross at less sensitive points (for example, fence posts).

Capacitance Sensors

Capacitance sensors operate on the same principle as electromagnetic systems but use electrical rather than magnetic fields. When intruders approach and physically touch the wires, they upset the electrical charge within the field and signal the sensors to react. A filter screens the signal and allows those within the range of an

capacitance sensor
detection sensor that uses an electrical field and signals an intruder when the charge is interrupted

intruder to be forwarded to activate an alarm. By increasing the sensitivity level, a presence in close proximity can also be detected without direct physical contact with the wires.

Though weather and EMI do not change the sensors' performance, any vibration—a stiff wind, birds flapping their wings as they settle on the wires—can appear to be intruders climbing the fence. To discourage birds and squirrels, nearby trees and shrubs should be removed. Even vegetation brushing the fence will change the capacitance so the grass close to the fence line must be kept short. In addition, blowing paper debris or anything making physical contact that changes the characteristics of the fence may generate an alarm. Tightening the tension of the wires at the termination points helps reduce this possibility.

Using this method of detection alone is not recommended because the main fencing remains vulnerable to intruders using wire cutters at ground level to slip under the fence.

Volumetric Motion Detection Devices

There are three types of volumetric motion detection devices: the active infrared system (AIRS), the passive infrared system, and microwave technology.

Active Infrared System

active infrared system
volumetric motion detection device that shoots a beam of infrared light from a generator to a sensor

The **active infrared system** (AIRS) is often called the "baseball" system. A generator shoots a beam of infrared light to a sensor, in much the same way as a pitcher throws the ball to the catcher. If the beam is blocked, the alarm sounds.

Passive Infrared System

passive infrared system
volumetric motion detection device that floods an area with invisible low levels of infrared light

It is more common to install **passive infrared systems** inside to protect valuable property such as you find in a museum or art gallery. Transmitters flood the selected area with low levels of infrared light. When a thief or some other object disrupts the invisible light patterns, the movement triggers an alarm.

Microwave Technology

microwave technology
volumetric motion detection device that relies on the Doppler effect to detect an intruder when the frequency of the microwave beam is changed

Doppler effect
increase or decrease in frequency of light, sound, or other waves as the source and the observer move toward each other

Whether used indoors or outdoors, **microwave technology** relies on the **Doppler effect** where the frequency of the microwaves issued is changed by the movement of an intruder through the field. When the sensor receives an unfamiliar frequency in the returned waves, it sets off an alarm. Most external systems, however, rely on the transmission of a microwave beam to a receiver. If the beam is interrupted or changed, an alarm sounds.

Two basic units, a transmitter and a receiver, make up an infrared or microwave sensor system. They are placed directly opposite each other. The transmitter generates a multi-wave straight-line beam to the receiver thus creating an infrared or microwave "fence" between them. The receiver passes the beam of energy through a collecting lens into a collecting cell, which converts the infrared or microwave energy into an electrical signal. The receiving unit monitors the electrical signal, and when an intruder passing through the field of beams interrupts the signal causing it to drop below a preset threshold for a specific period of time, the blocked signal generates an alarm.

When these systems are used as an outer security defence, the right conditions are necessary for them to work effectively. First, the sensors need clear lines of sight with no obstacles or obstructions between the transmitters and receivers to interrupt the infrared or microwave signal. Because infrared beams are so thin, they must also be properly aligned, so the ground must be the same level throughout the zone. Low spots in the terrain create "holes" in the surveillance pattern, while obstacles/obstructions disrupt the "coverage" pattern. Typically, active infrared sensors are combined with a single or double fence barrier, which defines the perimeter to be covered. A sensor zone length can extend up to 305 m.

Earth tremors, falling rocks or trees, even freezing and thawing of the ground can misalign detectors. Other sources of false alarms include animal activity; blowing debris or vegetation; and fog, heavy rain/snow, or dust storms. Where these conditions are likely to occur, it is more practical to choose another kind of system or to add a back-up system.

Taut Wire Sensors

Taut wire sensors are used to protect perimeter fence lines and operate like automatic breaker switches on an electric panel; only they work in reverse to initiate an alarm. Each switch swings from "off" to "on" instead of from "on" to "off" when the micro-switch sensors attached to barbed wiring on top of a chain-link fence sense the tension wires relax. Each switch contains a central arm suspended inside a cylinder. The switch remains "off" or in the "open" position as long as the inner arm does not touch the outer wall of the cylinder. As soon as the sensors register either an increase in tautness or relaxation of the tension wires, particularly when an intruder climbs, spreads, or cuts the wires in the fence to crawl underneath it, the arm inside the cylinder swings to hit the outer wall or "closes" contact to trip the alarm.

taut wire sensor
detection device that operates like breaker switches on an electrical panel only in reverse order to initiate an alarm

Taut wire sensors can be mounted in two different configurations: on top of an existing fence together with barbed wire outriggers to provide protection from climbing or as part of the fence itself.

Although this is one of the most expensive fence sensor systems to set up, combining both configurations for taut wire sensors produces a low false alarm rate (FAR) and low nuisance alarm rate (NAR), while getting reliable results for detecting intrusive climbing, cutting, and crawling under the fence. Taut wire sensors are typically used in high-risk facilities. Their only drawback is that the wires require regular tensioning to make sure the system works effectively.

Determined intruders can still breach this system by tunneling underground or leapfrogging the fence itself (for example, by parking a van beside the fence and using the roof to launch themselves over the protected area to safety). This is why the higher the fence the more effective it is. Where there is soft ground between fence posts, this invites tunneling as the other way to enter without detection.

For high-risk facilities, then, it is necessary to reinforce this system with in-ground sensors inside the protected fence area. To provide maximum protection, volumetric motion detection devices can be added, as can video motion detection surveillance.

Vibration Sensors

Vibration sensors detect the vibrations created from sawing, cutting, climbing, or peeling back fence material once the wires, mesh, or chain link are cut.

There are two basic types of fence vibration sensors: electromechanical sensors and piezoelectric sensors.

Electromechanical sensors work the same way as an electric circuit board where the switches remain open until significant vibrations close the contact and trip an alarm. Electromechanical sensors rely on either mechanical inertia switches (based on "on" and "off" circuit breakers) or mercury switches (based on the rise or fall of the mercury level to break the circuit and activate an alarm.

Piezoelectric sensors generate an analog signal that varies proportionally in amplitude and frequency to the vibration released by the source breaching or banging the fence. These signals are filtered through a process analyzer to be screened and interpreted before triggering an alarm.

It is vital that vibration sensors be installed properly on a fence and spaced correctly to be their most effective. The background noise from flapping, sagging, or swaying strips of loose fencing can set off nuisance alarms, as can stormy weather conditions. To offset this problem, it is possible to add a weather analyzer that feeds the latest forecast to the field processor, which then adjusts the alarm's sensitivity to the prevailing conditions to maintain a more effective level of detection reliability. Other sensing devices can be added to these sensors to refine their detection abilities even further to prevent false alarms. Still, vibration sensors should never be used on fence lines close to or on construction sites, railroad tracks/yards, highways, airports, or roadway activity. The level of noise and resulting vibration will continually set off false alarms.

electromechanical sensors
vibration-detecting device in which the switches remain open until significant vibrations close the contact and trip an alarm

piezoelectric sensors
vibration-detecting device that generates an analog signal that is filtered through a process analyzer before triggering an alarm

Fluid Pressure Sensors

A **fluid pressure sensor** is the final fence protection device to consider. A small diameter tube sealed at one end and filled with fluid is placed inside a fence wall. If something pushes against the fence, such as a person or vehicle, the pressure forces the sides of the tubes to squeeze together, which in turn places pressure on the monitored fluid. The change in fluid pressure sets off an alarm. This method helps detect persons crossing open ground and is commonly used in military installations, external bulk storage facilities, and tank farms.

fluid pressure sensor
small tube sealed at one end and filled with fluid that sets off an alarm when the fluid pressure changes

Protecting Outdoor Storage Structures

The protection of outdoor storage structures needs special attention for two reasons: the construction of these structures may make them especially vulnerable to intrusion, and the presence of outbuildings, garbage containers, sheds, and junk provides cover for intruders.

A messy storage yard can cause additional problems: it can make it hard to tell what is missing in the event of a break-in; and it can cause health and safety issues.

Order, discipline, and readiness, which are the hallmarks of security, include neatness. To promote an orderly environment, it's important to regularly inspect outbuildings.

Attention should also be paid to outbuilding construction. Where possible, construction should be sturdy and reinforced. Materials such as drywall provide very limited security protection, and false ceilings can hide unwelcome security surprises.

Security Considerations for Roofs

Roofs are often weak security areas constructed primarily for protection from the weather and not for access prevention. Roof construction normally consists of galvanized material covered with tar or pitch caulking. There are a variety of new types of material available that offer increased security. These should be considered. It is also important to remember that skylights, access hatches, and ventilation conduits are all likely points of entry for an intruder.

While everyone worries about break-ins through the doors and windows, it is useful to remember that roofs can be cut to gain entry. A professional thief often looks for an unprotected roof.

In addition, most building designs accommodate easy roof access for maintenance of the many mechanical systems that are traditionally installed there. These mechanical systems, which are central to a building's operation and maintenance, may be targeted by intruders either to disable the facility or to disarm the people working inside. Any access route to a roof must be secured and monitored.

DOORS, WINDOWS, AND GLASS

Moving from the perimeter, in this discussion of the four lines of security, we come to the exterior of buildings. Apart from issues of building construction, the primary considerations at this line of defence are the integrity of doors, windows, and other glass.

Protecting doors, windows, and glass is key, because statistics prove that approximately 50 percent of break-ins occur through glass, whether mounted in windows or doors.

The need for adequate security cannot be overemphasized, but it must be provided as part of an overall plan for the safe and efficient conduct of the business that security officers are charged to protect. If this balance is lost, two things happen: either the security function is downgraded in favour of a more immediate convenience, or the smooth flow of business is handcuffed to fit intrusive security standards. Neither of these conditions is acceptable, and it is up to the security director in partnership with the owner to determine the balance required in establishing systems that will recognize and accommodate both production and security needs.

Security Doors

One primary responsibilities on a site is to examine every door, whether exterior or interior, to determine the degree of security already used or required. This means carefully looking at the way a door is constructed as well as inspecting the locking system used.

Most doors to be secured in a facility fall into two groups: either "office" or "commercial." And each of these two groups have four levels of security. Their features are as follows:

Level 1   A steel face and a honeycomb core constructed of selected metals. This door has reinforced hinges and reinforced material around the lock area.

Level 2   A steel face with an inner bullet-resistant place. The core consists of vertical steel stiffeners and both the lock area and the hinges are reinforced.

Level 3   A steel face with a structural steel core designed in a hollow grid. The core is insulated and reinforced throughout.

Level 4   A steel face with a pressure-resistant steel core of vertical bars. The presence of an inner pressure-resistant steel plate offers added security to this door.

In protecting against unauthorized entry through doors, it is important to recognize the weaknesses of any doors in the facility.

Many doors are weaker than the doorframe that supports them. Thin panels or hollow cores may be easy to break, as can be glass panels. A poorly fitted doorframe can permit an intruder to unlock the door by using a lever to disengage the lock bolt. Soft doorjambs can allow for the locking mechanism to be torn out of place ("spreading/pulling the lock").

The placement of hinges on the exterior side of a door can allow an intruder to remove the door completely, in some cases, without leaving signs of forced entry.

Protective Devices for Windows

Windows are typically considered a facility's weakest point, because most break-ins occur through them.

In industrial facilities, windows are typically reinforced either by grilles/bars or screening (in some cases, alarmed screening). Where a window may be needed for use as an emergency exit, or to permit the entry of fire hoses, it may be necessary to consider a grille or screen that is removable; for example, that swings on hinges.

In commercial facilities, aesthetics (looks) are important as well as security— for example, retailers want passersby to be able to look into a store window to view the wares inside. In these kinds of applications, it is more common to use impact-resistant glass.

Glass

There are five types of glass used in the security industry—reinforced glass, tempered glass, safety glass, bullet-resistant glass, and privacy glass.

Reinforced Glass

reinforced glass
two layers of plate glass with a galvanized wire screen inserted between them

Reinforced glass consists of two layers of plate glass with a galvanized wire screen inserted between them. This type of glass is mainly used as an insert in door panels where breaking glass poses a significant danger. The wire screen holds the broken pieces of glass together and prevents shards from falling to the ground. Reinforced glass inserts are commonly used in schools, hospitals, swinging doors, and internal office doors.

Tempered Glass

Tempered glass is designed to break into small regular-shaped pieces to protect people from the danger of sharp glass. For example, a car windshield breaks into small cube-shaped pieces of glass when shattered on impact in an accident. As with reinforced glass, the primary feature of tempered glass is not security, but safety.

tempered glass
glass designed to break into small regular-shaped pieces

Safety Glass

There are two types of **safety glass**—laminate and film. They both use polymer-based materials to reinforce the glass itself.

safety glass
glass reinforced with polymer-based materials, either laminate or film

Underwriters' Laboratories (UL)-listed burglary-resistant glass is a laminate of two sheets of flat glass held together by a thin layer of polyvinyl butyral—a soft, transparent material. Laminated burglary-resistant glass is virtually indistinguishable from ordinary glass and is most often used in banks and retail stores where there is a need to prevent "smash and grab" raids on window displays and showcases. When burglars take a hammer or iron bar to break what they assume is a plate-glass window, they quickly realize the material is not penetrable after several unsuccessful blows. UL-listed burglary-resistant glass resists heat, flame, cold, picks, rocks, and most other weapons intruders use.

Unfortunately, even though such attackers may flee empty-handed, the owners in these situations are left with cracked windows, forcing them to replace the entire pane. In many cases, insurance companies require that laminated glass be clearly identified to discourage "smash and grab" attackers from making futile but damaging attempts.

While not as effective as laminate, some measure of resistance can be added to standard plate glass if it is covered with 4 mm- to 6 mm-thick Mylar film. Mylar needs to be replaced every five years. As little as a 2 mm cover of Mylar can keep glass from fragmenting. Mylar film applied to glass provides good protection from flying shards associated with bombings. This feature has led to an initiative in the security industry to work toward the recommendation of the use of Mylar in buildings that may be subject to the threat of terrorist attacks.

Bullet-Resistant Glass

Bullet-resistant glass is designed to stop bullets fired from various types of guns, including combat handguns, assault rifles, high-powered rifles, and assault shotguns.

bullet-resistant glass
composite of acrylic designed to withstand the impact of ammunition

Although described as glass, bullet-resistant glass is usually a composite of several types of acrylic. Acrylic glazing material is much stronger than true glass. It has many useful applications in window security. It is lighter in weight and cheaper than either safety glass or plastic glazing, and, at 3 cm thick, it is UL-approved as a bullet-resistant barrier.

Privacy Glass

Impact-resistant **privacy glass** is treated with a special coating that "frosts" when subjected to an electrical impulse. This unique type of security feature is usually applied to large glass surfaces where the option for allowing or denying visibility can be achieved with the flick of a switch.

privacy glass
glass treated with special coating that "frosts" when subjected to an electrical impulse

SECURITY LIGHTING

Security lighting serves three primary purposes: it promotes safety, by allowing enough light in which to work, patrol, etc.; it facilitates surveillance; and it discourages intrusion.

In planning security lighting, a security director seeks to give maximum advantage to security personnel and minimum advantage to intruders. In general, the weakest points of a facility, from a security perspective (such as entrances, window banks, and windowless stairwells) should be equipped with the most lighting, both to allow the proper operation of security cameras and to deter intruders who seek the cover of darkness. An ideal lighting standard, from the perspective of security, is for lighting to mimic levels of daylight even at night.

Good security lighting is also important to promote the quality of photographic and video evidence, and at access control points, to permit such activities as the checking of photo identification.

Areas of Use

There are four main areas of use for security lighting: at access control points, along fences, on internal structures, on outer storage areas.

Access control points in facilities are those that allow entry/egress for vehicles, pedestrians, waste, and deliveries. The lighting of fences is usually only essential for high-risk facilities.

Types of Lamps

Lamp bulbs used for protective lighting are incandescent, fluorescent, metal halide, mercury-vapour, quartz, and high- or low-pressure sodium. Each has specific purposes.

Incandescent Light

incandescent light bulb
white-hot light caused by an electrical current flowing through the filament in a light bulb

Incandescent light bulbs are commonly used in houses to provide general lighting. They turn on and off instantly in response to manual switching. Some are manufactured with interior coatings to reflect the light and others with built-in lenses that either focus light (as in task lighting) or scatter light over a larger area. Incandescent bulbs can be upgraded with a suitable fixture to focus or diffuse light.

Fluorescent Light

fluorescent lamp
cathode-ray tube containing a gas or vapour that produces light when acted on by an electrical current

Indoor **fluorescent lamps** are highly efficient. They emit 62 lumens per watt; but outdoors they react to temperature changes and are unsuitable in colder climates. Unfortunately, they also continually flicker, and this bright flickering not only bothers people's eyes, it can give some people migraine headaches and may be disorienting for others. Since security staff can be affected as easily as intruders, there is no advantage to using this lighting. A further disadvantage is that the ballast in the fluorescent lamp often interferes with radio reception.

Mercury-Vapour Lamps

More efficient than incandescent lamps, **mercury-vapour lamps** also last much longer. They are slow to activate, but allow for power dips of up to 50 percent. They create a pool of stark bluish light that reveals even small details.

mercury-vapour lamp
bluish light that can withstand power dips of up to 50 percent

Metal Halide Lamps

Metal halide lamps also tolerate power dips and take a long time to start up. But worse, a power outage of only one-twentieth of a second will completely knock them out of commission. These lamps are expensive and they perform inconsistently.

metal halide lamp
light generated by halogen and another element or radical

Sodium-Vapour Lamps

Mounted on tall concrete poles along highways, city parkways, and bridges, the soft yellow light of **sodium-vapour lamps** penetrates fog and mist well; thus, they are considered even more efficient than mercury-vapour lamps. These lamps need a long warm-up time.

sodium-vapour lamps
soft yellow light produced by means of an electric current passing through a tube of neon and sodium vapour

Quartz Lamps

Quartz lamps radiate a very bright white light of between 1,500 and 2,000 watts. They light almost as quickly as incandescent bulbs. As such, they provide the best illumination along perimeter barriers and in troublesome areas.

quartz lamps
a mercury-vapour lamp enclosed by an envelope made from quartz rather than glass

Lighting Design

Lighting bulbs can be organized into different systems, depending on the security application. The following four systems are those most commonly used in security—floodlights, Fresnel lenses, searchlights, and streetlights.

Floodlights

Floodlights broadcast beams of light to cover as wide an area as possible. When used without visors or shields, they tend to create glare, direct light inefficiently, and produce light pollution. Floodlights can be ordered in various beam widths, and with wattage between 300 to 1,000 watts.

floodlight
unit that produces a bright and broad beam of light

Fresnel Lenses

Unlike floodlights and searchlights, which project a focused oval beam, a **Fresnel lens** projects wide, long beams of light about 180° in the horizontal plane and from 18° to 30° in the vertical plane, not unlike the beam from a movie projector. Fresnel lenses are often used to light access routes to gateways, creating glare in a specific area, while leaving other areas in darkness. They normally come in 300 to 500 watt lamps.

Fresnel lens
thin optical lens consisting of concentric rings of segmental lenses

Searchlights

Searchlights are highly focused incandescent lamps mounted in a drum that can be swung in an arc, either automatically or manually, to pinpoint beams of light on

searchlights
highly focused incandescent lamps

a particular position inside or outside the property being protected. The intensity of the light beam depends on the width of the reflector, which typically ranges from 15 cm to 60 cm, and the wattage, which varies from 250 to 3,000 watts. The beam width is from 3° to 10°, although there are wider models. Searchlights are most often found on waterfront property to spot check incoming boats or ships, on lighthouses as directional beacons for ships, and in isolated mountain areas or on top of building towers to alert aircraft flying overhead to the danger of collision.

On board naval ships, searchlights can also be used to communicate signals as well as direct search beams. Besides holding the lamp, the drum provides a mounting for the signaling shutters, which open and close to interrupt the light beam to create a pattern of signals known as Morse code. Each signal represents a letter in the alphabet and, when they are combined in groups, they spell words.

Streetlights

streetlights
suspended lighting that is either symmetrical (in the centre of the zone) or asymmetrical (offset for maximum distance coverage)

Unlike floodlights, Fresnel lenses, and searchlights, which use reflection units with a set of mirrors to direct light, **streetlights** are suspended lighting units that overhang a street, laneway, route, or parking lot. They are either symmetrical or asymmetrical.

Symmetrical units spread light evenly over a large area such as a parking lot and are usually placed in the centre of each squared zone to illuminate the ground with a pool of light.

Focus on Technologies

Perimeter Lighting: Planning Considerations

The planning of perimeter lighting depends on many factors, including whether a site is remote or located in a high-density urban area and on the patrol needs of the facility.

In a typical free-standing, fenced facility, lamps are typically placed on posts installed about 9 m inside the security fence and about 48 m apart. They must be at least 9 m high to cast light in as wide an arc as possible on both sides of the fence to expose advancing intruders from outside the perimeter. When angling the reflectors in the lamps, make sure they direct the light beams toward the ground inside the fence to avoid throwing shadows or a glare into the officers' eyes; but expose the bulb in the lamp to the outside of the perimeter to create a deliberate glare for anyone approaching the fence from that position. This general rule will not apply to all situations, of course, but it works most of the time.

For more remote and isolated properties, the use of lighting along the fence lines changes. Here, some glare and illuminate should be created as far outside the perimeter as possible, so floodlights or Fresnel lenses are the best choice. The lamps are best set up 6 m inside the fence so their span of light can spread as far as 76 m outside the most isolated perimeters, if necessary. If, however, the driveway to a security property abuts highways, streets, or occupied residences, streetlights need to be installed that will not create glare along public places while adequately illuminating the approach.

Many buildings to be secured are located in high traffic areas like a city street and may have no fencing on which to mount security lighting equipment. In this situation, lamps can be mounted directly on the walls of the building or over doorways. Doorway lights should be set up so that shadows cast over the entrance by other nearby lighting are eliminated.

Asymmetrical units use reflectors in cases where the lamp must cast light some distance from the target area. Since the light beams are not concentrated on a specific spot, they do not create glare.

Streetlights are rated by power output (wattage) and by light output (lumens) and, in protective lighting applications, may range from 4,000 to 10,000 lumens.

Lighting Systems

There are four types of systems—continuous lighting, standby lighting, portable lighting, and emergency lighting.

Continuous Lighting System

The **continuous lighting** system may be controlled manually or by an automatic control and usually consists of Fresnel lenses providing glare projection. This system can also be positioned to provide controlled all-round illumination.

continuous lighting
a system that may be manually or automatically controlled to provide constant lighting

Standby Lighting System

The **standby lighting** system can be switched on when suspicious activity occurs or when a guard enters the area. It is an economical system to maintain and is usually equipped with searchlights.

standby lighting
a system equipped with searchlights that is turned on only when required

Portable Lighting System

The **portable lighting** system is usually battery or generator operated. This system can be mounted on a trailer or be carried by hand. It is usually moved to an area of operation as needed.

portable lighting
a battery- or generator-operated system that can be moved

Emergency Lighting System

The **emergency lighting** system works on auxiliary power. It is designed to provide minimum levels of emergency lighting in stairwells, hallways, and near emergency exits. In some facilities, where it is critical that specific areas continue to be lit, the emergency lighting system needs the capacity to generate power for the critical areas for a set period of time. Some examples of such areas are:

emergency lighting
a system that works on auxiliary power to provide lighting when other systems fail

- hospital operating rooms;
- computer facilities;
- stock exchanges;
- banks;
- telecommunications exchanges; and
- 911 services.

Maintenance

Regular maintenance is required to keep security lighting in tip-top shape. Electrical circuits and equipment should be checked for worn parts that have to be replaced.

Connections in switches and between circuits should be in working order. Any damaged or battered insulation should be replaced or repaired. Fixtures should be checked for rust and mirrored reflectors and lenses should be cleaned and polished. A log of operational hours for each lamp should be kept and when it reaches 80 to 90 percent of its rated life, the bulbs should be replaced.

Step Aside

Tips for Security Lighting

- Avoid glare unless intended.

- Keep glare or light from public places.

- Make sure lights are reliable with regular maintenance.

- Overlap arcs of light to eliminate shadows.

- Position lights so they are easy to service and maintain.

- Protect lights against attack or vandalism.

- Have a back-up power supply.

- Have emergency lights available.

SUMMARY

In thinking about security, it is useful to remember the concept of four lines of defence: grounds perimeter protection, building perimeter protection, interior space or area protection, and object protection. Each line constitutes a barrier through which an intruder must pass. There exist different security strategies for protecting each line.

Typically, the perimeter of a site that includes outdoor grounds is protected by fences. Fence protection devices are a part of this package, and understanding how they work—their strengths and weaknesses—as well as the susceptibility of outside storage sheds and building roofs to intrusive manoeuvres or break-ins is what prepares security officers to operate most effectively.

Beyond the perimeter fences lie windows and doors. In best-case scenarios, the ones in use are designed specifically for security purposes. Where windows and doors have weaknesses, it is important for security personnel to know how these are most commonly taken advantage of by intruders.

Finally, security lighting completes the perimeter security picture, providing both the necessary illumination for surveillance technologies and patrols and an effective deterrent for intruders.

KEY TERMS

active infrared system

bullet-resistant glass

capacitance sensor

concertina wire

continuous lighting

Doppler effect

electromagnetic cable

electromechanical sensors

emergency lighting

fibre optic cable

floodlight

fluorescent lamp

fluid pressure sensor

four lines of defence

Fresnel lens

incandescent light bulb

metal halide lamp

mercury-vapour lamp

microwave technology

natural barriers

passive infrared system

perimeter barrier

physical defences

piezoelectric sensors

portable lighting

privacy glass

quartz lamps

reinforced glass

searchlights

sodium-vapour lamps

standby lighting

streetlights

structural barriers

taut wire sensor

tempered glass

PERFORMANCE APPLICATION

1. What are the four lines of defence?

2. What special challenges does perimeter protection present?

3. List three natural barriers that can promote site security.

4. What are some of the reasons a facility might decide *not* to fence its perimeter?

5. List six points in a building that pose an increased risk for unauthorized entry. Describe strategies to protect each.

6. Many different situations require temporary barricades and fencing. Give three examples, besides those provided in this chapter, where they would work.

7. Describe, in simple terms, how fibre optic technology can be used to protect/alarm a fence.

8. What is the minimum size of an industrial window that must be protected with a grill? What type of safety glass would you use and explain why?

9. From a security planning perspective, pick one feature of security lighting that you feel would be your top priority and explain why.

10. Perform an Internet search for two large light fixture manufacturers, select a single type of security bulb, and compare each manufacturer's approach to design and security application. Which manufacturer would you recommend and why?

17 Safes, Vaults, and Locks

INTRODUCTION

In chapter 16, the concept of the four lines of defence was introduced. While protecting a building's grounds and inner and outer perimeters is the first step against property loss and damage, it is equally important to keep the interior of a facility secure.

Securing the contents of a building depends in large part on access control. Various technologies have emerged to help organizations control the movement of employees, customers, and individuals into and through a facility.

Depending on their nature, valuables are best secured with cabinets, locks, safes, or vaults, or a combination of these devices. This chapter will introduce technologies used on the two innermost lines of a facility's defence.

ELECTRONIC ACCESS CONTROL

Technology is advancing rapidly, and keeping abreast of it is a never-ending challenge for security managers whose top priority is access control. Many businesses and industries must continually invest in new access control products to keep ahead of criminals working just as fast to defeat today's systems. Purchasing decisions depend on the size, function, number of buildings to manage within a complex, and location of the facilities that security officers are protecting.

The most effective access control systems must

- identify who wants in and verify their admission;

- permit access to those who have authorized admission only into their designated areas of work;

- prevent access to unauthorized personnel and limit access to designated work areas;

- trigger alarms for any security breaches of access or invalid identity;

Chapter Objectives

When you have completed this chapter, you will

- have a thorough grounding in the way electronic access control systems work and the role they play in total facility protection.

- have a basic knowledge and understanding of the important role filing cabinets, safes, and vaults play in protecting valuable assets.

- have a basic knowledge and understanding of mechanical locks and the role they play in protecting property.

- record every entrance and exit passing through an access point; and

- support and retrieve all evidence intact and in an easy-to-understand format.

Types of Access Control Technologies

There are three types of electromechanical locks: code-operated, key-operated, and card-operated.

Code-Operated Locks

There is no key used to open a code-operated lock. A series of numbered keys are pressed in a preset sequence to activate an electromagnetic switch that releases the door. For some code-operated locks, an alarm sounds if a wrong number is keyed. The sequence combinations can be quickly changed in an emergency. One drawback is that more than one person can slip behind the person cleared to enter. This is called **tailgating**. So, to be truly effective, this type of access requires the presence of a security officer or receptionist.

tailgating
to gain access by slipping in behind a person cleared to enter

Key-Operated Locks

Electronics enhance the best features of a regular pin-tumbler lock with a key that activates an electric switch (**solenoid**). The solenoid draws power from a battery to move a strike plate or keeper to open the lock. Unfortunately, intruders can bypass the key-operated lock by tailgating or using a dry-cell battery.

Use a voltage shroud or voltage discriminator to make a key-operated lock more reliable. A voltage shroud protects the lock from attack by an intruder using a dry-cell battery. It channels the electric current away from the solenoid and dispels it harmlessly. A voltage discriminator blocks any incoming voltage, except the specific voltage level designed for the lock and thereby prevents access. This prohibits an intruder from using a dry-cell battery to "jump start" the lock.

solenoid
electric switch that draws power from a battery to open a lock

Card-Operated Locks

Card-operated locks are mainly electromagnetic. The key is a plastic card with a magnetic stripe, notches, or holes. It looks and feels like a credit card and contains coded information. When the card is passed through an electronic reader, it matches the name on the card with its authorized list of users and records the time of entry. This card is also used for company identity. The code can be changed at the door or from a remote location using a PC. There are two flaws with this system: an intruder can tailgate through an access point, and because the reader identifies only the card and not the person, an intruder can steal or borrow a card to get in. There are several types of card-operated systems on the market.

Magnetic-Coded Cards

There are two basic designs of magnetic-coded cards: one contains a flexible magnetic sheet sealed between two sheets of plastic, and the other contains a magnetic strip along one edge of the card.

The code is contained in magnetized spots on the sheet or strip. If the card is exposed to a strong magnetic field or is stored in a wallet or purse with the magnetic side facing another magnetic-coded credit card, the code will be erased from both cards. The flaw with this card is that it is easy to copy the magnetic pattern onto a duplicate card.

Wiegand-Effect Cards

Up to 26 magnetic wire bits are imbedded in Wiegand-effect cards. These bits of magnetic wire can store millions of code combinations. The card is immune to demagnetization and difficult to copy.

Optical-Coded Cards

Bar codes, similar to those found on products in most grocery stores, are implanted in optical-coded cards and are scanned in the same way as products are. Originally the bar codes were visible, which made it easy to copy them. Now the bar codes are visible only under ultraviolet or infrared light.

Proximity Cards

Proximity cards send a code to a receiver via magnetic, optical, or ultrasonic pulses. A reader or scanner is not required.

BIOMETRIC ACCESS CONTROL

Dwayne Mercredi is director of engineering for SAFLINK in Edmonton, Alberta. In "Beyond Passwords and Pins," in the October 2003 issue of *Canadian Security*, he noted that: "According to Meridien Research, between 500,000 and 700,000 people are affected by identity theft each year in the United States alone."

Identity theft—one person's misuse of another's identity for an illegal purpose (such as fraud)—has led to increasing support for **biometrics**, a class of security technology that recognizes a person's unique physical characteristics: fingerprints, hand geometry, signature, voice print, iris, and retina (see figure 17.1). No password, PIN number, or identification is required.

The reliability of facial imaging is still in development. Nonetheless, the error rate for a retinal scan is one out of every 10 million individuals identified. The iris scan is less accurate: one out of every 131,000. Fingerprint and hand geometry recognition follow with one error out of every 500. The least accurate is signature and voice recognition with one error out of every 50 for each. This is because their recognition is based on behaviour rather than physical characteristics. How you write and how you speak varies from situation to situation, and from mood to mood, and affects the result, so that it is possible for a good imitator to mimic your voice pattern, and a good forger to duplicate your signature, though the scanner is so sensitive it usually defeats such attempts because it's almost impossible to imitate the precise timbre of a voice and pressure applied in a signature.

Of the various biometric techniques, retinal scanning is the most accurate access control method available today. Accuracy in detecting intrusions through fingerprint verification also increases if two fingers are registered and compared for identification. Overall, the more biometric elements used to verify identity, the more accurate the results are, making biometric technology the most reliable for access control of high-risk facilities.

identity theft
misuse of another person's identity for illegal purposes

biometrics
branch of security technology that allows access based on recognition of a person's physical attributes

FIGURE 17.1 Current Biometric Methods

Physical attribute	Biometric method
Fingerprints	Fingerprint recognition systems optically scan a chosen fingerprint area and compare the scanned area with the file of the person to be admitted.
Palm recognition	Hand geometry recognition systems use the geometry of the hand. The system basically measures finger lengths and compares them with the authorized files.
Signature	Signature recognition systems rely on the fact that no two people write with the same motion or pressure. Although forgers can duplicate the appearance of the signature, the amount of pressure and motions used in creating the signature will differ.
Voice print	Speaker verification systems use the uniqueness of voice patterns to determine identification and control admittance. The system uses soundproof booths and requires that the person to be identified repeat a simple phrase, usually four words in length.
Retina	Retina recognition systems analyze the blood vessel pattern in the retina of the eye. These patterns vary widely, even between identical twins. The chance of false identification using this system is one in 10 million.

Source: Thomas Ruggles, "Comparison of Biometric Techniques," Biometric Technology, Inc., May 2002.

If there is any drawback to the use of biometrics, it is that people change, either because of age, injury, stress, illness, or fatigue. Technical experts recommend that biometric records be updated on a regular basis or after a significant change in any employee's life.

EMERGING TECHNOLOGIES IN ACCESS CONTROL

Card manufacturers now provide "modules" of coded information that can be added to one access card. This technology is based on the smart card technology for retail credit cards. In the not too distant future, it will be possible for people to carry one card that will include all their information: birth certificate, social insurance number, passport, banking data, credit information, medical records, shopping discounts, tax payments, employment authorization, and everything else that comprises one person's life—one card for all purposes. If nothing else, a one-card system will further simplify security processes, but one thing technology can never do is replace all security officers in any access control system. Someone has to answer the alarms and deal with the people, both those individuals they are protecting and any intruders breaking in.

CABINETS, SAFES, AND VAULTS

Cabinets, safes, and vaults provide a means of protecting valuables by enclosing them in a (hopefully) secure container. The concept of secure containment is ancient—consider the example of a pirate's locked treasure chest.

The art of lock breaking is equally ancient, and as thieves have grown more sophisticated, safe technology has had to remain continually one step ahead. When safe crackers used explosives to shatter locks and security systems on safe doors, safe manufacturers introduced anti-explosive devices that automatically secured the bolts of the safe to the door. Security experts estimate there is a three-month window between the introduction of the newest security device and the introduction of the resilient criminal's counter tool or technique to overcome it.

Serious thieves carry what is called a safecracker's tool kit, and today's tools are quite sophisticated. They range from hand-picking tools to electric drills, saws, jackhammers, and **plastique**, to digital decoders and gas-powered circular saws. Security personnel who work with key valuables should understand the most common safe-breaking techniques, and should understand the limitations of the technology in place at their worksites.

plastique
plastic explosives

Safe-Keeping Needs

It is important to remember that theft is not the only adverse event against which safes are meant to protect. For some valuables, fire, flooding, and natural disaster present an equally serious threat, and many container technologies are designed specifically to protect against these.

Understanding which type of filing cabinet, safe, or vault that best suits the security needs depends on what valuables are to be protected from fire or thieves. For example, a storekeeper protecting his or her inventory and cash receipts worries more about fire and petty theft, while a financial institution is more concerned about keeping cash deposits, investment bonds, and highly valued objects out of the hands of sophisticated burglars. The protection of sensitive and valuable documents is an issue for all companies, large and small, and cabinets, safes and vaults play a critical role.

The most common items security services are asked to protect are cash, jewellery, investment metals such as gold and silver, photography equipment and films, coin and stamp collections, antique collectibles and heirlooms, deeds and wills, firearms and ammunition, and confidential papers and ledgers.

Unfortunately, many security or loss prevention managers let the price tag of a protective container guide their choice of purchase, and it is only after a fire or burglary occurs that they pay attention to the flaws of the safeguard that failed. To ensure that they do not fall into this trap of wrong thinking, security officers should learn everything they can about how security containers are built, the materials used and why, and the standards set by the industry.

Types of Filing Cabinets, Safes, and Vaults

Filing cabinets, safes, and vaults are three expressions of the same concept: a locked metal container used for storing valuables. There are many shapes and sizes, but in general, they are classed according to their use.

There are five main types:

1. safes designed specifically for in-wall mounting;

2. floor safes designed to be imbedded within a floor;

FAST FACT

Insurance Considerations
Increasingly, insurers are refusing to pay claims for loss where safes or vaults described in the policy do not meet actual industry standards.

3. chests or cabinets that stand alone on a floor;

4. depositories designed with a hopper or slot for easy deposit of valuables without allowing access;

5. vaults large enough for walk-in entry.

Security Filing Cabinets

In most organizations, everyday administrative files are stored in filing cabinets. Though some contain confidential information, most do not. Losing these paper files to a fire would be a nuisance, but as long as the computer files are not also lost, everything is recoverable. Because filing cabinets are normally located in busy traffic areas of offices, someone wanting to steal something from a locked filing cabinet would need about a half an hour to pry it open undisturbed. That's not a likely scenario. So, in general, when it comes to everyday files, fire is the biggest concern. A standard filing cabinet that can withstand a fire for one hour and is fitted with a lock meets most office needs.

What works for paper files, however, does not work for preserving computer data files. Floppy disks, microfilm, microfiche, and CDs are highly vulnerable to humidity, dust, and magnetic fields. They also self-destruct in temperatures over 52 °C (125 °F). These items are too sensitive to store in a standard filing cabinet and must be stored in an indestructible fireproof container known as a security filing cabinet or a safe.

Focus on Technologies

Gardex Filing Cabinet

The Gardex filing cabinet is typical of current security filing cabinet technology. It has

- fire-resistant insulation;

- a ULC-listed key-operated plunger lock system;

- a selective locking system that allows any combination of drawers to be locked while leaving the remainder open;

- an inner steel jacket that prevents access to a locked drawer from an unlocked compartment; and

- independent insulation for each drawer so that if one drawer is left open, the others remain fire-protected.

Safes

For larger items of value, most organizations will need to consider safes and vaults. They are more expensive than security cabinets, with cost increasing with the number of protective features. Most safes protect against either fire, or burglary, or both.

In burglary-resistant safes, the key is preventing access. Doorjambs are angled in such a way that the safe door cannot be driven inward; the doorway works like a set of puzzle pieces, with doorway edges fitting into the matching pieces of the frame on both sides. Burglars can also break into the walls of a safe. To prevent this, quality safes incorporate offset panel seams along the sides of the safe.

Fire-Resistant Safes

Protecting valuables from fire becomes more complicated. It is critical to understand how fire resistant the physical composition of the items to be stored in the safe are before the components of the safe that are designed to preserve them are selected. For instance, the insulation designed to line the walls for most fire safes have compounds that suspend moisture in them. The insulation looks like plaster, and in an Underwriters' Laboratories of Canada (ULC) test, where the safe is placed inside an oven and the temperature is set at 982 °C (1,800 °F) to mimic an actual fire, the insulation inside the safe must cool and sustain a temperature of 177 °C (350 °F) (which burns paper) for over an hour. At the same time, it releases the trapped moisture in the form of steam. After an hour, if the cash and papers stored in the safe are still intact, it receives the basic ULC paper rating. An hour would give the fire department sufficient time to put out the fire in most emergencies of this kind.

Storing a combination of paper and computer disks presents a problem because the disks can't tolerate humidity and they self-destruct at 52 °C (125 °F). Thus, dry insulation to keep the temperature under 52 °C (125 °F) for at least one hour and a special surround that seals the safe against water leaking through from the firefighters' high-powered hoses are required.

High-Security Composite Safes

The best solution for most situations is a composite safe that protects contents from burglary and fire. These, however, are the most expensive because they exceed all industry standards.

Industry Standards for Security Safes in Canada

The safety ratings originally introduced for safes were introduced as a guide for setting premiums for their customers in the event safes were lost due to fire, theft, or some other irreparable damage. For want of another guideline, these ratings set the industry standards.

In Canada, the testing authority for safes is ULC, located in Scarborough, Ontario. The international label of equivalent authority is the Chicago-based Underwriters' Laboratories Inc. (ULI). Insurance charts list levels of acceptable insurable standards. To qualify for a class 2 raing, a burglary-resistant filing cabinet or safe, for instance, must meet either a minimum materials standard of a 3.8 cm (1.5 inch) steel plate body and a minimum 2.5 cm (1 inch) steel plate door with combination lock or a minimum performance standard. The remaining qualifying classes from 3 to 5 must pass a performance test in the ULC labs. Once a safe manufacturer achieves a ULC standard, its products are randomly tested to make sure they continue to meet that level of guaranteed performance.

These performance tests measure three things: how long a safe will resist the most recent tools in a safecracker's kit, how long it will resist fire damage, and how well it resists explosive devices.

Step Aside

Cover All the Bases

Constable Henri Bérubé of Peel Regional Police in Brampton, Ontario always ends his burglary workshops for security managers with this eye-opening anecdote: "When none of the tools worked that thieves used to break into a safe in a Kingston-area department store, they simply lifted it up and hauled it away. The safe provided excellent protection, but the retailer's detection system did not."

So, always remember, nothing done in security can be done in isolation. Every step between outer and inner defence lines is connected.

How To Select a Safe

In an article in the August/September 2000 edition of *Canadian Security*, industry experts combined to give the following advice in selecting the right filing cabinet, safe, or vault to suit a facility's needs:

- Analyze the physical properties of the assets to be protected.
- Start with realistic specs based on the budget, not a wish list.
- Look for a safe with interior features, such as multiple compartments, filing drawers, shelving, or custom racks that best match the facility's needs.
- Choose a safe with only the accessibility needed.
- Be aware that basic ULC standards may not be sufficient for the situation and that they represent only a minimum.
- Choose a safe with the most affordable security features.
- Check out the dealer's reputation and service record for safes.

LOCKS

Consider this statement: "There is no locking device on earth that can't be opened." True or false? It's true.

Lock pickers on the Internet not only brag about how they can open "anything with a keyhole, dial, or access port" with their picking tools, they have posted a manual telling any criminal who wants to know how to do it. Under these conditions, how can any security manager ever be confident of locks as a means of defence against break-ins?

The difference between a standard lock and a high security lock is how long it takes to open the lock using lock pickers' tools. For instance, a high security Medeco lock can take up to two hours or longer to pick open. If the rest of your security system is working effectively, the thief should be detected and apprehended long before he or she finishes unlocking the door under attack. So, the deterrent aspect of using a high security lock is the length of time it takes a thief to open it using criminals' tools.

Mechanical Locks

Ancient Egyptians introduced the first known locks over 4,000 years ago, and like the invention of the wheel, little has changed in their basic design today. A lock consists of a key, the operating mechanism, and a bolt. The key is inserted into a slot and turned to align with spring tumblers to unlatch the bolt.

FAST FACT

Insurance Considerations

An important feature of a quality safe or lock is that it should show evidence of tampering if it is broken. Insurers will resist paying for losses where there is no adequate evidence of break-in.

Warded Locks

Warded locks are generally found in pre-World War II construction. A warded lock has a single plate that includes both the doorknob and the keyway. The security value of these locks is almost nil.

Lever Locks

First used in the 18th century, lever locks are difficult to define in terms of security because they vary greatly in effectiveness. In this type of lock, there are usually four or five levers. When the key is inserted, it lifts each lever to a different height to allow the notch in the lever to align with the post of the bolt. As the key continues to turn a full 360°, it moves the locking bolt through the notch into the second gate and opens the lock. The best lever locks are used in safe deposit boxes and are nearly pick proof. The simplest of these locks are used in desks, lockers, and cabinets and are generally less secure than pin tumbler locks.

Pin Tumbler Locks

Over half the locks in use today are the pin tumbler locks that you see on house and garage doors, padlocks, and mailboxes. Invented by Linus Yale, this design has five tumblers, which provide about one million different key combinations for each lock. When the key is inserted, the grooves along both sides of the key edge connect with the five tumblers to align them in a straight line, which then allows the plug to turn to release the locking mechanism. Despite multiple key combinations, the delay factor for picking a pin tumbler lock is only 10 minutes or less.

If the wrong key is inserted, some of the pins will not rise to the correct level while others will rise too high. Without alignment, the cylinder cannot turn.

Wafer or Disc Tumbler Locks

Wafer or disc tumbler locks are less secure than pin tumbler locks. The tumblers are shaped like thin flat wafers instead of pins but are similarly spring-loaded with less distance between the wafers. They are used for garage and trailer doors, desks, padlocks, filing cabinets, most autos, window locks, and older vending machines. The life of these locks, however, is limited because of their soft metal construction. Although these locks provide more security than do warded locks, they cannot be considered very effective. The delay afforded is approximately three minutes. A higher security version is a double-wafer lock used in old pop and candy machines, gas caps, filing cabinets, and window locks.

Tubular Cylinder Locks

Tubular cylinder locks are pin tumbler locks arranged on a circular plane. Unlike conventional pin tumbler locks, all of the pins are visible to the eye. The central section of the lock rotates to operate the cam when all of the seven pins have reached their breaking points. When the proper key is entered into the lock, the tumblers are pressed into position so that the central plug can be turned. This manual operation of inserting the key places the tumblers in position so that the lock can be operated and ensures that frost, dust, salt, or unfavorable climatic conditions will not affect the smooth operation of the lock. Used for alarm control systems, newer vending machines, car-wash control boxes, and higher security applications for protection of property, merchandise, and cash, they comprise about 25 percent of locks in use today. They provide the maximum amount of security for their price range.

Lock Evaluation

The strength of a lock is determined by how well it resists forcible entry and concealed entry. Overall, the factors that determine how effective a lock really is depend on four things: design, construction, installation, and maintenance

Design

A good security lock is designed to be functional and is in a style or design that suits the selected task.

Construction

A good security lock is constructed of solid forged materials with reinforced moving parts for durability and resistance to impact.

Installation

Installation of a good security lock is easy to do with a minimum of special tools. If the installation process is difficult or lengthy, there is a risk that the lock will not be installed correctly.

Maintenance

Maintenance of a good security lock should be simple and require simple tools. The design of the lock and its functional parts need to support this.

Pick-Resistant Features

Pin tumbler locks can be designed with improved security features. These are known as pick-resistant features. Here are some of the more popular examples found in the security industry today.

Mushroom-Head Pins

The rounded shape of the head on the pin fools the lock picker into thinking it is picked when in fact it isn't. When upward pressure is applied, the pins seem to be aligned with the spring tumblers in the keyway, but the additional spools or mushroom heads above the pins are not. They continue to block the cylinder from turning all the way to release the lock.

Six- or Seven-Pin Tumblers

Most pin tumbler locks carry five pins. High-security pin tumbler locks are available with six or seven pins, and the additional pins offer an increased level of pick resistance.

Medeco Lock Sidebar

This security feature allows the key to move each of the pins in sequence as well as the side bar when the key is inserted.

Multiple Direction Pins

An even greater level of pick resistance is afforded when the pins are mounted at right angles to each other. Only the most expensive locks carry this feature.

Biaxial Pins

Biaxial pins are cut out at an angle of about 45° and form a "V" within the cylinder. This feature makes them extremely difficult to pick.

"MIWA" Four Pins and Magnetic Discs

Designed on the principle of magnetic polarities, each "key" or plastic card contains a set of small magnets arranged in a coded pattern to attract and repel other magnets in the lock, thereby allowing the spring-loaded bolt or cam to open the lock and allow entry. These are used in access control systems.

Security Applications for Mechanical Locks

There are three main types of pin tumbler locks used for security applications: rim, mortise, and deadbolt.

Rim Lock

The rim lock is a pin tumbler lock that is activated entirely by the action of the key being turned. It has no external latch, bolt, or handle. Rim locks can be keyed from both sides of the door.

Mortise Lock

The mortise lock is widely used on doors where a combination of aesthetics (looks) and security are required. Operating with a pin tumbler system, this lock is inserted into the frame of the door so that only the handles and keyway are visible on the surface of the door. Mortise locks have a very slim profile that allows them to be fully inserted into the thin width of the door.

Deadbolt Lock

Used for higher security applications, deadbolt locks are those mounted on a door above the knob, are not spring-loaded, and cannot be opened by sliding a plastic or metal card through to the bolt so as to work it open. The deadbolt design uses the basic pin tumbler lock with one important addition. When the lock is in the closed position, the person occupying the interior of the room can turn a latch or shift a button/lever that will engage a separate bolt into the frame of the door. This bolt cannot be disengaged using the key from outside the room. The only way to disengage the bolt is to activate the lever or latch from the inside of the door.

Key Control

Although selecting the right lock is an important concern, it's not the whole picture. You also need to consider who controls the master key and how custody and use of the key will be managed.

Alan Heaney, director of Canadian operations for Medeco Canada, quotes an alarming statistic:

> More than 75 percent of thefts occurring today happen internally. In hospitals, for instance, it's not people breaking in causing thefts. They are caused by employees or patients who have keys or access to places they shouldn't.

Here are a few things security officers can arrange to do to ensure security keys stay in the hands of authorized personnel only.

Copying Restrictions

In this case, someone wishing to cut a copy of a key would be required to produce written authorization, as the original keys to the lock would bear a manufacturer's stamp advising "Do Not Copy." In addition, the lock may have an extended warranty as well as an individual serial number.

Key Accountability

In buildings where a cleaning service requires keys to clean the offices, it is foolhardy to issue pass keys for an extended period of time to all workers. In such settings, there is often a high turnover of workers, and workers usually clean offices and stores at night when they are unoccupied.

The best policy is to have the cleaning service report to the security reception desk where specific interior keys are issued only to the housekeepers cleaning these areas. When the housekeepers have completed their work, they sign out and return the key they used.

Also, because tenants or employees who are issued entrance keys can lose them or forget to return them when they leave the company's employ, it is wise to change the lock cylinder in the entrance every few months and issue new keys to the authorized personnel.

Key Inventory

When a key is issued, security should maintain strict records, showing the name of the person who received a key, the employee number, position, the date issued, department, and the date the employee returned the key on leaving the company's employ.

Keys issued during non-working hours to temporary or contracted staff should be kept in a locked location and accounted for daily by the security officer on duty; the log should be checked and signed by the security supervisor at the end of each shift.

Lost Key Policy

When a key is reported lost, security personnel should write up an investigative report. They should check to see if the key was used to access a sensitive area. If it was, or if there are other suspicious concerns that arise during the investigation, the locks should immediately be changed and new keys issued.

SUMMARY

Access control systems are designed to control the movement of individuals into, and within, a protected facility. The most common systems include keypad systems, electronic keys, and card-based systems. Biometrics is a cutting-edge class of technology based on the principle of unique physical characteristics. Technology that measures these characteristics can be designed to control access based on features of the individual.

Today's thieves are very sophisticated criminals, who know the strengths and weaknesses of every make of security filing cabinet, safe, or vault better than most owners, bankers, and security managers. When it comes to preserving a company's assets and critical data or designs, security personnel need to look beyond the obvious and provide the best-made security, filing cabinet, safe, or vault the company can afford.

Mechanical locking systems are among the most widely used security devices in the world. Understanding how they should be used, as well as their strengths and weaknesses, will allow security officers to provide a higher standard of protective services during their career.

KEY TERMS

biometrics

identity theft

plastique

solenoid

tailgating

PERFORMANCE APPLICATION

1. Why do some facilities incorporate automated access control? List three common access control systems.

2. What are two pitfalls of a system based on cards with electromagnetic strips?

3. What are the advantages of an access control system based on biometrics? List three forms of biometric systems.

4. Locate five Canadian manufacturers of security filing cabinets, safes, and vaults. In your role as a security officer, select one specific brand for each of the following for your employer:

   - security filing cabinet

   - burglary-resistant safe

   - fire-resistant safe

   When selecting the brand for each of the above, what was your primary consideration? Why?

5. If you had a restricted security budget for a small developing company making major breakthroughs in space technology, the safety of what assets would concern you the most? Explain what storage solution you would recommend and why you think it is the right solution for this company.

6. Find four manufacturers of mechanical security locks in Canada on the Internet and, in your role as a security supervisor or manager, select one sample brand name for each of the basic locks and describe their features:

   - warded locks

   - lever locks

   - pin tumbler locks

   - wafer or disc tumbler locks

   - tubular cylinder locks

7. Find lock manufacturers on the Internet for each of the three high-security locks discussed in this chapter: rim, mortise, and deadbolt. List which brand name you would recommend for each type and explain your choice.

8. Why is key control even more important than the locking system itself?

INTRODUCTION

This chapter will introduce three classes of security technology and will explain how each works, and how each can be integrated with the others and with the human security system.

ALARMS

An alarm is a means of giving early warning of intrusion or any other condition the system is designed to detect. There are three standard categories: intrusion alarms, fire alarms, and special-use alarms.

Intrusion alarms warn of entry of trespassers beyond authorized zones. They are commonly found in homes, businesses, and vehicles.

Fire alarms warn of smoke, heat, carbon monoxide, or fire, depending on their nature. They may sound an alarm and/or trigger the operation of a sprinkler system.

Special-use alarms warn of other dangers, including changes in temperature and humidity, toxic fumes, and machinery malfunctions.

Alarm System Capabilities

Alarm systems can be designed to provide total facility protection. Accordingly, there are elements of each system that provide the best security protection for certain areas. These elements have been developed to complement the four lines of defence—grounds perimeter protection, building perimeter protection, space/area protection, and object protection—introduced in chapter 16.

Elements of an Alarm

Alarms serve to warn you that something is happening and that your immediate attention and reaction are required. Alarm systems are of many types, but all have three common elements: a sensor detector, a circuit or sending device, and an enunciator or sounding device.

Chapter Objectives

When you have completed this chapter, you will

- have a security officer's basic knowledge and understanding of alarm systems; internal access control devices; and closed-circuit television and surveillance systems and the role each system plays in providing intrusion detection, special alarm functions, and access control.

- have an understanding of the advantages and challenges involved in integrating physical security with automated functions into one system that is centrally controlled.

intrusion alarm
warning that an unauthorized person
has gained entry

fire alarm
warning that smoke,
heat, carbon monoxide,
or fire has occurred

special-use alarm
warning that a danger,
such as toxic fumes or
machine malfunctions,
has occurred

Alarm Sensor Detector

A detector must initiate an alarm when sensing a condition to which it was designed to react, even if primary power fails, and back-up power fails to come on immediately.

Circuit or Sending Device

The circuit or sending device transmits the alarm to the sounding device, where it will be heard or seen by security personnel.

Enunciator or Sounding Device

The enunciator or sounding device is a light, a bell/buzzer, or a punch tape located at the monitoring station. It alerts security personnel that the alarm sensor has detected something.

Alarm System Monitoring

There are several different ways that an alarm system can be monitored for response purposes. A facility's choice of monitoring system is usually based on perceived risk, cost issues, and facility size.

A large facility will most likely have a proprietary alarm monitoring station—alarms of all kinds (intrusion, fire, and specialized) are set up to trigger a signal at a central location, from which the facility's own security and/or fire personnel will be deployed. This kind of system permits a very rapid response.

Residences and small commercial facilities without 24-hour security personnel may choose an alarm that sends a signal to a remote-control station that is staffed by contract security. When the alarm is triggered, the monitoring station sends personnel to the scene (and in some cases, contacts on-site security personnel). The response time with such a system is slower than with a proprietary system.

Somewhat similar to this kind of alarm is a system designed to dial one or more contact phone numbers when triggered. This system can lead to delayed response times and its reliability is contingent on the unimpaired operation of the public phone system.

A third kind of alarm may be localized to a specific area or zone within a facility. This kind of alarm will sound or light up only in the vicinity of the disturbance. It's designed to alert security personnel working close by. To the extent that it may take extra time to get back-up for a major emergency (since local guards may have to call or radio other personnel), it has limitations; however, there are advantages: it is more discreet than a building-wide alarm, and therefore less likely to trigger panic among people in the building, or to disrupt operations unnecessarily in other areas.

INTRUSION DETECTION SENSORS

Controlling unauthorized intrusion into a facility is a key function of security. Security personnel must work to allow unimpeded access to employees and other authorized entrants, while excluding trespassers. Effective internal access control can be achieved by the application of a combination of three forms of security coverage. These are:

1. security officers for static guard and patrol duties;

2. a key, card, or other electronic access system; and

3. appropriate response to intrusion sensors and detectors.

Types and Characteristics of Alarm Sensors and Intrusion Detectors

A wide variety of intrusion detection systems are available. The choice of a particular system for a facility depends on many factors, including facility size, incident history, and the nature of the facility (administrative office, manufacturing facility, etc.). A summary of the most important intrusion detection systems is provided here; once security officers know which type is in use in the facility in which they are working, they can study that system in greater detail so that they are familiar with its operation, its advantages, and its weaknesses.

Mechanical Switches

Mechanical switches are spring-loaded or plunger-style devices that change position to trigger an alarm when a door or window is disturbed.

When patrolling an area equipped with mechanical switches, security officers should check for ill-fitting doors or windows that create conditions for unreliable detection. Loose mountings can allow random movement of a door or window in windy weather or high humidity, triggering a nuisance alarm, or allowing an intruder to take advantage of the device's erratic operation to gain entry.

Mechanical switches, if not properly concealed, are relatively easy to defeat. Holding the switch in the "normal closed" position while opening the door or window will preclude the initiation of an alarm. Also, taping the switch in the "closed" position during daytime operations can allow an intruder to return after the alarm has been activated and open the door or window without generating a new alarm.

Magnetic Switches

Magnetic switches are contact switches used to detect the opening of a door, window, or container. They depend on the direct physical operation/disturbance of the sensor to generate an alarm.

Magnetic switches are composed of two parts:

1. a two-position magnetic switch mounted on the interior of a door, window, or container frame; and

2. a two-position, magnetically operated switch.

The standard switch is designed to be either normally open or normally closed, depending on the design. When the door/window is closed, the magnet pulls the switch to its "normal" non-alarmed position. When the door/window is opened, the magnet releases the switch, breaking the contact to activate the alarm.

While patrolling an area equipped with magnetic switches, security officers should check for any loose attachment of the door, window, or gate to its framework because this can cause unreliable detection and nuisance alarms.

A skilled criminal can sometimes penetrate a door or window equipped with a magnetic switch without moving the magnet switch mechanism to bypass the alarm device. Some criminals use a second, free-moving and stronger magnet to imitate the mounted magnet, so they can open the door without generating an alarm. One way to avoid this is to place the switch where a potential intruder cannot see it.

Balanced Magnetic Switches

Balanced magnetic switches (BMSs) consist of a switch assembly with an internal magnet that is usually mounted on the door/window frame and a balancing (or external) magnet mounted on the moveable door/window.

Typically, the switch is balanced in the open position within the magnetic field of the two magnets. If the movement of the external magnet disturbs the magnetic field, the switch moves to a "closed" position. When the door is closed, the magnetic field generated by the balancing magnet interacts with the field created by the switch magnet, so that the total net effect on the switch is stable. When the door is opened, the switch falls to one of the contacts, becoming unstable, and generates an alarm.

BMSs provide a higher level of security for windows and doors than magnetic or mechanical switches.

Again, security officers should check for loosely fitting doors and windows that can cause nuisance alarms. Extreme weather conditions that cause a door, window, or access gate to move back and forth excessively can add to the nuisance alarm rate (NAR).

Pressure Devices

Pressure devices transmit an alarm when they detect pressure, usually at a threshold between an authorized and an unauthorized zone. For security purposes, these devices are most often concealed in floor mats, either visible or hidden under carpeting.

False alarms can occur if the wiring is faulty or if weather conditions cause doors to swing or other objects to move and disturb the sensors.

Photoelectric Devices

A common motion intrusion detector is a photoelectric device, which, using regular, infrared or ultraviolet light, transmits a beam across a threshold to a receiver. Disruption of the beam (by a person or an object crossing the threshold) triggers an alarm.

The main vulnerability of this kind of system is that, if an intruder can determine the trajectory or pathway of the beam of light, he or she can step over or crawl under it without triggering the alarm. For this reason, it's essential that the transmitter and receiver are properly concealed and that the beam of light cannot be detected. In some applications, concealment can be achieved by using mirrors to redirect the beam of light.

Depending on the type of device, intruders can sometimes also gain entry by using a flashlight or other device to maintain light going into the receiver. Using an infrared- or ultraviolet-based system can make this more difficult.

Microwave Sensors

Microwave sensors are motion detection devices that transmit or flood a designated area or zone with an electronic field. A movement in the zone disturbs the field and sets off an alarm. Microwave sensors may be used in exterior and interior applications.

Microwave sensors transmit microwave signals in the "X" band. These signals are generated by a Gunn diode operating within preset limits that do not affect humans or the operation of pacemakers. Although very little power is used, the system provides enough energy for a detector to project a signal up to 120 m in an uninterrupted line of sight. The detection of intrusion is directly related to the Doppler frequency shift principle. Most sensors are tuned to measure the Doppler shift between 20 Hz and 120 Hz. These frequencies are closely related to the movements of humans. Objects that fail to produce a signal or produce a signal outside the tuned frequencies are ignored. Objects that fall within the range cause the sensor to generate an alarm signal.

There are two basic types of microwave sensors. In monostatic sensors, the transmitter and receiver are contained in a single dual-function unit. The antenna is mounted within the microwave cavity and can be configured or shaped to cover a specific area or detection zone. In bistatic sensors, the transmitter and receiver are two separate units creating a detection zone between them. A bistatic system can cover a larger area and would typically be used if more than one sensor is required. The detection zone is created between the two units. The antenna can be configured to alter the signal field (width, height), creating different detection zones.

Microwave sensors can be used to monitor both exterior areas and interior confined spaces, such as vaults, special storage areas, hallways, and service passageways. In the exterior setting, they can be used to monitor an area or a definitive perimeter line, as well as to serve as an early warning alert of intruders approaching a door or wall.

To further enhance detection, video motion detection equipment can be installed to complement the microwave sensor. The use of a companion system not only provides a second line of defence, but also provides security personnel with an additional tool to assess alarms and discriminate actual or potential penetrations from false alarms or nuisance events.

Because of the high frequencies at which microwaves travel, the signal or sensor is not affected by moving air or changes in temperature or humidity. However, the high frequency allows the signal to easily pass through standard walls, glass, sheet rock, and wood. This can cause false alarms to be generated by movement adjacent to, but outside the protected area.

Within the detection area, it is essential to test for, note, and compensate for any dead spots (areas of no detection) created by metal objects such as dumpsters, shipping crates, trash cans, and electrical boxes. These dead spots create ideal areas for intrusion attempts. In addition, signals reflected off these metal objects can "extend" sensor coverage to areas not intended to be covered, thus creating the potential for false alarms.

Ultrasonic Motion Detectors

ultrasonic motion detector

intrusion detecting sensor that emits ultrasonic sound energy into a monitored area and reacts to a change in the reflected energy pattern

The **ultrasonic motion detector** operates in much the same way as the radio frequency unit does, except that it consists of a transceiver that both transmits and receives ultrasonic waves. The active ultrasonic sensor emits ultrasonic sound energy into a monitored area and reacts to a change in the reflected energy pattern.

The sound uses air as its medium and travels in a wave-type motion. The wave is reflected from the surroundings in the room or hallway, and the device "hears" a pitch characteristic of the protected environment. When an intruder enters the room, the wave pattern is disturbed and reflected more quickly, thus increasing the pitch and signalling an alarm.

Typically, ultrasonic sensors are mounted on the wall or ceiling. Ultrasonic energy is easily contained within a selected area, avoiding the problem of the energy passing through walls and detecting activity outside the protected zone.

The disadvantage is that ultrasonic energy will not pass through most solid objects and material, thus creating dead zones within the coverage area where the sensor is ineffective. The sensor must be positioned so dead zones are minimal. Also, extreme changes in temperature or humidity from the initial calibration may cause a reduction in detection reliability.

Some of the most common stimuli that cause ultrasonic sensors to false alarm are air movement from heating and air conditioning systems, drafts from doors and windows, hissing from pipes, and ringing of telephones. These stimuli can create noise near or in the ultrasonic range, thus triggering an alarm. Also, anything non-human that moves, such as animals, has the potential to cause an alarm.

Slow horizontal movement by an intruder across the area of coverage is often difficult for ultrasonic sensors to detect. Proper calibration is needed to ensure that slow-moving intruders will be detected. In addition, a knowledgeable and properly equipped intruder can use special "test lights" to detect coverage patterns and circumvent these areas.

Passive Infrared Detectors

As the name implies, passive infrared (PIR) sensors are inactive. The sensor does not transmit a signal; the sensor head simply registers an impulse when received. The sensor head is typically divided into several sectors or zones, each defined with specific boundaries. Detection occurs when a heat-emitting source (like a human body) crosses two adjacent sector boundaries or crosses the same boundary twice within a specified time. PIRs "see/detect" infrared images by sensing the contrast between the "hot" image and the "cooler" background. Infrared energy is measured in microns, with the human body producing energy in the region of 7 to 14 microns. Most PIR sensors are focused on this narrow bandwidth. When the radiation change captured by the lens exceeds a certain preset value, the thermal sensor produces an electrical signal, which is sent to a built-in processor for evaluation and possible alarm.

Because the PIR looks for thermal radiation projected against a cooler background, detection is based on temperature. As the environment approaches the same temperature as the intruder (about 37 °C), the detectors become less sensitive. This is especially true for environments ranging between 30 °C to 38 °C. Theoretically, if a person was radiating the same temperature as the environment, he or she would be invisible to the sensor.

Heat radiating from small animals and/or rodents can cause false alarms. Time-activated space heaters, ovens, and hot water pipes, as well as car headlights can also cause false alarms if they are in the field of view. Although infrared energy from sunlight is filtered by ordinary window glass, objects in a room can become heated over time and subsequently begin emitting and reflecting infrared energy. If this energy is "turned off/on" (such as by the movement of clouds), it can create a random "on/off" situation, thereby generating nuisance alarms.

Shadowing, cloaking, or masking the intruding heat source, whether a person or a machine, from the field of view, decreases the probability of detection because it reduces the possibility of sufficient radiated and emitted heat being focused on the thermal sensor. In addition, knowing the dead spots of the detection pattern can permit an intruder to bypass active regions. Walking toward the sensor rather than across the sensor's field of view can also reduce the detection capability by not allowing the boundaries of the detection beams to be broken.

Active Infrared Detectors

Interior active infrared sensors generate a curtain pattern of modulated infrared energy and react to a change in the modulation of the frequency or an interruption in the received energy. Both of these occurrences happen when an intruder passes through the protection zone.

Interior active infrared sensors are made up of a transmitter and receiver encased within a single housing unit. The transmitter uses a laser to create a detection zone. The laser plane is projected onto a special retro-reflective tape that defines the end or edge of the protection zone. Energy is reflected off the tape to the receiver, which is located in the same housing unit as the transmitter.

Upon reaching the receiver, the energy passes through a collecting lens that focuses the energy onto a collecting cell, which converts the infrared energy to an electrical signal. The receiver monitors the electrical signal and generates an alarm when the signal drops below a preset threshold for a specific period of time. An intruder passing through the field of detection will interrupt the signal and temporarily cause the signal to fall below the threshold value.

Depending on which type of tape is used as the reflective medium, coverage patterns can be between 4.5 m to 7.6 m wide by 5.2 m to 9.1 m long. In addition, the laser plane angle can be adjusted from 37° to 180°. This system has a high probability of detecting intruders. Speed or direction of the intruder, and the temperature of the environment, have no effect on detection characteristics.

Dust or other particles collecting on the surface of the reflective tape can hinder the detection capabilities. The reflective tape must have no gaps and be continuous to ensure reliable detection, and the angle from the sensor to the ends or corners of the tape must not exceed 45°.

Incandescent light shone directly into the sensor itself can generate a nuisance alarm, as can sunlight or incandescent lights reflected off the tape into the receiver. While infrared technology has a high detection rate, a knowledgeable intruder can deduce the detection field from the location of reflective tape and plan his or her movements to avoid detection.

Capacitance Sensors

This detection system is based on the principles of electromagnetics. An ungrounded metal object (such as a safe) is wired to two oscillator circuits that oscillate in balance, creating a stable electromagnetic field around the object. When the field is disturbed, an alarm is triggered. The system is commonly used to protect metal containers and high-security storage areas within a fenced enclosure. False alarms can be triggered by anything (vibrations, wind, animal movements) that disturbs the detection field.

Sonic Alarm Sensors

ambient noise
normal background sound

Known sometimes as noise detection, sound, or audio alarms, sonic alarm systems operate on the principle that an intruder will make enough noise in a protected area to be picked up by microphones that will activate an alarm. This type of system has a wide variety of uses, limited only by the problems of **ambient noise** (normal background sound) levels.

Audio detectors listen for noises generated by an intruder's entry into a protected area. They are generally, but not exclusively, used in internal applications. For example, they may be used to alert security about someone's movement from a public foyer into a restricted storage area.

The sensor is made up of two devices: pick-up units and an amplifier.

Pick-up units (receivers) mounted on the walls or ceilings of the monitored area and an amplifier that contains processing circuitry. The pick-up units are basically microphones that listen for noise. These microphones collect sound for analysis by the processor circuit, which can be calibrated to a noise threshold that is characteristic for an intrusion attempt. If a certain amount of noise is detected from a monitored area within a selected time period, an alarm signal is generated.

Audio sensors should be mounted in areas where the predicted intrusion noise is expected to exceed that of the normal background noise. If background noise does exist, and if calibration is not set to compensate for it, the microphone may be unable to detect or differentiate an intrusion noise.

Typically, audio sensors are used in conjunction with another type of detection system (PIR, ultrasound, microwave) to improve probability of detection. Because an audio sensor is unaffected by changes in the thermal environment and light levels, its use with a thermal imaging or a light-based motion detection system can provide multiple ways to detect an intrusion.

Principal causes of unreliable detection include excessive background noise, such as airplanes, trains, or thunderstorms. Also, an intruder who moves very slowly and takes measures to muffle the normal sounds of movement may avoid detection.

Vibration Sensors

Vibration sensors are designed to be mounted on walls, ceilings, and floors to detect mechanical vibrations caused by chopping, sawing, drilling, ramming, or any type of physical intrusion attempt that would penetrate the structure on which the sensors are mounted. Vibration sensors are not appropriate for walls of limited structural integrity, such as sheet rock, plywood, or thin metal, because these types of walls are very prone to vibrations caused by sources other than intrusion actions. Poor placement, for example, near machinery or in an area subject to noise from trains or airplanes is another cause of nuisance alarms.

Security personnel patrolling an area equipped with vibration sensors should check for unstable or improper installation.

The system can be defeated by an intruder's selection of a point and method of entry in a segment of a wall, roof, or floor that will permit the suppression or diffusion of the intrusion vibrations.

Conductive Foil

Conductive foil, usually available in strips or sheets, is designed to be applied to the interior surface of glass. The foil contains electrical filaments that, when broken, break a circuit and trigger an alarm.

Grid Wire Detectors

This intrusion detection system is designed to protect areas with walls of hollow or soft construction (such as drywall). An intruder may attempt to cut or smash through drywall to avoid triggering a door alarm. To protect the walls, a system of wires is installed inside the walls between rooms, and disruption of the wires triggers an alarm.

Another defeat measure, which is also applicable to many other sensors as well, is the generation of a persistent but random number of false alarms over a long period of time, causing the alarm to be ignored or the response time to be greatly diminished.

SECURITY SUPPORT FOR INTRUSION DETECTION

While the intrusion detectors discussed in this chapter are designed to identify and report unwanted activity, they are useless without the support of an appropriate human response.

Appropriate Alarm Maintenance and Response

Security personnel must support the technology in place. They should

- respond promptly and appropriately to all alarms;

- patrol alarmed areas to check on the integrity of the alarm system; check that the system is engaged, that the sensors are in their appropriate places, and that they are working correctly; look for any nuisance alarm triggers, such as high winds, or excessive background noise;

- promptly report all technical problems to control, and/or arrange for maintenance by technicians;

- be alert to a system's vulnerabilities and monitor for signs that an intruder is seeking to circumvent the system; and

- respond appropriately to any nuisance alarms by determining and eliminating their cause.

It is worth remembering that one way a patient intruder can evade almost any detection system is by triggering regular nuisance alarms, in the hope that security personnel will eventually either ignore the alarms or respond slowly and/or carelessly to them, providing the intruder an opportunity to enter undetected.

Finally, closed-circuit television equipment, discussed below, can provide an additional level of intrusion protection, by allowing security personnel to visually monitor the premises.

Security of Systems Control Panels

It is vital to the security of a facility that the control panels for an intrusion detection system function properly. Security personnel must be vigilant about protecting these control panels. Here are some points to consider:

- The control panels for the intrusion detection system must be protected from vandalism, unauthorized use, and intentional attack.

- The "activity" state of the alarm system has to be controlled with a shunt key or code number.

- The system should incorporate 30- to 90-second delays for authorized entries and exits.

- The system has be connected to an enunciator by hard-wire, transmission lines, AC/DC, tone, or digital signals to ensure that signal output will be available when required.

- The panel must be equipped with a back-up power source in the form of NiCad (nickel cadmium) batteries, a solar-pack, or Gel-Cel batteries.

- The control panel must also be equipped with a voltage discriminator that sets the alarm off in one-second intervals if the amplitude, frequency, or phase of the carrier signal is off by plus or minus 10 percent. This protects the panel from someone disconnecting the signal transmission wire to prevent the audio alarm from being activated.

CLOSED-CIRCUIT TELEVISION SYSTEMS

"The Sleuth that NEVER Sleeps," an article in the November 2000 issue of *Canadian Security*, conveyed the advantage of closed-circuit television (CCTV) technology very nicely.

In the early days of CCTV technology, only banks and high-end industrial and commercial facilities could afford to install CCTV systems. In the 21st century, modern video and web cameras have become an essential feature of the security landscape. Government, law enforcement, correctional institutions, the military, civil defence, the media, airports, seaports, train stations, emergency response agencies, and banks along with the private sector use CCTV surveillance because it is by far the most versatile security tool available today.

Step Aside

CCTV and Personal Privacy

Other pioneers of the CCTV age included eccentric millionaires. During the late 1970s, one very wealthy building developer in Burlington, Ontario installed sensors and covert camera surveillance throughout his headquarters building—not to guard against intruders or vandals, but to monitor the efficiency of his employees. His office looked like a *Star Trek* set with a bank of monitors that swept two-thirds of the room. A little sensor under his secretary's seat told him how long she was away from her desk.

The capacity of CCTV to invade personal privacy has been a matter of controversy since the technology was introduced. Attitudes toward surveillance in the workplace change constantly, in response to social changes. Since the September 11, 2001 terrorist attacks in the United States, public attitudes toward surveillance have taken a more tolerant turn, but privacy continues to be an important issue in the workplace.

For security personnel working in high-risk enterprises, CCTV has become an essential component in the overall security scheme. While alarms are useful for intrusion detection, surveillance cameras permit security personnel to determine the nature of the intrusion, thus limiting dangerous "surprises" when an alarm response is required.

CCTV BENEFITS AND LIMITATIONS

Benefits

Effective surveillance systems have three primary functions:

1. They allow security personnel to view an intrusion from a remote location.

2. They collect evidence of an intrusion for later use in court.

3. They discourage would-be-thieves or vandals.

A fourth, more indirect benefit of CCTV is a reduction in insurance rates for businesses employing the technology. Some statistics suggest that the mere presence of CCTV technology in a facility reduces the incident rate by up to 60 percent.

Limitations

Four challenges—cost, standards, maintenance, and employee morale—can limit the effective use of CCTV and surveillance devices.

Cost

While CCTV technology represents a considerable expense for an organization, the technology costs must be considered by reference to the costs of *not* using it. Where the risk to the organization from unauthorized intrusion is very high, the cost of

---

Step Aside

CCTV Applications

CCTV technology has many different applications. It can be used to monitor activity

- in unprotected areas,
- in remote areas of a facility,
- on the perimeter of a facility,
- in amusement parks,
- on waterways and around marinas,
- on wireless highway traffic systems, and
- outside a residence through a selected television channel.

CCTV can be used to monitor cash transactions and to identify shoplifters and white-collar theft. Having this technology in place protects a facility from vandalism and deters intrusions and theft.

---

the equipment may be well warranted. Because of its ability to cover much of a facility simultaneously, the cost of CCTV should also be compared with the cost of having enough security officers to continually patrol the same territory. Where continual security coverage is needed, quality CCTV equipment will almost invariably be less expensive than maintaining a large patrol force.

Standards

The CCTV technology market is not widely regulated. Only British Columbia and Quebec license electricians who serve the security market. Ontario, to date, has no regulations governing those who sell or service security products, nor standards to guarantee the quality of security products. This means that it is fairly easy for business owners to be misled into purchasing a system that is of poor quality.

Maintenance

CCTV technology must be carefully maintained to work properly. Tape heads and service motors of VCRs must be cleaned to keep them in working order. In older analog systems, cable wiring also needs periodic repairs. While digital technology eliminates both the time and annual cost of this maintenance, a trend to wireless links further reduces system maintenance, except to computers and monitors within security networks.

Employee Morale

Regardless of the positive impact that a well-designed CCTV system has on the safety of a facility, there will always be employees who feel victimized or imposed upon by being subjected to surveillance. The onus falls on management and the security team to assure these people that the system is there for their protection and safety.

CCTV TECHNOLOGIES

Equipment

Because of early experiences where an intruder could not be identified adequately when "the picture resolution was too poor" or "the camera angle was wrong," CCTV equipment offered today provides better performance with more choices at more affordable prices. The more common types of equipment now used for security applications can be broken into three types: motion-picture cameras, sequence cameras, and video cameras with CCTV monitors.

Motion-Picture Cameras

- use high-speed 16 mm film,
- provide fast shutter speeds,
- can be alarm-activated,
- are limited to the amount of film in the can, and
- are noisy and expensive.

Sequence Cameras

- record still pictures at regular intervals,
- take a sequence of shots in rapid succession,
- adjust interval between shots,
- take shots in darkness using infrared film,
- use any type of camera from 8 mm to 70 mm, and
- can be used to verify checks because print quality is excellent.

Video Cameras with CCTV Monitors

- replace motion- and still-picture cameras,
- provide real-time video images and instant identification,
- use VCR technology to store images,
- allow flexible movement of a camera from any angle with zoom lens,
- convert **analog** signals to high-resolution **digital** images that are transmitted via modem over phone lines,
- trigger immediate police response,
- provide irrefutable evidence,

analog
represented by a continuous physical variable

digital
represented by digits using discrete values of a physical quality

- are more cost-effective (for example, reusable videotapes), and

- adapt easily to the environment, specific size requirements, specific tasks, and image requirements.

Operating Modes

There are several standard operating modes for CCTV in security applications. Here are a few examples.

The simplest operating mode is a single CCTV camera with one video monitor. This one-to-one system is typically used in a convenience store.

Figure 18.1 illustrates the capability of the monitoring system to view the images from several cameras at the same time on one monitor. For example, the monitor displayed in the middle of the top row shows a screen split into four smaller screens, also known as a "quad." Within each smaller screen a separate image from different cameras can be viewed.

A typical multicamera system routed to a central security location is shown in figure 18.2. This combination is used almost exclusively in small retail and commercial businesses. It is made up of several cameras connected to a video switcher, which in turn is connected to a CCTV monitor. Some models can support 21 cameras.

The combination shown in figure 18.3 is used to display the image from one camera to several different locations. The distance between the camera and each of the monitors can be metres or kilometres. This operating mode is used for reasons of response when the area being monitored is under extreme risk.

The combination of many cameras with many monitors shown in figure 18.4 is the most common security application for large facilities, especially those that consist of several buildings spread out over an extended area.

FIGURE 18.1 Images from Several Cameras Can Be Viewed in Many Different Ways on One Monitor

FIGURE 18.2   A Multicamera System

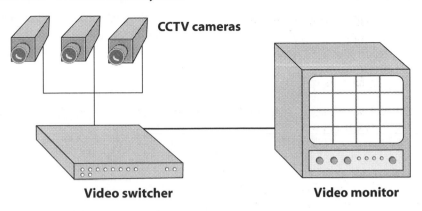

CCTV cameras

Video switcher

Video monitor

When a video switcher is connected to the cameras and the monitor, views from any camera can be selected either manually or automatically.

Up to 21 different images can be viewed on some monitors.

FIGURE 18.3   A One-Camera, Multimonitor System

The distance between the camera and the monitors can be metres or kilometres.

When an amplifier is connected to the camera and the monitors, identical images can be viewed simultaneously over several monitors.

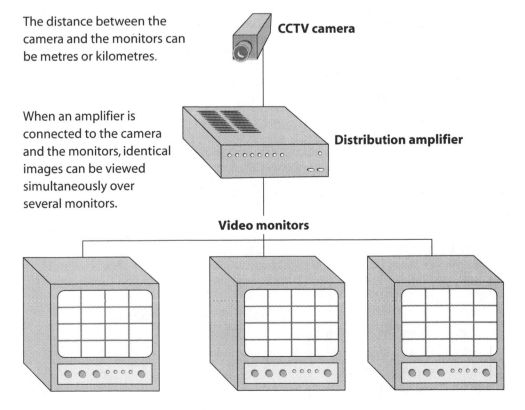

CCTV camera

Distribution amplifier

Video monitors

FIGURE 18.4 A Multicamera, Multimonitor System

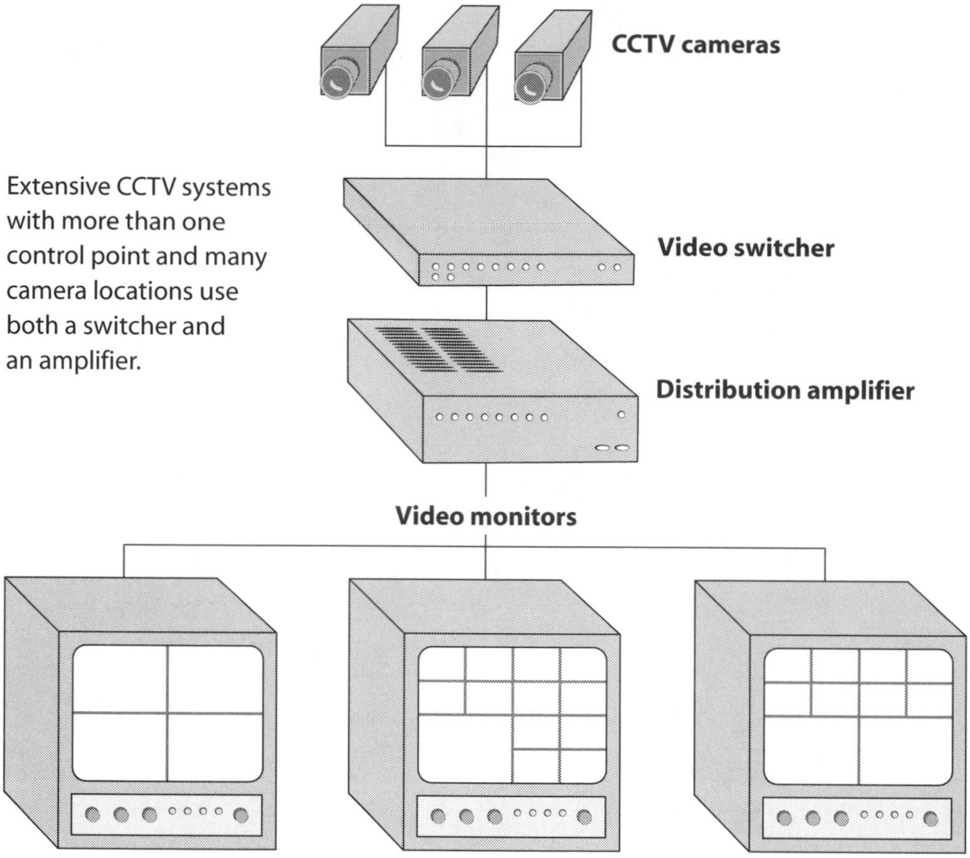

Extensive CCTV systems with more than one control point and many camera locations use both a switcher and an amplifier.

CCTV cameras

Video switcher

Distribution amplifier

Video monitors

Covert Applications

Covert CCTV cameras are designed to be hidden easily. A camera can be smaller than a quarter and can be designed to fit into almost any space so that it blends with the surroundings. Cameras can be hidden on surfaces, or in objects, such as wristwatches, sunshades, pens, mannequins—even the eye of a stuffed toy. Some cameras can be operated by remote control, using line of sight (LOS) activation or a signal frequency, or they can be wired directly into a building system as part of a security surveillance network. Specialized cameras can operate in extreme climactic conditions, low light (or even total darkness), underwater, or in the high-impact environment of a professional football player's helmet.

MAINTENANCE OF CCTV SURVEILLANCE SYSTEMS

Lack of maintenance is perhaps the biggest obstacle to CCTV effectiveness. There have been many instances where a crime has been committed within view of a security camera and, due to a faulty camera, dirty or poorly focused lens, or poorly maintained recording equipment, the recorded video image has been of no evidentiary value. Failure to carry out required maintenance will degrade the equipment and produce images unsuitable for evidence. The inspection, cleaning, and other maintenance of the CCTV system should be built into the patrol function, and

What Would You Do?

Video Surveillance for Work Performance Purposes

Read the following scenario, and answer the questions.

You work in the security department of a large school bus line. The depot/dispatch facility covers almost two hectares, with four separate buildings, a large parking area, and a repair centre. After a run of three serious occupational accidents on the site in the past year (two collisions with pedestrians, and one explosion in the repair shop) the bus line decided to install a video surveillance system. The system was intended to help increase workplace safety and to manage bus traffic on the site.

Your primary duty is to monitor the CCTV surveillance system. A senior executive in your employer's human resources department approaches you one morning and asks a favour. He suspects that an employee, mechanic Sara Smith, has been taking unauthorized smoke breaks during her shifts on duty. She is entitled to three breaks per eight-hour shift, including lunch, and she is required to leave the work premises to smoke. The human resources staff person asks you to monitor Ms. Smith's movements on and off the site and to keep a log of her smoke breaks over the course of a week.

1. Will you do as you have been asked? Why or why not?

2. Is monitoring employee breaks a part of the security staff's role?

3. Would your answer be different if you'd been asked to monitor the employee's smoking inside the repair shop? Why or why not?

4. Is it legal to monitor employee breaks using CCTV technology?

5. If you were uncertain about what you should do in the situation, whom might you ask for advice?

security personnel should have training on how to troubleshoot the technology and maintain it in good working order.

INTEGRATED SECURITY SYSTEMS

In the 21st century, converging physical security with information technology is no longer a *Star Wars* fantasy, but a growing reality in our efforts to increase safety for everyone. When an incident occurs, we want to hear an alarm, examine a point of intrusion immediately from every angle, see and understand what is happening, record the date and time, capture the incident on video, store the information in a central database, and directly transfer these pictures of the security breach to the police for their rapid response. We need to know everything possible, instantly. This takes a coordination of security functions and services with information technology that only integrated systems can meet, especially for security managers who are managing multiple sites.

In the digital world of today, we have the Internet and high bandwidth telephone lines and cable to provide immediate communication, and immediate communication is the cornerstone of the security industry. The question is, how do we tie the independent technologies of alarms, access control, and surveillance to the space-age wonders of wireless and cable communication?

Advantages and Challenges of Integration

Security today thrives in a complex technological environment. No matter what the application is, there are a number of different vendors and stakeholders involved in a system implementation. A security planner must work with equipment manufacturers, service providers, cable and conduit services, people who do the hard wire infrastructure installations, security device manufacturers, design agencies like security contractors and electrical engineers, information technology (IT) technicians, and programmers who set the standards and say, "Your product needs to conform to this kind of environment." A security planner must also work with facility managers who are concerned with the operating budgets and operational procedures in managing a building or a suite of buildings. Each service provider is an expert in his or her own field, but often knows little about the others. Coordinating all of these approaches and technologies is a significant challenge for the security planner, who needs to be much more of a generalist. He or she must be able to identify the integration points between each system and provide a vision that brings the information technology and security organizations together.

Early security systems integration was achieved through a collection of independent systems loosely connected through an **interface**. It meant that evidence was stored in separate databases and had to be correlated manually. Often critical information was overlooked or couldn't be retrieved if, for instance, videotape recordings weren't triggered because old tape hadn't been replaced. The pitfalls of this imperfect integration led to the evolution of a new specialist, the integrator, who custom designed and installed a seamless system.

Part of the integrator's job was to analyze the compatibility between existing systems and new add-ons and select only equipment and software that fit together. This allowed for real-time linking of events through the subsystems—action in one system setting off a snowball reaction in the others—and the data captured through the sequence could be transferred and stored in a central database. Now the guesswork was taken out of any investigation, and the necessary evidence could be collected with a click of a mouse.

With today's convergence of physical and network security, the information trail is even more seamless, but it brings another dimension into the picture. The information technology department within an organization has to become equally involved in a company's security design and procurement process.

In order to successfully integrate security technologies, you need, on the buyer's side, the chief decision makers—the security director, business administrator, company controller, and IT director; and on the seller's side, representatives from the product and communications suppliers and the integrator. The security director describes the problem and how he or she thinks it can be solved. The product suppliers explain which products will do the job, but these have to be linked into the company's existing IT network to get the fastest response from the police, so this requires products and software that are compatible with Internet **protocols**. The communications supplier then explains to the IT director what changes need to be made to the company network to accommodate the products. Together, the parties analyze the needs and create the integrated system. At the same time, those financing the implementation both see how the security problem is going to be solved and what return on investment they can expect to achieve.

interface
device that allows independent systems to interact

protocols
set of rules or conventions that allow sending and receiving computers to understand the messages being transmitted

Changing Roles

Patrol officers are no longer the centre of the security universe. There is an ever-increasing need for technologically skilled personnel who can understand, run, monitor, and fix the "brains" of integrated systems.

Integrated security systems can reduce the number of security officers deployed through a facility and can free up security personnel to serve other duties. The growing complexity and expertise required in the security industry directly raises the standards for skill and knowledge in new hires. Higher standards, in turn, increase the prestige of the profession, and command higher pay.

SUMMARY

While no technology will ever replace the eyes, ears, and other senses of security personnel, the complex needs of today's security clients mean that security departments must take full advantage of appropriate technologies to support their protective efforts.

This chapter introduced the three main security systems: alarms, intrusion detectors, and CCTV surveillance systems. The various types of available technologies within these categories were discussed, as were their advantages and disadvantages. Because there is such a wide range of technologies available in the market and in workplaces, it is the responsibility of security personnel to become as familiar as possible with the specific technologies in use in their workplaces. In order to provide proper maintenance and monitoring of these systems, it is important to understand how they work, and how to avoid potential pitfalls.

Finally, the chapter discussed the integration of security systems. In many workplaces, more than one system is required to meet the organization's security needs. In such cases, it's necessary to integrate the systems so that they work together for maximum efficiency. Systems must also be integrated with computer technology, which means that an organization's IT department must work in partnership with the security department and external providers of security technologies to assess the organization's particular needs and to implement appropriate and cost-effective solutions.

KEY TERMS

ambient noise

analog

digital

fire alarm

interface

intrusion alarm

protocols

special-use alarm

ultrasonic motion detector

PERFORMANCE APPLICATION

1. Describe the elements of an alarm.

2. What reasons might a facility have for *not* installing an alarm system?

3. Why is an effective communications system essential if a remote/centralized alarm monitoring system is chosen?

4. List five kinds of organizations for which intrusion detection is a key concern.

5. List two disadvantages/weaknesses of intrusion detection systems based on photoelectric sensors.

6. What other security technologies make appropriate companion systems for intrusion detectors? Why?

7. Why has CCTV become an essential technology in today's security environment?

8. What maintenance challenges are associated with a CCTV system?

9. What does systems integration mean?

10. Who is charged with the integration of security systems? What kind of skills and knowledge must this person have?

PART V EXERCISE

1. Design a high-risk facility, using the four lines of defence: grounds perimeter protection, building perimeter protection, space and area protection, and object protection.

   a. Suggest the various devices you would select to defend the perimeters and explain why.

   b. Indicate any concerns you might have about outside storage structures, and how you would secure them.

   c. Give specific recommendations for making the roof of the facility secure?

   d. Suggest the various ways you would secure the building's perimeter. For example, indicate the type of doors, windows, glass, and security lighting you would use.

   e. Indicate the alarm system you would install to protect the interior space.

   f. Indicate how you would protect the valuables that will be stored in the facility—that is, the type of safe or vault you would install.

2. Imagine a fishing lodge that caters to world leaders. It is landlocked on a peninsula with a lighthouse overlooking the open sea and bay. A rocky dam blocks the river. How does the location of the exclusive lodge in this natural setting help to secure it from an intruder's attack?

PART VI

Workplace and Retail Security

19 Identity Control

INTRODUCTION

Many businesses leave the matter of access control to a receptionist or a security officer stationed at the entrance of the facility. But in plants with over 50 employees per shift or in high-turnover businesses, this type of access control is simply not sufficiently secure.

In today's uncertain climate, employers are justified in having their receptionist or security officer request check an unknown visitor's photo ID or driver's licence before allowing them access to secure employee areas.

However, this can be intrusive. Instead, to protect their personnel, place of business, and their assets, most larger employers issue some form of positive photo identification. This allows them to exclude all but authorized personnel, as well as control their movement once they are inside the facility.

Chapter Objectives

When you have completed this chapter, you will

- have a basic knowledge and understanding of the use of identity (ID) cards, badges, and passes and the role they play in providing a measure of security and access control for a facility.

ELEMENTS OF A GOOD ID SYSTEM

The type and quality of ID card chosen typically depends on the sensitivity of the facility. A good security ID policy should include provisions that cover the following:

- When, where, how, and to whom passes should be displayed;
- What is to be done in case of loss of the pass;
- Procedures for retrieving badges from departing employees;
- A system for periodic cancellation and reissue of all passes in response to security concerns.

Vulnerabilities

Unfortunately, ID cards are open to abuse. They can be bought or stolen, forged, and produced internally without authorization.

Bought or Stolen ID

Purse snatchers and pickpockets have been known to sell employee ID cards to other criminals.

Forged ID

Employee ID cards and visitor passes can be forged using computers and colour printers in an effort to gain access to restricted areas for criminal activity.

Unauthorized ID

An employee with access to the equipment and blank card stock can produce an unauthorized ID card, badge, or pass, and use it to gain access to restricted areas. These cards and passes can also be given to an accomplice for future activity.

STANDARDS FOR ID CARDS

Before considering the specific types of identity cards that the security industry provides today, note some general criteria for ID card effectiveness.

- Cards and badges should be tamper-resistant—difficult to alter or reproduce. For example, they may be printed or embossed on a distinctive stock that incorporates designs that are difficult to reproduce.

- They should contain a clear and recent photograph of the employee, preferably in colour. The photograph should be at least 6.5 cm sq. and should be updated every two or three years, or when there is any significant change in facial appearance, such as the removal or growth of a beard or moustache.

- ID cards should incorporate vital statistics such as the employee's name and number, date of birth, height, weight, hair and eye colour, gender, employee's signature, and, where required, a fingerprint.

- They should be wallet-sized, computer-generated on special paper, and laminated.

- In facilities where there are areas with different access restrictions, cards and badges should be colour-coded to reflect specific access privileges.

- ID cards should be unique to the facility, containing the company name and logo and a serial number.

- Cards should have a date of issue and expiry and bear an authorizing signature, preferably in a different colour.

Visitor Passes

Like employee ID cards, visitor passes should be unique to the facility and tamper-proof. Passes should be laminated, recognizable from a distance, and prominently displayed on a clip or chain. In some facilities, visitors are required to exchange a piece of personal identification before a pass is issued. When passes are returned, they should be kept in a secure place.

Passes should contain the company name and logo and an expiry limit. Some passes may be issued for a designated area to be visited, such as the warehouse. The authorized area may be indicated with a letter or colour coded on the pass.

TYPES OF IDENTITY CARDS AND THEIR USES

Identification cards can generally be grouped into four categories or types: simple laminated cards, light-sensitive badges, time-sensitive badges, and high-security, computer-generated cards and badges.

Simple Laminated Card

This form of ID card is widely used for small businesses, schools, health clubs, and the retail industry. Made of paper or cardboard, this form of ID card is printed on coloured paper or "stock," using an approved layout that contains the employee's basic information. The employee and the department head usually sign it. A photograph is usually taken separately, cut to size, and attached to the card before it is sealed in the laminate pouch.

Light-Sensitive Badges

Light-sensitive badges are created with a chemically treated insert or patch that reacts to sunlight. When exposed to sunlight, the patch changes colour, and the word "VOID" appears in a pattern across the patch. This renders the card useless for future use. Used mainly as a form of visitor ID, this badge is normally issued with instructions to return to it to security before the visitor's departure from the facility.

Time-Sensitive Badges

Time-sensitive badges are also used primarily for visitor access. This badge or pass consists of two portions. The base is pre-printed and can be filled out with the visitor's information by the security officer. A small patch is applied to a chemically treated "red" section of the badge. A chemical reaction takes place over a specific period of time when the "Front/Visitor" portion of the pass is applied to the "red" or expired portion.

Depending on the period of time granted for access, time-sensitive badges may be used

- by new employees, while an official employee ID is being prepared;

- by contractors, when multiple entries are required over a specific period of time;

Time-sensitive badges can be designed so that different patches take longer to change colour to indicate when they are void—one day, two days, or seven days.

High-Security, Computer-Generated Cards and Badges

When designing a secure employee ID card, there are three primary considerations to keep in mind: security, functionality, and appearance.

Card Security

If security concerns are relatively low, a digitally printed card with a clear or holographic "topcoat" may provide plenty of protection. Clear topcoats and laminates made of durable polymers provide an extra line of defence against forgery or alteration of cards. Topcoats feature edge-to-edge protection across a card surface, while laminates provide greater thickness for extended durability. If a strong line of defence against forgery and alteration is required, there are several advanced card security technologies available.

laser engraving
technology that embeds data into ID cards to guard against forgery

Laser engraving technology embeds data into ID cards to guard against forgery. A laser beam permanently engraves (or burns) data into the inner core of the card. The information cannot be mechanically or chemically removed without damaging the surface of the card, providing an extremely effective, tamper-evident barrier. Laser-engraved data can also be printed to "disturb" the outer surface of a card, creating a tactile effect. This high-resolution technology supports "microprinting," or printing of extremely small characters invisible to the naked eye, as an added measure against counterfeiting.

ghost printing
technology that adds a lighter reproduction of an image on an identity document

Ghost printing technology is used to create a substantial level of tamper-resistance by adding a lighter reproduction of an image on an identity document, typically in the same area of the document as personalized data. The second image appears as a light background to text data, significantly increasing the difficulty of altering the photo image or the data.

Any attempt at photo substitution would require altering the printed data as well as the ghost image. Ghost images can be printed in full colour or one colour in a wide range of inks, including laser and UV.

computer-generated image modification
use of digital printing technology to pre-print or variable-print advanced computer-generated graphic elements on identity documents

Computer-generated image modification uses digital printing technology to pre-print or variable print advanced computer-generated graphic elements on identity documents. With a special reader or viewer, certain elements become visible—elements that disappear when the document is reproduced with a copier or scanner.

The latest entry into badge protection is holography. The introduction of holography into badge control systems reduces the chance of counterfeit ID cards being produced. Holograms, together with other technological advances, have produced an identification card system that is almost forgery-proof.

Functionality

To secure ID cards beyond visual verification, smart card chips, magnetic strips, bar codes, or proximity capabilities (radio frequency) can be added.

"Smart" cards offer the highest level of security for storing machine-readable data on a card. Information on these chips can be protected with passwords and PINs, or integrated with biometric technology that requires matching cardholder profiles to gain access to information on the chip. Smart cards can store vital cardholder data that can be accessed offline and offer you a secure method for conducting online transactions with government agencies.

Appearance and Branding

Some card providers offer the option of printing full-colour images, text, and other graphics on identification cards. These options support company branding initiatives.

THE ABCs OF VISITOR CONTROL

The following guidelines are appropriate for most reception area security personnel and receptionists:

1. Greet all visitors. A friendly "good morning" or "good afternoon" relaxes the visitor and makes it easier to ask questions later.

2. Question all visitors. Depending on the company's security needs, certain questions will be appropriate. Security officers and receptionists should be encouraged not to hesitate to ask for appropriate information if it is necessary for a security purpose. For example:

   ▪ What is your name?

   ▪ Who are you here to see?

   ▪ Do you have an appointment?

   ▪ What company do you represent?

   ▪ May I see some identification?

3. Announce all visitors to the person being visited. In many cases, the person receiving the visitor will want to come down to reception to escort the visitor to the meeting room. If this is the company's policy, ensure that it is followed.

4. Confirm that the visitor has parked in the appropriate area and has a parking permit if required.

5. Ensure that the visitor wears an identification badge. Some companies issue repair and temporary personnel with their own identification badges instead of a visitor badge.

6. Collect all badges upon a visitor's departure. Record all uncollected and/or lost badges.

7. Record all visits in a visitor log. The log should record the following:

   ▪ visitor's name,

   ▪ date,

   ▪ visitor's signature,

   ▪ arrival time,

   ▪ name of employee being visited,

- departure time, and

- purpose of visit.

The security director may require additional information such as:

- department/area visited,

- security personnel signature/initials confirming that the visitor's ID was checked,

- visitor's company phone number, and

- vehicle licence number.

8. Ask any visitor claiming to be a federal or provincial law enforcement officer for identification. Government and law enforcement agents always have photo ID. Take the time to examine the ID carefully. Record the badge or ID number.

9. Ask any person leaving the premises with company property (such as office equipment) to show a property pass dated and signed by authorized personnel, along with a list showing the contents that are being removed.

10. If a visitor seems nervous or hostile or if he or she is sweating or pacing, looks unkempt, distraught, or disoriented, do not allow that person access to the premises. If you are the receptionist, call a security officer immediately. Better safe than sorry!

Step Aside

What about your *own* ID?

- Carry your ID card/cards at all times.

- Display your ID card/cards in the required location on your uniform as per site instructions.

- Replace worn, outdated, and damaged ID cards as soon as possible.

- Request a replacement card if you have altered your appearance significantly—for example, if you are no longer wearing eye glasses (using contacts/had eye surgery), have removed or grown a beard or moustache, or changed your hair colour.

- Secure your ID card when it is not in use.

- Leave your ID cards in a locked container in the security office when you go on vacation.

- Report any lost or stolen ID cards to the shift supervisor immediately.

Temporary ID Cards

The following guidelines for the issuance of temporary ID cards are appropriate in most facilities:

- Ensure that all required forms are filled out when issuing the card.

- Get a signature before issue.

- Confirm identification of a temporary employee from an approved Canadian photo ID.

- Advise temporary employees to wear their ID card visibly at all times while on site.

- Advise temporary employees of any areas to which their cards do not allow them access.

- Make temporary employees wait for their escort (if required). Do not send them or allow them to find their escort on their own.

- Ensure that all cards are returned as required.

- Follow up on all outstanding cards immediately.

- Protect/secure blank cards.

SUMMARY

If a badge/card/pass system is introduced, it can only be as effective as the level of compliance with the policies supporting it. Facility security officers are responsible for administering the system, but they must have the cooperation of the majority of the employees and the full support of management.

For the most part, the use of high-quality ID cards and passes is the simplest method of access control. Nevertheless, as with any form of security, you get what you pay for, so it only makes sense to implement a level of security consistent with the threat or risk involved.

KEY TERMS

computer-generated image modification

ghost printing

laser engraving

PERFORMANCE APPLICATION

1. Describe four types of identity cards and how they work.

2. What are the three primary considerations you have to remember when designing an employee ID card? Explain fully.

3. How are ID cards vulnerable to criminal use?

4. What are the standards an ID card system must meet to be effective?

5. If you were assigned security duty at the reception desk of the CN Tower, what are 10 security procedures for administering and controlling ID cards, badges, and passes you would expect to see in place? Give reasons for each procedure.

20 Retail Security

INTRODUCTION

Retail security forms one of the basic duties of many security officers, and a major chain store that employs professional security personnel can save hundreds of thousands of dollars annually.

Our discussion of retail security is in two parts. The first part discusses the principles of retail security and the conditions that support retail theft. In part two, the specifics of asset protection and the resources available to combat theft and shoplifting are considered.

The statistics on retail crime reveal how serious the problem is and how much it affects Canadian business. In the October 2000 issue of *Canadian Security*, Jim McDermott, the director of security for Cadillac Fairview's Eaton Centre in downtown Toronto, brought the point home when he said, "Shoplifting is more lucrative than robbing banks."

How could that be? Shoplifting appears, at first glance, to be such a petty crime. But petty or not, when the losses are totalled, McDermott makes a significant point. According to the Retail Council of Canada, in 1999, Canadian retail outlets were losing more than $2.3 billion per year to shoplifting, break-ins, vandalism, and employee theft. In 2000, this figure rose to a staggering $3.1 billion or 1.8 percent of total national sales. At the time of printing, figures were not yet available for 2002 **shrinkage**, but if the annual rate continues to grow at the pace set in 2000, everyone will suffer, not just the merchants.

Demands from consumers for the freedom to roam through store aisles to buy goods on open display presents a significant challenge to security professionals, who must focus not only on apprehending criminals, but also on developing strategies to prevent retail crime.

> ## Chapter Objectives
>
> When you have completed this chapter, you will
>
> - have a basic knowledge and understanding of retail security and how merchants can protect themselves from the losses due to theft and shoplifting.

shrinkage
retail inventory losses attributed to shoplifting, employee theft, and administrative error

PRINCIPAL SOURCES OF LOSS

There are five principal sources of loss to retailers.

1. *External theft.* 38 percent of losses stem from shoplifting, break and enter, and robbery.

2. *Internal theft.* Employees who steal from employers, including that innocent "extra box of pencils or bottle of nail polish," contribute to $3 million nationally per day or 33 percent of retailers' total losses.

3. *Carelessness or mismanagement.* Paperwork errors made in the way retailers record and keep account of their inventories contribute to 21 percent of retailers' total losses.

4. *Vendor fraud.* Suppliers who overcharge or double-charge shipments or in some way cheat retailers contribute to 8 percent of their total losses.

5. *Return fraud.* A more recent type of threat, costs of losses are just being tracked where people "borrow" merchandise to use it and then return it, or thieves return stolen goods without a receipt to get a refund. Stores with return policies are often too lenient in favour of keeping customer loyalty.

Step Aside

Special Challenges

Some retail businesses face special challenges when it comes to internal theft. Retailers who do most of their business in a particular season often hire short-term, seasonal staff who may be less committed to the employer (and thus less honest) and less traceable than permanent staff.

Also, especially where wages are low, the retail sector in general experiences high staff turnover. The need to continually hire new staff and the frequent staff changes that result create a climate of staffing impermanence in the retail industry, which poses a significant challenge from the perspective of curtailing employee theft. Retail employers should be aware of these factors, and need to take extra steps, including closer observance of staff by security personnel, to offset the increased risks.

THE NATURE OF RETAIL CRIME

The following statistics from the Retail Council of Canada may help to illustrate the problem of retail crime:

- Female shoplifters outnumber male shoplifters 5:1.

- 90 percent of shoplifters are under the age of 30.

- The shoplifter's average age is 19–21 years.

- Only 2 percent of shoppers enter a store to steal.

- Only 1 in every 35 shoplifters is caught.

- 20 percent of losses are due to organized theft rings.

- 86 percent of retailers now have pre-employment criminal screening in place.

Average Losses

The value of thefts depends largely on the type of store:

- $3 to $7 each theft on low-end goods

- $37 to $260 each theft on high-end goods

- $152 average loss per customer theft incident

- $609 per employee theft incident.

The types of stores most likely to be affected by shoplifting are large supermarkets, department stores, music and video/electronics stores, and gift and novelty stores.

National Figures

In 2000, the Canadian retail industry suffered $3 million per day in losses. In 1999, the Retail Council of Canada reported total annual losses of $2.3 billion. In 2000, the Retail Council of Canada recorded $3.1 billion in total annual losses, and this was described as the "tip of the iceberg" in its 2001 Canadian Retail Security Report:

> Shrinkage does not include the cost for retailers to train staff in ways to prevent losses, investment in asset protection personnel, and technology such as closed-circuit television and electronic article surveillance tags.

All crime combined costs Canadians about $46 billion per year, according to the 2001 Canadian Retail Security Report.

Focus on Technologies

Disposable Surveillance Tags and Strips

Whereas the electronic surveillance tags of the past used to be bulky and occasionally interfered with the appearance of merchandise, new technological innovations have led to the development of very small and unobtrusive tags and strips which, instead of being removed at the point of purchase, are simply de-activated and left on merchandise packaging. These tags seldom interfere with the customer's ability to examine and/or try on merchandise, and provide some measure of security against theft.

One of the main disadvantages of such tags is that they are often designed to be applied not to merchandise itself, but to packaging; so if a thief manages to remove the article's packaging before leaving the store, the theft may well go undetected.

CATEGORIES OF SHOPLIFTERS

Professional shoplifters account for 20 percent of all shoplifters and for very high dollar losses. They target small items with high resale value, such as jewellery. Often working in organized groups, they sometimes use children as decoys. Professional shoplifters are well rehearsed, aggressive, and difficult to detect. When they are detected, they often resist capture.

Amateurs (including kleptomaniacs and the poor) make up 80 percent of shoplifters and are responsible for the bulk of losses. Motivated by greed or need, they usually steal on impulse when opportunity presents itself.

Among the pool of amateur shoplifters are addicts—who may steal based on a need for money or for substances to which they are addicted—and thrill seekers (often youth) who steal on a dare or just to see if they can get away with it.

ASSET PROTECTION

There are eight basic countermeasures employed throughout the retail industry to combat shoplifting and theft. These are human surveillance, closed-circuit television cameras (CCTVs), electronic article surveillance, CheckInk 11, tamper-evident seals, signs, mirrors, and merchandise display.

Human Surveillance

Store employees trained in surveillance are the single most-effective deterrent to shoplifters, according to the Eaton Centre's Director of Security Jim McDermott. First on his list is the "power of observation." He trains his employees to be attentive and alert.

Closed-Circuit Television Cameras

Properly sited CCTVs used in a retail store are an integral part of the retail security plan. These cameras come in many forms and sizes and may be used in almost any environment. They can be hidden or camouflaged, for instance, inside the clothing of a store mannequin, or openly visible, such as domes mounted on a ceiling or monitors angled so that customers can see themselves as they walk into a bank or store. The use of CCTVs is discussed in chapter 18.

Electronic Article Surveillance

Electronic article surveillance (EAS) systems have at least three components: tags, sensors, and alarms. Tags are of various types, but two systems and their tags dominate the industry.

One is a VHF/microwave system. In this system, the tag contains a semiconductor chip that, when radiated by the transmitter frequency, reflects a signal to the receiver.

The other system uses a magnetic field rather than radio waves. Here the tag contains a strip that is sensed by a magnetometer. Most systems are recyclable, but some newer systems have tags that can be desensitized and thrown away.

The most popular EAS system uses a large plastic tag that is attached to the clothing with a metal pin. It can be removed only with a special tool and can be reused. These tags not only aid apprehension but also serve as loss-prevention devices. The systems serve as a deterrent by decreasing the opportunity to steal.

Members of the Retail Council of Canada's Resources Protection Network reported an overall reduction of 0.8 percent in inventory shrinkage over three years once they introduced the EAS system into stores. They claim they had made a return on their investment within the first year, they were better able to identify employees committing internal theft, and they were able to increase sales of merchandise that they used to keep under lock and key. The director of loss prevention for the Hudson's Bay Company, Don Jobe, reports that "EAS provides us with an opportunity to protect our merchandise in a way that is unobtrusive to our honest customers."

CheckInk 11

CheckInk 11, a non-sensor-based system, is an ink-based "denial" system. When the tag is removed without the use of a special tool, ink explodes out of the tag to deface the attached clothing.

Tamper-Evident Seals

Some merchandise may carry seals that reveal tampering when they are removed. For example, in the case of a leased laptop whose hard drive may be exchanged for a less expensive type, the seal cannot be re-affixed, because it would now read "Void."

Signs

There are conflicting viewpoints as to the usefulness of signs that warn against shoplifting. Many merchants feel that such signs are an insult to the great majority of honest shoppers who may become angry and take their business elsewhere. Others believe that such signs have no effect on honest people because they have no criminal intent. On the other hand, the people who intend to steal will be reminded of the seriousness of their actions and perhaps change their mind. There are no recorded figures that show how signs affect actual theft, but there is no denying the enormous psychological impact that signs convey.

The most common types of anti-shoplifting signs are the following:

- Signs that warn of the presence of "store investigators."
- Signs that warn of "prosecution."
- Signs that warn of the use of CCTV.

Mirrors

Many types of mirrors may be used to enhance security within a retail environment. Security personnel must be very careful when positioning mirrors, because a distorted image of an individual can lead to an illegal arrest, which may end up hurting the reputation of the store and damaging customer relations. Mirrors must be sited according to the layout of the store, and care should be taken to select the type most suited to the immediate area. Remember that although curved mirrors can enlarge the viewing area, they also distort the image. Flat mirrors are best for direct observation and offer the least distortion.

Mirrors most often used for security purposes are convex, regular, and one-way.

Convex full-dome mirrors provide full 360° visibility and are usually positioned above a lane intersection.

Convex half-dome mirrors afford 180° visibility and are usually positioned above a three-way "T" intersection.

Convex quarter-dome mirrors afford 90° visibility and are usually positioned above a two-way "L" intersection.

Merchandise Display

Merchandise displays must be attractive to customers, while at the same time protecting the items from theft. There are several strategies used by merchants to accomplish this. The following are a few important ones:

Secured Samples

Thin, almost invisible wires that do not detract from the appearance of the item are sometimes used. Different styles of chain and flexible straps are also used.

Lockup Display

One of the most widely used forms of display security is the lockup display. The lockup display is mostly used when small valuable items need to be displayed. Jewellery, watches, expensive sunglasses, personal electronics, and perfumes are some of the items protected in this manner. This ensures that the items are handled only in the presence of a salesperson.

Choice of Location

Where the items are displayed within the store also has an effect on whether they will be more likely or less likely to be stolen. Items close to the store exit invite a snatch attack. In small leather goods stores, leather jackets near the exit are often chained together as well as to the rack. This reduces the possibility of a snatch attack. Inexpensive items can be placed in the areas of the store that are hardest to observe by the staff.

Symmetry

This simple technique works on the principle that our eyes are drawn naturally to any break in a pattern. Anything different tends to stand out. Consequently, if items are displayed close together in a distinct pattern, when one or more are removed, we tend to recognize the difference in the pattern (symmetry) very quickly. This allows employees and security staff to react quickly to a loss, possibly before the thief has left the premises.

Packaging

From meat to video games, the technology of packaging for security has developed to keep pace with the increase of losses from stores. Several techniques are employed in the design and application of security packaging. Here are a few examples:

- Large plastic sleeves (which make it harder to conceal small merchandise in a pocket or jacket) are often used on video game cartridges, CDs, and cassettes. They are removed at point of sale.

- Bulky cardboard packaging may be used for small items, again making it difficult to hide the item under clothing or in a pocket.

- Plastic packages with EAS bar codes printed on as part of the design of the package. This makes it difficult for a thief to remove the item without completely removing the packaging.

Store Layout

The overall design and layout of the store itself can complement security. Here are some points to consider:

- Ensure that there are clear lines of sight from the cash point to all expensive item display areas.

- Avoid isolated corners where shoppers are hidden from sight.

- Have adequate shelving and rack space to avoid cluttered displays.

- Use symmetry whenever possible to display items.

- Use lights and mirrors to create the illusion of space and to assist with visibility.

- Position EAS gates to maximize exit points.

- Use a combination of overt and covert cameras (including dummies) to create the desired psychological effect.

- Select signage appropriate to the aesthetics of the store.

Fitting Room Policy

Good fitting room management can help reduce losses. The privacy afforded by fitting rooms provides customers with an excellent opportunity to steal. Employees must be trained to control the fitting room environment to minimize this risk.

Physical

Rooms should be kept clean and clear of all merchandise and minimally furnished. Floor-to-ceiling walls will prevent shoplifters from passing garments to an accomplice in an adjacent cubicle.

Procedural

Store policy should limit the number of items allowed in a fitting room at one time. Clerks should watch for items concealed within garments and note any items with big price differences or with obviously wrong sizes.

Other Tips

The fitting room area should have only one monitored entrance. Fitting rooms should be locked and only opened on demand. Cracks around mirrors and wall should be repaired to help eliminate hiding places for price tags.

Refund Procedures

Refunds on the return of merchandise should be issued with the original sales slip only. Quite often, the person requesting a cash refund is not in possession of the sales receipt. In this case, the full particulars, including name and address of the customer, should be entered on the refund form. Paperwork should be processed at a different location within the store to avoid the possibility of collusion between the customer and the refund clerk. Copies should be checked against a refund audit carried out by the security department. Letters to refund recipients asking for their opinion about how their refund was processed may help in later investigations of discrepancies.

SPECIAL TIPS AND STRATEGIES

Employees and security officers can benefit from improving their observation and procedural skills. Developing specific practices is effective in detecting retail theft. Security officers should watch for:

- people loitering either inside or outside the store for long periods of time;

- people entering the store just to "browse";

- professionals, who have many ways to distract store security, such as using children to sidetrack cashiers and salespeople while they steal something;

- baby carriages, which provide excellent cover for stolen merchandise;

- customers wearing out-of-season clothes, such as people wearing bulky sweaters or long coats in the summer, under which they can hide items;

- people with lots of bags or packages—offer to keep these while the customer shops or tries on garments;

- people who appear nervous;

- people who walk with an awkward gait, which can signify that merchandise is hidden somewhere on their person;

- people who move items from one area to another to enable an accomplice to retrieve them later—items should be returned to their proper location as soon as possible; and

- non-paying customers who ask for store bags.

Training Tips

1. Do not identify new employees with "Trainee" tags.

2. Create attentive clerks.

3. Post photos of repeat shoplifters in an employee area of the store.

4. Develop a "zone" system that makes each employee responsible for security in particular areas.

5. Develop a code system to alert other employees.

Undercover Security Tips

Security officers should

- dress like they belong in the particular environment;
- rehearse a communication plan with employees;
- have physical back-up available;
- ensure that there is unbroken observation of the event—that is, that observation does not have to stop to call for back-up; and.
- arrest the offender off the property.

In loss-prevention audits or checks, security officers should look for

- empty containers/boxes on the sales floor;
- empty hangers on clothes racks;
- empty hangers in the fitting rooms;
- discarded price tags in washrooms;
- switched price tags;
- a missing piece of a set;
- an increase in refunds compared with sales; and
- merchandise returned for refund instead of exchange.

SUMMARY

The retail industry is an excellent example of an area where the application of total security can be clearly observed. Security personnel can make a difference in reducing and preventing losses from theft and shoplifting. With the application of the various retail security strategies discussed here, it is possible to create a retail establishment that welcomes honest shoppers, encourages good customer relations, emphasizes employee awareness, and discourages theft and shoplifting.

KEY TERM

shrinkage

PERFORMANCE APPLICATION

1. Why must a security officer arrest a shoplifter outside the premises where the theft occurred?

2. What are the five principal sources for retail losses today? Explain how these losses affect the Canadian economy.

3. How would you profile a shoplifter? Which type of shoplifter causes the greatest losses?

4. Explain eight countermeasures that retail security implements to prevent shoplifting and theft. Which one is the least effective?

5. How can you train new store employees to be an effective part of your security team?

CHAPTER 21

Internal Theft

INTRODUCTION

In chapter 20, we learned that internal theft accounts for 33 percent of Canadian retailers' total losses each year, or $3 million nationally per day.

    While some studies suggest that up to one in three employees is dishonest, even employees not directly involved in theft are partly to blame for losses. When managers fail to establish controls or don't follow procedures established to prevent internal theft, their negligence encourages pilfering. While reluctance to establish controls or enforce procedures is an understandable failure on managers' parts because they don't want to appear to mistrust their employees, it also demonstrates a very shortsighted and self-serving attitude. By failing to prevent internal loss, such managers play a key role in the erosion of their companies' profits. Because it is profitability that keeps a company afloat, failing to play a part in preventing theft can, in the end, undermine a person's own job security. All honest employees should consider whether they should put loyalty to dishonest colleagues above their own employment interests.

    To combat retail losses, the Retail Council of Canada sponsors a team of leading resources protection experts from large and small businesses that it calls the Resources Protection Network. The goal of this team is to work together to reduce internal theft and fraud nationally, and as a result more retailers are forming strategic partnerships with police, suppliers, and other merchants to tag goods on display and to pool their investigative forces in gathering evidence against organized rings of professional shoplifters. To read more about the network, see www.retailcouncil.org/rpn.

Chapter Objectives

When you have completed this chapter, you will

- understand the issue of internal theft and how to help protect merchants and other businesses from the heavy losses that employee theft produces.

UNDERSTANDING INTERNAL THEFT

Why do employees steal? The answer seems to reside in human nature. Philosophy and psychology teach that there are two things that form the cornerstone for people taking any action: motive and desire. In committing a crime, there is one more element: opportunity.

Motive

Motive means having a reason, but the act of reasoning does not necessarily mean one's logic is sound. Reasoning that leads to a decision to steal is necessarily flawed. In most cases, a thief's reasons amount to an attempt to justify that which the thief knows is an inappropriate action.

Desire

Desire equals wish or fantasy. Desire is based on an emotional and physical need to have something that a person imagines will satisfy or gratify that need. If wrong thinking provides motive, then fantasizing about getting what one wants further feeds his or her desire to take self-serving actions.

Opportunity

Opportunity, in the context of internal theft, is a loophole or weakness in security that permits a thief to act on his or her motive and desire without fear of being caught.

While desire and motive are beyond any manager's control, opportunity is not. Security can close the door on giving a thief the opportunity to steal.

Reasons for Stealing

While everyone's motives are unique, studies of internal theft reveal certain recurring themes. Employees who steal may do so because:

- they feel resentment over a real or imagined injustice that they blame management for;

- they need to maintain status and to augment their income for financial reasons;

- they desire to indulge in something they may not normally purchase or cannot normally afford;

- they want to help others;

- they feel nobody cares;

- they think no one is looking;

- the absence of or inadequate theft controls eliminate their fear of being caught;

- they want excitement;

- they have a drug or gambling habit.

With these motives and desires in mind, it is easy to understand why, when an opportunity arises for employees to indulge their fantasy, temptation may be too great for them to resist. According to most experts, all that prevents most people from breaching the border of crime at that moment when opportunity tempts them is the fear of their boss catching them. If the security system is lax or their supervisors seem indifferent, their fear is neutralized. So, guess what? They steal.

Indicators of Employee Theft

In determining whether losses relate to internal theft, employers must look for symptoms, much like a doctor would. For example:

- patterns of financial irresponsibility;

- garnishments of pay;

- inquiries by creditors;

- constant requests for payroll advances;

- sudden acquisition of expensive cars or clothes that are clearly beyond the employee's earnings;

- financial difficulty owing to family illness;

- recurring or long-term medical expenses;

- income tax problems;

- evidence of regular gambling on or off the premises;

- excessive drinking or signs of other drug use;

- persistent borrowing, especially from other employees; and

- bouncing personal cheques or post-dated cheques.

Theft Targets

Dishonest employees will steal anything that is available, useful, or has resale value. Company funds may be stolen in a variety of ways, including:

- false receipts for goods never received;

- falsifying inventories;

- payroll padding;

- expense account padding;

- manipulation of computer records;

- overcharging or undercharging;

- gaining access to petty cash;

- collusion with vendors or outside thieves;

- fake invoices; and

- false certification of overtime.

Employees may also steal company furnishings, such as desks, chairs, paintings, cabinets, rugs, and ornaments. Office supplies, like pens, pencils, stationery, CDs, and floppy discs are another favourite, especially for those employees with children.

Employees may "borrow" office equipment, such as calculators, computers, computer peripherals, and software programs. They may also steal products that the company manufactures.

METHODS

Because an estimated 7 to 30 percent of business failures are the result of internal theft, it is important to understand how employees work to rob their employers—their *modus operandi*, so to speak, or method of operation. It is impossible to figure out every type of crime or fraud undertaken against companies, but the following list shows how widespread the problem really is and how clever some employees can be in their subterfuge.

Payroll and personnel employees may

- collaborate to falsify records by using non-existent employees or by retaining terminated employees on the payroll;

- pad overtime reports and kick back part of the extra, unearned pay to the authorizing supervisor;

- pocket unclaimed wages;

- split increased payroll that has been raised on signed, blank cheques for use in the authorized signer's absence.

Maintenance personnel may remove equipment and merchandise with the trash or collude with contract service people to steal and sell office equipment.

Receiving clerks and truck drivers may collude to falsify merchandise counts and sell the extra merchandise.

Purchasing agents may collude with vendors to falsify purchase and payment documents. The purchasing agent authorizes payment on goods never shipped after forging shipment receipts. The purchasing agent may also conspire with vendors to pay an inflated price.

Mailroom and supply personnel may pack and mail merchandise to themselves for resale.

Accounts payable personnel may

- pay fictitious bills to an account set up for their own use;

- commandeer cheques made out to cash;

- increase the amount on cheques after voucher approval or raise the amount on vouchers after their approval;

- pay creditors twice and pocket the second cheque;

- manipulate accounting software packages to credit personal accounts with electronic account overages; and

- forge cheques, destroying them when they are returned with the statement from the bank, and then change their cash account records accordingly.

Cashiers, sales clerks, or service clerks may

- take incoming cash without crediting the customer's account;

- pocket small amounts from incoming payments and apply later payments on other accounts to cover shortages;

- invoice goods below regular price and get a kickback from the purchaser;

- issue (and cash) cheques on returned merchandise not actually returned.

MANAGEMENT'S OBLIGATIONS

By reducing the potential for internal theft, management not only protects its assets, but also withdraws the temptation to steal by otherwise honest employees. Management is in a position to be proactive in two ways: through education and controls.

Education

Employers can demonstrate the impact of theft by evaluating profit losses and showing employees the affect these losses have on production and the employment opportunities.

Controls

Employers can begin being proactive by doing thorough background checks on new employees and fostering loyalty to the company by promotion on merit. To prevent theft, employers can remove opportunity by involving company personnel in creating loss prevention procedures. They can also protect profits by establishing loss prevention audits and surveys of items lost. Finally, employers can set up procedures that lead to prosecution.

Step Aside

Aims of an Internal Theft Prevention Program

An internal theft prevention program is designed to provide management and security personnel with information that will:

- explain how to predict which employees will steal,
- explain why they steal,
- show how they steal, and
- explain what employers can do about it.

CONTAINING CORRUPTION

The company's finance department is best suited to introduce special policies and procedural controls to prevent internal loss. Accounting is responsible for auditing assets, cash control, and handling daily receipts. The following breakdown of duties suggests what these policies and procedures might be.

Auditing Assets

When auditing assets, the accounting department reviews all financial transactions and compares the transaction volume with the inventory. To prevent loss, surprise audits should be conducted by the finance department and outside auditors should be invited to check the accounting records annually.

Cash Control

Although it is unusual, a company might have a bonded supervisor who deals with cash receipts, handles cash-by-mail transactions, and records the receipts on numbered forms.

Petty cash should be kept separate from cash receipts and should be replenished with a cheque drawn on an authorized account. Receipts and authorized vouchers should be issued.

Daily Receipts

To contain corruption, employers should match the daily cash register tally with cash in the till and record cash deposits meticulously.

Bank Statements

A non-money handler should be assigned to check vouchers, statements, and cheques.

Handling Cash

There are several factors that an employer should consider with respect to handling cash. After determining the minimum amount of cash needed for daily operations, a minimum float should be provided for each cash register. Throughout the day, large bills should periodically be removed from the registers. On the premises, cash should be kept in a three-way safe in the cash room.

The cash room should have good physical security, including a closed-circuit television system. The room should be opened by two people in case of trouble and a call-in procedure with a varying code word should be established. At the end of the day, the receipts should be tallied by two people and all systems should be checked before departure.

Transporting Cash

Large amounts of cash should be moved off the premises by two people or under the escort of an armoured car service. Routes and times should be varied to confuse anyone monitoring the schedule.

Company-Wide Strategies

There are tactics and organizational structures that a company can follow to discourage internal theft and to build a positive relationship between management and employees. Here are a few suggestions:

- Keep accounts payable, accounts receivable, and payroll separate.
- Keep control of purchasing, receiving, warehousing, and shipping in different hands.

What Would You Do?

Petty Cash "Borrowing"

Consider the following scenario and answer the questions that follow.

The owner of a large independent coffee shop, who does not normally employ security personnel, decides to host a showing and sale of paintings by a local artist, as a promotional strategy. The owner decides that because of the value of the artwork being displayed, it would be wise to hire security for the event.

You are a contract security officer. Your employer enters into a contract with the coffee shop owner to provide your services for the three-hour event. Your primary duty is to keep an eye on the works of art with a view to preventing vandalism and theft.

The art show turns out to be a huge success. The coffee shop is packed throughout the showing, and the employees bustle about trying to keep up with demand. At one point, the employees discover that they are likely to run out of soya milk. The discussion of the soya milk crisis takes place within your earshot, as you stand unobtrusively near the cash. The employees make the decision to send one server to the corner store for soya milk. Because the cash register is electronic and will open only when the appropriate sale code is keyed in, supplies emergencies like this one are handled through a petty cash system. The cashier retrieves the cash box from under the till, but when she opens it she finds it empty. She does not appear alarmed, but simply calls out "Hey? Who owes petty cash?" Another employee looks up and says "Oh, yeah, sorry, me—lunch money." He hands the cashier two 20s.

You ask the cashier about the significance of this, and she explains that the employees have a longstanding practice of "borrowing" money from petty cash on a short-term basis for personal use, usually at mealtimes, returning the money before the end of the shift. "It's no big deal," she says. "It's just sitting there, and this is the first time in the two years I've worked here that we've ever even used petty cash for something. The money always gets paid back." You ask whether her employer, the coffee shop owner (and your client) is aware of this practice. She says "no."

1. Is this practice a "big deal"? Why or why not?

2. Because your responsibilities were intended to relate to protecting the artwork, should you do anything about this? Why or why not?

3. What would you do?

4. What are the public relations implications of this incident between your employer (the security company) and the client?

- Have department audits done by someone from another department or by security.

- Promote deserving employees to raise morale.

- Rotate tasks to augment crossover skills, to reduce boredom, and to discourage theft. Switching positions removes control from a would-be thief and often uncovers evidence in a review of records/practices when someone new on the job cross-checks paperwork.

- Insist that employees take their vacation when due.

- Provide a paper trail for inventory.

- Support audits of payroll and invoices.

- Institute a clear and consistent company policy for handling loss prevention.

If the usual controls of internal loss fail, consider reliability tests and undercover investigation.

HANDLING OFFENDERS

Most companies have a clear policy about what they will do when security catches an employee in the act of stealing.

Only about 10 percent of employees caught stealing are criminally prosecuted or sued under civil law. There are valid reasons for this low rate.

Prosecution is time consuming and costly, especially if the employee belongs to a union. In a civil action, the employee may be acquitted and ordered rehired. If acquitted in a criminal trial, the employee may sue the company for wrongful dismissal, false arrest, and/or defamation.

Prosecuting a former employee is also bad for a company's image. However, the occasional prosecution is necessary to send a message that theft will not be tolerated.

Ninety percent of employees caught stealing are simply dismissed based on "performance" with no letter of recommendation. This means, of course, that they may go on to steal again in another organization.

On rare occasions, an employee may be retained and given counselling. This option usually applies only to senior members of the company.

SUMMARY

Once a company institutes an internal theft prevention system, the finance department and security must monitor it to keep it effective. With the addition of "resources protection" teams sponsored by the Retail Council of Canada, retailers have additional help to cut retail losses and improve sales.

REFERENCE

Robert J. Fischer and Gion Green, *Introduction to Security*, 6th ed. (Burlington, MA: Butterworth-Heinemann, 1998).

PERFORMANCE APPLICATION

1. Create 15 tips to help new retail store employees deal with potential shoplifting.

2. a. How do companies contribute to employee theft?

   b. Outline 10 ways employees cheat, defraud, or steal from their companies.

3. What company strategies can retailers implement to control their internal losses? Discuss at least eight in detail.

4. What do you think is the most important countermeasure in handling cash to prevent employee theft? Give a detailed explanation for your answer.

5. Why do companies prosecute only 10 percent of employees who are caught stealing from them?

PART VI **EXERCISE**

Assignment: Read this scenario and answer the questions that follow.

Little Co. Grows Up

A small research group has been working to develop a line of ergonomic computer peripherals (keyboards, mice, etc.). To date, the group has consisted of a computer programmer, two designers, and two office staff.

After a successful prototype launch, the group has incorporated and is moving into the manufacturing stage of the enterprise. The company is moving from a two-room office to a large factory building with an assembly area, a shipping centre, and business offices. The number of workers will grow, in a matter of months, from 5 to 70 employees.

The group has contacted your security company to consult about security needs. Specifically, the principals are interested in issues of access control/employee identification, and internal security, including protecting against internal theft of company funds, products, and equipment.

What advice would you give? Specifically:

1. Identify a list of security issues you might anticipate for this company.

2. Identify steps that they can take during the hiring process to minimize exposure to employee criminality.

3. What kind of identification system (ID) would you recommend for a company like this? Why?

4. Give the company recommendations with respect to how the business functions will be organized.

5. How can the company protect its equipment and products from theft?

6. How can the company improve its chances of early identification of internal fraud?

7. How can the company educate its employees to minimize employee dishonesty?

8. What other steps can the company take to promote a climate of employee accountability and honesty?

PART VII

Workplace Safety

CHAPTER 22

Workplace Safety

INTRODUCTION

Work can be a dangerous place. While most people can readily identify the hazards associated with certain high-risk occupations such as construction or mining, all work carries with it certain risks. Statistics published by the Workplace Safety and Insurance Board (WSIB) indicate that two Ontarians die as a result of preventable work-related causes every week.

Workplace health and safety is a highly complex and diverse workplace issue. There are several pieces of legislation in place in Ontario alone (in general, workplace safety is a provincial responsibility) to govern the promotion and enforcement of safety in the workplace. The Ontario *Occupational Health and Safety Act* (OHSA) creates what it describes as an internal responsibility system (IRS), which is a partnership of all workplace parties (including management, supervisors, employees/workers, and unions) for the promotion of workplace safety.

Security personnel, because of their role in providing workplace surveillance and responding to workplace emergencies, are often the first to discover workplace hazards or to respond to workplace accidents. As such, the issue of workplace health and safety is especially pertinent to the security department, and all good security personnel must embrace the enforcement of workplace safety as a core duty.

This chapter will introduce the legislation governing workplace health and safety, and, in particular, the OHSA. It will outline the basic roles of workplace parties and the essential procedures relating to the investigation of workplace accidents.

Chapter 23 will provide a closer look at workplace hazards, the regulations in place for classifying hazardous materials, and the goals of a workplace safety inspection.

Objectives

When you have completed this chapter, you will

- have an understanding of the goals and basic structure of the *Occupational Health and Safety Act* and the various roles of people in the workplace with respect to supporting the principles of the OHSA.

- have a basic knowledge of the principles of workplace accident investigation.

THE ONTARIO OCCUPATIONAL HEALTH AND SAFETY ACT

First introduced on October 1, 1979, the OHSA has been revised many times and is published in tandem with the Workplace Hazardous Materials Information System (WHMIS) regulations. (WHMIS is considered in more detail in chapter 23.) The latest full-scale revision occurred in 1990.

Introduction

Margaret Hunt, the environmental health and safety officer for the University of Guelph, explains the function of the OHSA as follows:

> Workplace hazards can best be dealt with through communication and cooperation between employers and workers. Fundamental to the operation of the Act is what is called the *internal responsibility system*: a concept that employers and workers must share the responsibility for occupational health and safety, and that both parties must strive to identify hazards and develop strategies to protect workers. The internal responsibility system affords all workers three basic rights: the right to know about workplace hazards; the right to refuse to do work that is unsafe; and the right to participate in occupational health and safety decisions. Within the internal responsibility system, workplace safety is monitored by workers and employers through the creation of joint health and safety committees and the appointment of health and safety representatives as required, and by regular workplace inspections by the Ministry of Labour.

Under the OHSA, corporations face potential fines of $600,000 per offence for violations of the rules. Individuals face potential fines of $27,500 or 12 months in jail. The courts have proved willing to levy substantial fines against employers, regardless of company size, for violations of health and safety statutes.

For small and medium-sized businesses on limited budgets and with a few personnel—which describes many contract security services—trying to adhere to complex health and safety laws as well as many other laws is daunting in light of the severity of fines. This is why security officers need to stay abreast of the basic rights and responsibilities of owners, employers, directors, managers, supervisors, and workers by checking regularly on the Canadian Federation of Independent Business (CFIB) website for OHSA bulletin updates at www.cfib.ca/research/businfo/din0064_e.asp.

Regardless of size, every corporation can take steps to avoid OHSA violations through effective **due diligence**: showing that every precaution has been taken in the circumstances.

due diligence
taking every reasonable precaution to avoid an undesirable consequence

Six essential elements of a safety due diligence program are as follows:

1. workplace hazard analysis/audit;

2. corporate safety policy and implementation program;

3. specific critical task policies and procedures;

4. training procedures for workers, supervisors, managers, officers, and directors;

5. enforcement of health and safety procedures; and

6. ensuring supervisor competence.

It is important to note that Ontario's OHSA does not apply to employees of the federal government, banks, communication companies, or transportation companies. These are covered under part II of the *Canada Labour Code.*

Today, in Ontario, both large and small companies recognize the need for safety coordinators, but most companies cannot afford to pay for one. As a result, a volunteer usually assumes the responsibility, but if there is no volunteer, administering safety duties often falls to the company's security officer or manager. For this reason, understanding occupational health and safety is an essential part of security training.

Structure of the OHSA

Some of the most important sections of the OHSA from the perspective of security officers are

- the rights and responsibilities of the worker;

- the responsibilities of the employer; and

- policies and regulations that govern the workplace.

The Act comprises 10 parts. Although it is not necessary to know these parts in detail, it is important to have an understanding of what they cover in case the need to research an issue in further detail arises.

Health and Safety Representation

Depending upon the size of the organization, the OHSA requires the nomination of either a health and safety representative or a joint health and safety committee (JHSC) made up of members representing both management and workers. Only very small organizations are exempt from the need for representation. Figure 22.1 explains the requirements.

FAST FACT

Structure of the OHSA

- Part I (ss. 2–4) describes the application of the Act and the agencies responsible for decision making.

- Part II (ss. 5–22.1) covers administration.

- Part III (ss. 23–32) outlines responsibilities and duties.

- Part III.1 (ss. 32.1–32.4) describes codes of practice.

- Part IV (ss. 33–42) covers toxic substances.

- Part V (ss. 43–49) covers work refusals.

- Part VI (s. 50) prohibits reprisals by employers.

- Part VII (ss. 51–53) contains special notices.

- Part VIII (ss. 54–65) covers enforcement.

- Part IX (ss. 66–69) outlines offences and penalties.

- Part X (s. 70) covers regulations.

Health and Safety Representatives

In small workplaces, a health and safety representative, chosen by the workers, is required instead of a committee. The representative's duties include, but are not limited to, inspecting the workplace, obtaining health and safety information from the employer, and being involved in testing equipment and products.

Joint Health and Safety Committees

A JHSC comprises people who represent the employees and the employer. Together, they are committed to improving health and safety conditions in the workplace. Their duties include, but are not limited to, identifying hazardous and dangerous situations, recommending improvements for the improved health and safety of workers, and obtaining information about existing hazards in the workplace.

FIGURE 22.1   Breakdown of Health and Safety Representation by Company Size

Number of employees	Health and safety representative	Joint health and safety committee
0–5	Not required	Not required
6–19	One, selected by the workers	Not required
20–49	Not required	Two members (minimum): one represents workers, one represents management
50–plus	Not required	Four members (minimum): two represent workers, two represent management. Two members must be certified.

Certified Members

All workplaces with 50 or more workers must choose four members to sit on the JHSC: two representing the employer and two representing workers. At least two of the four members must be certified, which means that they have received occupational health and safety training as prescribed by the Act. In many cases, security personnel are chosen to represent management on the committee and receive certification training. The duties of certified members include, but are not limited to, inspecting the workplace, participating in investigations of serious or fatal injury, requesting an investigation of dangerous circumstances in the workplace, and recommending a work stoppage where dangerous circumstances are confirmed.

More About the JHSC

Term

It is recommended, in the interest of building expertise at the JHSC level, that JHSC members serve terms of at least one year. All vacancies on a JHSC must be filled as soon as possible to maintain compliance with the legislation.

Security Department Participation

It is very common for a security director/manager to serve as an employer member of a JHSC. It's also possible for a security officer to serve as a worker member.

Confidentiality

In the course of conducting committee business, confidential company and personnel information may become known to committee members. It is a legal responsibility that members keep such information confidential.

Duties

The Canadian Centre for Occupational Health and Safety lists specific JHSC duties and responsibilities as:

- complying with OHS legislation;

- holding meetings and keeping minutes;

- obtaining information;

- identifying hazardous situations;

- participating in development and implementation of programs to protect the employees' safety and health;

- dealing with employee complaints and suggestions concerning safety and health;

- participating in all safety and health inquiries and investigations;

- consulting with professional and technical experts;

- participating in resolving workplace refusals and work stoppages;

- making recommendations to management for accident prevention and safety program activities;

- ensuring the maintenance and monitoring of injury and work hazard records;

- following up hazard reports and recommending action;

- monitoring effectiveness of safety programs and procedures;

- being consulted on the inventory of hazardous materials and hazardous physical substances;

- setting up and promoting the development and review of instruction and employee training;

- being consulted on safety and industrial hygiene testing; and

- being consulted about assessment and control programs for designated substances.

Functions and Powers of Worker Members

Worker members of the committee have certain legislated roles that are applied to them. For example, the JHSC may:

- designate one worker member to conduct workplace inspections at least once a month;

- ask a worker to accompany a Ministry of Labour inspector during physical conditions inspections;

- designate one or more worker members to investigate critical injuries and/or fatalities;

Focus on Technologies

Designed for Safety

Manufacturing is a sector that has struggled with frequent workplace injuries, due to the need for mechanized equipment and repetitive assembly work. The machines used on assembly lines are frequently the subject of innovative engineering modifications designed to encourage safe work practices.

For example, a common source of manufacturing injuries is the use of presses, which can cause crushing injuries if a finger or hand strays into the press during operation. In an attempt to remove this possibility, many presses are now designed so that the pressing action can only be activated if the user presses *two* separate buttons, placed shoulder-width apart. This procedure requires the use of both hands and ensures that the worker cannot have a hand in the press when it is activated.

- designate worker members to be present at the beginning of industrial hygiene testing; and

- assign a worker member to represent a worker in a refusal-to-work situation.

Employer Responsibilities with Regard to the JHSC

Employers are required by the Act to provide whatever assistance and cooperation are necessary to the committee in carrying out its role. Their main responsibilities are

- to establish a committee;

- to post the names and work locations of the committee;

- to give committee members time for preparation, attendance, and to carry out their duties;

- to pay committee members for carrying out above duties at regular or premium rate as required;

- to respond in writing, within 21 days, to written recommendations by the committee;

- to pay members for becoming certified at regular or premium rate as may be proper;

- to post a copy of the annual summary of data from the Workplace Safety and Insurance Board on the company's accident experience;

- to provide assistance and cooperation to committee members;

- to provide the committee with the most recent inventory of hazardous materials and hazardous physical agents, along with copies of the material safety data sheet (MSDS);

- to provide a copy of the written assessment for hazardous materials;

- to provide information to the committee on hazardous physical agents; and

- to ensure that at least one management and one worker member are certified members.

Step Aside

OHS Representation Across the Nation

The Canadian Centre for Occupational Health and Safety (CCOHS) summarizes the legislative requirements for Health and Safety Committees for each of the provinces and territories in figure 22.2. You can find government updates at the Centre's website: www.ccohs.ca/oshanswers/hsprograms/hscommittees/whatisa.html.

Duties of an Employer

The Act imposes duties on "the employer," which in practice means management—those who have some degree of control over the workplace, the materials and equipment in the workplace, and the direction of the workforce. Included in these duties are

- ensuring that measures and procedures prescribed by the Act are carried out;
- ensuring that everyone performing work complies with the Act and regulations;
- protecting the health and safety of workers;
- acquainting a worker with any hazard in the workplace;
- ensuring that equipment, materials, and protective devices prescribed are provided, maintained, and used as prescribed;
- providing information, instruction, and supervision to workers to ensure their safety; and
- appointing only competent people to take the position of supervisor.

Duties of a Safety Supervisor

"Supervisor" means a person who has charge of a workplace or authority over another worker. According to the Act, safety supervisors should ensure that workers

- work safely;
- use protective devices and clothing when required;
- follow established safety procedures;
- are advised of any actual or potential hazards of which the supervisor is aware; and
- receive every protection reasonable in the circumstances for the protection of the worker.

FIGURE 22.2 Legislation Requirements for Health and Safety Committees

	When do I need one?	Size of committee	Representation
Canada	Mandatory: 20 or more employees	At least 2	At least half to represent employees
British Columbia	Mandatory: when there are 20 or more employees or when "required by order"	Not less than 4	At least one-half must be worker representatives
Alberta	As directed by the minister	At least 3 and not more than 12	At least two employees and one employer or at least half employees
Saskatchewan	Mandatory: when 10 employees or more	At least 2 and not more than 12	At least half to represent employees
Manitoba	Mandatory: 20 or more employees as designated by lieutenant governor	At least 4 and not more than 12	At least half to represent employees
Ontario	Mandatory: 20 or more employees, when ordered by minister, or where a designated substance is in use (no minimum number of employees)	At least 2 (fewer than 50 employees); At least 4 (50 or more employees)	At least half to represent employees
Quebec	Mandatory: 20 or more employees and where regulated	At least 4	At least half to represent employees
New Brunswick	Mandatory: 20 or more employees	As agreed upon by employees and employer	Equal representation
Nova Scotia	Mandatory: 20 or more employees	As agreed upon by employees and employer	At least half to represent employees
Prince Edward Island	Agreed upon by employees and employers	Not specified	At least half to represent employees
Newfoundland and Labrador	Discretionary: 10 or more employees	At least 2 and not more than 12	At least half to represent employees
Yukon	Mandatory: 20 or more employees	At least 4 and not more than 12	At least half to represent employees
Northwest Territories	As directed by chief safety officer	Not specified	Equal representation

Duties of a Worker

Workers also have several general duties under the Act.

- They must take responsibility for personal health and safety insofar as they are able and be aware of issues (and avoid taking actions) that might affect the safety of others.

- They must work in compliance with the Act and regulations.

- They must use and wear protective equipment or other safeguards required by the Act.

- They must report all hazards to their employer or supervisor.

- They must report any contravention of the Act.

The Act also makes certain limitations very clear to workers. They must *not*

- remove or make ineffective any protective devices;

- use or operate any equipment, machine, device, or thing in a manner that may endanger themselves or another worker;

- engage in any prank, contest, horseplay, etc., that could endanger the health and safety of themselves or another worker.

WORKPLACE ACCIDENT INVESTIGATION

As noted in the introduction, workplace accidents are, unfortunately, commonplace. Security personnel, regardless of formal health and safety roles (such as JHSC membership), are typically "first responders" in such situations. Consider, for example, the widely reported accident of December 9, 2003 during the demolition of Toronto's landmark Uptown Theatre at Bloor and Yonge streets. Instead of imploding, part of the building collapsed on the neighbouring Yorkville English Academy, killing one person and injuring 14 others. In this case, the demolition company's security management team along with provincial investigators and fire marshals participated in finding out what went wrong.

Reporting Requirements

Part XV of the Canadian Occupational Safety and Health Regulations requires reporting of an accident by the employer to a Labour Canada safety officer if the accident results in any of the following:

- death;

- disabling injury;

- permanent impairment of a body function;

- fire or rupture to a boiler or pressure vessel;

- any damage to an elevating device; or

- an explosion.

Purpose of a Workplace Accident Investigation

The purpose of a workplace accident investigation is to determine the cause of the accident, the extent of injury, any damage (or loss) to property, and to recommend corrective or preventative measures.

The cause of an accident is "any behaviour, condition, act, or negligence without which the accident would not have happened." It is essential that the security officer investigating the accident focus on "fact finding" and not "fault finding."

Analysis of workplace investigation reports suggests that most accidents fall into one of six general categories. These are: organizational errors, technical data insufficiency, material failure, design deficiency, human failure, and natural phenomena.

Organizational Errors

An accident may occur through failure of the organization to properly manage planning, training, supervision, or work practices.

Technical Data Insufficiency

An accident may occur when a hazard is not well understood because of inadequate technical data, incomplete operating instructions, omissions in data, or erroneous data.

Material Failure

When the physical breakdown or chemical deterioration of any part, structure, or component contributed to the accident, the accident can be attributed to "material failure."

Design Deficiency

When a part or component is designed so that failure can or should occur under predictable circumstances, the accident can be attributed to design deficiency.

Human Failure

An accident is deemed to be caused by human failure when a person, whether due to physical or psychological limitations, including illness, fails to perform an assigned task properly and contributes to an accident.

Natural Phenomena

An accident is attributed to natural phenomena when unusual acts of nature (such as an earthquake or hurricane) cause the accident; but this attribution of cause is not appropriate when there is evidence of failure to take normal precautions against these contingencies.

Procedures for a Workplace Accident Investigation

As the first responder to an accident scene, the security officer must first focus on the need for medical attention for any injured worker(s) and the prevention of further injuries. The procedures are covered in CPR/first aid training. Once these matters have been dealt with, the workplace accident investigation must begin. The following guidelines explain how the investigation might proceed:

Step One: Respond to Emergency

Control the accident scene, by:

- *Erecting barriers*: Barriers of some kind must be established in order to prevent and/or control the movement of people and vehicles into the accident scene.

- *Shutting down machinery*: Any machinery that is in operation within the accident area, including any machinery that may have been involved in the accident, must be shut down safely and treated as evidence.

- *Following standard operating procedures (SOP)*: The investigating security officer must follow the SOPs that govern that specific area of the workplace affected at all times.

- *Locating and identifying witnesses*: Find out what happened from those witnesses who saw the accident.

Step Two: Collect Information

Collect information through:

- *Interviews*: Conduct interviews as soon as possible in a place that is non-threatening for the people being interviewed.

- *Photographs*: The use of a Polaroid camera is recommended as the photos are available immediately, and information can be inserted on the tab of the photograph for future identification. A digital camera or a camcorder is also useful. Be aware, however, that in court, the defence may object to any evidence that can be (or may have been) manipulated.

- *Block diagrams*: Block diagrams are useful for recording the layout of an accident scene in addition to showing the following information:

  - the sizes of objects in relation to their surroundings;

  - the position of objects or people in relation to other objects;

  - the distance (to scale) between fixed objects within the scene;

  - the recorded location of objects and people prior to their removal from the accident scene.

- *Removal of material or equipment for testing*: It may be necessary to remove tools, substances, machinery, or other items to have them tested for any operational malfunction or physical deficiency. In many cases, the worker may have been injured due to some fault of the tools or equipment he or she was using.

Step Three: Analyze Information

The initial analysis of an accident scene begins as soon as the security officer arrives. It is very important that the officer specifically write down all observations along with the facts obtained from the answers to his or her questions. In gathering information about the accident, the who, what, where, when, how, and why questions should always be asked.

Who was involved? The security officer should get the names of everyone who witnessed the accident and events preceding or following it, including supervisors. Workers who do the same job as the injured worker may be able to describe it in a step-by-step way. Names, phone numbers, and work locations should be recorded in case the witnesses need to be interviewed at a later stage in the investigation.

What was involved? Physical evidence can be removed or destroyed. For this reason, it should be one of the first things the security officer examines and records. Materials and equipment involved should be described and checked for any defects. If the officer is unfamiliar with the equipment, one of the workers may be able to assist in the examination. If safety guards were missing or were not being used, the security officer should find out why. The officer should check for defects or other equipment problems that might have contributed to the accident and examine the general housekeeping, weather conditions, and any other hazardous conditions that might have been a factor in the accident.

Where did it happen? A description of the exact location and circumstances that led to the accident must be fully provided as part of the accident report. The description should include reference to hazardous conditions such as overcrowding, noise, poor lighting, fumes, and other potential factors. It is also important to note what other jobs are carried out in the same work area. Making a rough drawing and taking photographs of the accident scene from several angles is an effective way of recording information.

When did it happen? The day and time that the accident occurred must be recorded and it is important to note any relevant details that might have a bearing on the accident, such as whether shift work was a factor. The responding officer should note whether the injured worker was on overtime and if he or she was working alone. The weather conditions at the time should also be noted if relevant to the accident. The security officer should write down the time of arrival at the accident scene. The lapse of time between the accident occurring and the investigation beginning can make an important difference in some cases.

How did it happen? Because the security officer was not at the scene of the accident, asking the injured worker questions is the best way to find out what happened. The officer should ask about any near misses prior to the accident and whether any changes have recently been made to the job or work environment. The injured worker or a witness should be asked to describe the job process in detail, noting events immediately before, during, and after the accident. A review of these descriptions may indicate ways that the accident could have been prevented.

Why did it happen? This is the big question that everyone wants to know and the hardest thing to find out. It is important to record suggested reasons from witnesses or employees even if they are hypothetical rather than factual. Every theory should be investigated until discounted. The security officer must find out all the causes, both direct and indirect, that contributed to the accident. Most accidents are not caused by a single problem, but by a combination of factors.

Things to consider are

- the adequacy of health and safety training;

- job procedures, quotas, labour relations;

- supervision issues;

- previous complaints about equipment safety;

- the effects of toxic substances and poor indoor air quality; and

- other work conditions that might be related to the accident.

In order to conduct an effective investigation, it is important to look behind what appears to be the primary cause, (for example, "faulty equipment") to determine what really caused the accident.

Initial impressions should be followed by questions until the security officer is satisfied that he or she knows all the causes of the accident.

Not all the information needed for a thorough investigation will necessarily be available at the accident scene. Often, information about the accident can be found in:

- reports of past accidents and hazardous occurrences reports;

- material safety data sheets (MSDSs);

- maintenance reports and inspection reports;

- training reports;

- first aid reports and workplace safety and insurance claims;

- blueprints and floor plans of the workplace;

- specifications of equipment and engineering reports;

- reports of similar incidents from other workplaces in the same industry with similar working conditions;

- reports supplied by the union or other labour organizations; and

- newspaper articles about the accident being investigated.

Any pertinent information should be examined to see what can be learned about other factors that might have contributed to the accident and what changes might be recommended to prevent a recurrence. This background information must be assembled and examined before doing a final analysis and reaching a conclusion about how the accident happened.

Step Four: Write Report

The investigative report should be thorough and accurate and must include specific recommendations to management. Recommendations need to cover such areas as how to avoid a similar accident, safety precautions or improvements, along with information on compliance with provincial health and safety laws and regulations. The report should then be posted in the workplace in every area where workers congregate, such as the staff cafeteria, lunch rooms, change rooms, notice boards, the personnel office, and the security office. Copies of the investigative report should be sent to the site manager, security manager, union representative department supervisor, the injured worker, the Ministry of Labour, and the joint health and safety committee.

Step Five: Follow Up

Every workplace accident report should have a suggested timetable for the implementation of the recommendations. The security manager will usually advise the security officer on how to schedule the timetable. The timetable should have realistic achievable deadlines and be submitted in writing. The security manager usually reviews the health and safety training done on site after an accident has occurred. The recommendations compiled in the complete workplace investigation submitted by all official parties are adopted and an effort is made to raise awareness in all the workers about the cause of the accident. This helps to avoid a recurrence of the accident.

Step Aside

Accident Investigation Checklist

Check the working environment. At the place of the accident, what was the state of the lighting, temperature and humidity, noise level, dust and fumes, workplace layout, flooring, and housekeeping?

Check the training, job experience, and supervision of the injured worker. Consider these questions:

- How long had the worker been on the job?
- What safety training had the worker received?
- What supervision was present?
- What safety training had the supervisor received?

Other aspects of the accident to consider are:

- Was information available on the safe use of equipment and the handling of materials?
- Was all plant and equipment maintained to standard?
- What do maintenance reports reveal about the state of any equipment?
- Did protective clothing hamper communications in any way?
- If protective clothing was issued, was it suitable for the individual and the job, and properly maintained?
- Are there records of other accidents or dangerous occurrences in the same work area or job? If yes, are there any common factors that could link them?
- Is there any evidence of previous unsafe practices being condoned by management?

Investigative Pitfalls

Listing "carelessness" as a cause of an accident is a direct admission that the investigation was worthless.

Basing the cause solely on the type of accident or injury indicates a lack of completeness. For example, listing "faulty electric wiring" as a fire cause without elaboration provides no information upon which future prevention efforts can be based.

Security officers should be careful not to assume that one single cause will be found in each and every investigation. All possible causes indicated by the evidence should be listed so that corrective action can be taken to eliminate every one of them.

SUMMARY

Occupational health and safety is probably the most important safety issue in modern workplaces. Since security personnel are employed by a company to protect against both external and internal risks, responsibility for occupational health and safety is a natural part of the security role. In recognition of this "fit," many companies choose security personnel to play key roles with respect to occupational health and safety, such as JHSC membership. Even when not assigned formal roles, security officers are usually the first responders when there is a workplace accident.

Security officers are expected to understand the general principles of the OHSA, the roles of workplace parties, and how the internal responsibility system is supposed to work. They may also be given responsibility for the investigation of workplace accidents. This chapter has provided an overview of the steps to take to ensure that accidents are investigated fully, with a view to prevention of future problems.

KEY TERM

due diligence

PERFORMANCE APPLICATION

1. Why do security officers also have to assume the responsibilities of a safety supervisor under the OHSA of Ontario?

2. Explain the duties of a safety supervisor under the OHSA.

3. As a worker, what are your responsibilities under the OHSA?

4. What is a JHSC? Why do you think that the OHSA stipulates that half its members come from management, and half from among the workers?

5. What role does a JHSC play in promoting occupational health and safety in the workplace?

6. What is the primary purpose of determining the cause of a workplace accident?

7. List three common general causes of workplace accidents.

8. Who will read the investigative report prepared in response to a workplace accident? List four different audiences for such a report.

9. List three kinds of *historical* evidence (i.e., dating before the accident) that might be relevant to the investigation of a workplace accident.

10. Why does the security department have a special interest in preventing workplace accidents?

CHAPTER 23

Workplace Hazards and Safety Inspection

INTRODUCTION

Regular workplace inspections are vital in any company or work environment for overall health and safety. These inspections may range from a short, start-up equipment check to an investigation of the entire workplace. Recording and monitoring hazards that may cause injuries or accidents is an essential part of an organized workplace inspection.

Understanding the range of hazards in the workplace is an important part of a security officer's responsibilities. This chapter will cover the identification of hazards in general, and also the classification of hazardous materials under the **Workplace Hazardous Materials Information System (WHMIS)**.

WORKPLACE SAFETY INSPECTION

The Ontario *Occupational Health and Safety Act* (OHSA) mandates that the workplace inspection must be carried out as a part of the employer's compliance with its moral and legal responsibility for the protection of the safety of employees. A workplace inspection identifies and records potential and actual hazards associated with buildings, equipment, the environment, procedures, and processes.

Selection of the Inspection Team

The joint health and safety committee (JHSC) members who have received training or certification are usually named to a workplace safety inspection team, but often the security officer or supervisor is a certified member and is automatically assigned to the team or to conduct the inspection alone.

Types of Workplace Inspection

There are five types of workplace inspections. These are scheduled inspections, spot checks, inspections in response to a complaint, new equipment inspections

Chapter Objectives

When you have completed this chapter, you will

- be aware of the purpose of workplace safety inspections.

- understand how workplace hazards are identified and classified.

- be aware of the role of legislation and regulations, particularly the Workplace Hazardous Materials Information System, in promoting a safe workplace.

Workplace Hazardous Materials Information System (WHMIS) symbols found on hazardous products that identify the type of danger associated with the product and that provide information on safe handling prior to operation, and critical parts inspections, which are usually specifically related to dangerous activities or to parts that degrade quickly or need special maintenance.

Role of the Workplace Inspection

Workplace inspections are designed to identify hazards within the workplace and to provide the means with which to avoid or correct these hazards while ensuring workers and management they can work together to prevent any reoccurrence. These inspections are not isolated functions, but relate to major objectives—namely, to identify hazards, set standards and related procedures, measure performance against standards, evaluate health and safety performance, and correct deficiencies and commend successes.

The Canadian Centre for Occupational Health and Safety (CCOHS) lists the following hazards that an inspection team or appointed inspector should look for:

- Safety hazards such as inadequate machine guards, unsafe workplace conditions, and unsafe work practices.

- Biological hazards caused by organisms such as viruses, bacteria, fungi, and parasites.

- Chemical hazards caused by a solid, liquid, vapour, gas, dust, fumes, or mist.

- Ergonomic hazards caused by anatomical, physiological, and psychological demands on the worker, such as repetitive and forceful movements, vibration, temperature extremes, and awkward postures arising from improper work methods and improperly designed workstations, tools, and equipment.

- Environmental hazards caused by noise, vibration, energy, weather, heat, cold, electricity, radiation, and pressure.

Planning an Inspection

It makes sense to plan an inspection. The team or security officer may want to see documents in advance, such as previous inspection reports, accident investigations, maps of the work area, inventories of equipment and chemicals used, or maintenance reports for reference.

There are three separate sources of information that should be reviewed in preparation for a hazard inspection. These are the facility, safety standards, and safety profile.

The Facility

It is important to have knowledge of the layout, function, and process of the facility if an inspection team is to conduct a systematic inspection in order to identify hazards. Here are some of the essential areas that should be covered:

- all buildings and structures;
- the internal layout, showing equipment placement;
- the process flow, showing how work is done;

- all hazardous materials (WHMIS) used;

- storage facilities; and

- traffic flow and location of all exits.

Safety Standards

There are several sources of safety standards that apply to the conduct of a workplace inspection. The inspection team must consider the OHSA; the fire code; company policies, bylaws, and regulations; Canadian Standards Association (CSA) specifications, manufacturers' specifications, personal protective equipment (PPE) standards; engineering controls; and emergency procedures.

Safety Profile

Before conducting a workplace safety inspection, it is important to have information about the safety history of the company. Some of this information can be found by examining the following:

- new experimental experience rating (NEER);

- accident statistics from the Ministry of Labour (MOL) and/or the Workplace Safety and Insurance Board (WSIB);

- previous inspection reports;

- employee complaints;

- MOL inspection orders; and

- safety spot map.

Sample Inspection Checklists

To help security officers understand what things are examined in a workplace safety inspection, there are two sample checklists available on the Internet. Figure 23.1 is provided by the Canadian Centre for Occupational Health and Safety. The CCOHS advises:

> While many ready-made checklists are available in safety literature, it is best to adapt these to local conditions. The JHSC should participate in the preparation of these tailor-made checklists.

Figure 23.2 is the workplace safety inspection guide/checklist used by the University of Western Ontario.

Typical Workplace Inspection Report

Following a workplace inspection, the inspection team must provide a report so that all parties affected can be aware of its findings, and to allow for an employer response to problems requiring remediation. Management is required to respond in writing to all recommendations within 21 days. Figure 23.3 shows a CCOHS workplace inspection report form.

FIGURE 23.1   Sample Inspection Checklist from the CCOHS

Date   _____

Location/Department   _____

Yes = Satisfactory

No = Unsatisfactory, needs attention

Yes	No		Yes	No	
		Safe Work Practices			**Fire Protection**
		Use of machine guards			Fire extinguishers
		Proper manual lifting			Proper type/location
		Proper use of air hoses			Storage of flammable materials
		No horseplay			Other_____
		Other_____			
					Tools and Machinery
		Use of Personal Protective Equipment			Lawn mowers
		Eye/face protection			Power tools
		Footwear			Hand tools
		Gloves			Snow blowers
		Protective clothing			Machine guarding
		Head protection			Belts, pulleys, gears, shafts
		Aprons			Oiling, cleaning, adjusting
		Respirators			Maintenance, oil leakage
		Other_____			Other_____
		Housekeeping			**First aid**
		Proper storage areas			First aid kits in rooms/vehicles
		Proper storage of flammable material (oily/greasy rags, etc.)			Trained first aid providers
		Proper disposal of waste			Emergency numbers posted
		Floors (clean, dry, uncluttered)			All injuries reported
		Maintenance of yards, parking lots			Other_____
		Other_____			
					Miscellaneous
		Electrical Safety			MSDS/Labels
		Machines grounding/GFI			Dust/vapour/fume control
		Electrical cords			Safe use of ladders/scaffolds
		Electrical outlets			New processes or procedures carried out
		Other_____			Other_____

Notes

_____

_____

_____

_____

_____

FIGURE 23.2   Sample Inspection Checklist from the University of Western Ontario

UWO Joint Occupational Health and Safety Committee
Workplace Safety Inspection Guide/Checklist

Date: _____   Department: _____   Location: _____

JOHSC Member: _____   OH&S Member: _____

Supervisory Responsibilities

Y   N   N/A   Has a workplace (and campus) orientation been given to all workers?

Y   N   N/A   Has training on special hazards been given (and documented) by the supervisor?

Basic Safety

Y   N   N/A   Are aisles, walkways, and exits clear and all walking surfaces slip-free?

Y   N   N/A   Is the access to all emergency equipment and services clear?

Y   N   N/A   Are shelves, bookcases, etc., sufficient for the intended load and well secured?

Y   N   N/A   Are records kept of workplace equipment inspection and maintenance?

Y   N   N/A   Is all mechanical, cutting, chemical, and/or ionizing equipment properly shielded?

Y   N   N/A   Are all vacuum and/or pressure systems properly shielded or guarded?

Y   N   N/A   Are proper Dewars being used for cryogenic liquids (i.e., liquid nitrogen)?

Y   N   N/A   Does all electrical equipment have approval stickers/plates (CSA, ULC, etc.)?

Y   N   N/A   Is all equipment connected directly to the supply without the use of extension cords?

Y   N   N/A   Are ground fault interrupters being used in potentially wet environments?

Y   N   N/A   Are compressed gas cylinders individually and securely restrained?

Y   N   N/A   Is the proper regulator being used for each compressed gas?

WHMIS

Y   N   N/A   Is the laboratory/emergency equipment posted according to UWO guidelines?

Y   N   N/A   Are all hazardous materials labelled according to section 8.3?

Y   N   N/A   Is there a current inventory of all hazardous substances in the lab?

Y   N   N/A   Do the workers know where to find current (<3 yrs.) MSDSs for materials being used?

Y   N   N/A   Have all workers received the prescribed training from OH&S?

Hygiene Practices

Y   N   N/A   Are chemicals stored and segregated according to UWO regulations?

Y   N   N/A   Is waste segregated/streamed/stored/labelled properly?

Y   N   N/A   Are large/heavy containers stored less than 2 metres above the floor?

Y   N   N/A   Are explosion-proof refrigerators used for the storage of flammable liquids?

Y   N   N/A   Are there <10 litres of flammable liquids outside an approved (yellow) cabinet?

Y   N   N/A   Are fume hoods being used as required and free of storage and clutter?

Y   N   N/A   Is the fume hood flow alarm indicator present and working properly?

Y N N/A   Is proper personal protective equipment being worn by all lab personnel?

Y N N/A   Is the lab free of all evidence of food consumption in hazard areas?

Emergency Equipment and Procedures

Y N N/A   Do personnel know the location of the closest first-aid kit and spill kit?

Y N N/A   Is there an eyewash station and safety shower (< 25m) available as needed?

Y N N/A   Are the fire extinguishers appropriate and checked regularly (monthly)?

Y N N/A   Do personnel know the emergency evacuation plan and route of exit from the workplace?

Y N N/A   Is an emergency contact sign posted with names and numbers of key personnel?

Y N N/A   Are UWO accident/incident forms available and accidents/incident procedures posted?

Source: Revised September 11, 2001, courtesy of the University of Western Ontario.

According to the CCOHS,

During the actual inspection, both work conditions and procedures should be observed. If a hazard that poses an immediate threat is discovered, preventive action must be taken right away, not after the inspection. Notes are made, specifying details of the hazard, including its exact location. When completing the inspection report, it is a good idea to classify each hazard by degree of possible consequences (for example: A = major, B = serious, C = minor). In this way, priorities for remedial action are established.

The CCOHS notes:

Inspections serve a useful purpose only if remedial action is taken to correct shortcomings. Causes, not symptoms alone, must be rectified. Corrective action should be taken immediately, with the emphasis on engineering controls, management failures, or need for worker education, whatever applies.

HAZARDS

hazard
anything that might injure or harm a worker

A **hazard** is anything that can cause injury to or illness in a worker.

Hazard Classification

There are three levels of hazards: class A, B, and C.

Class A

A condition or practice likely to cause permanent disability, loss of life, or body parts, and/or extensive loss of structure, equipment, or material.

- Example 1: A barrier guard is missing on a large press brake.

- Example 2: A maintenance worker is observed servicing a large sump pump in an unventilated deep pit, using gasoline.

FIGURE 23.3   CCOHS Workplace Inspection Report

Location _____

Department/areas covered _____

Date of inspection _____

Time of inspection _____

Item (location)	Hazards observed	Repeat item Yes/No	Priority	Recommended action	Responsible person	Action taken	Date
Analysis and comments:							

Priority Codes: **A** – do immediately; **B** – do within 3 days; **C** – do within 2 weeks; **D** – other

> ## Step Aside
>
> ### Inspection Etiquette
>
> During a workplace inspection, the inspection team should
>
> - allow enough time for inspection;
> - try not to disrupt work unnecessarily;
> - avoid assigning blame; and
> - note the good points as well as the bad.
>
> After a workplace inspection has been completed, the inspection team should:
>
> - discuss findings;
> - use a formal report format;
> - be sure of its facts; and
> - use appropriate language.
>
> The team should circulate the report to the facility manager, department managers, supervisors, and the health and safety coordinator and committee. The report should also be posted on the workplace notice boards.
>
> To promote an open and productive atmosphere, a safety inspection team should avoid being confrontational with management.

Class B

A condition or practice likely to cause serious injury or illness (resulting in temporary disability) or property damage that is disruptive, but less severe than class A.

- Example 1: Slippery oil condition observed in main aisle.
- Example 2: Frayed carpeting at bottom of office stairs.

Class C

A condition or practice that is likely to cause minor (non-disabling) injury or illness or non-disruptive property damage.

- Example 1: Carpenter observed handling rough lumber without gloves.
- Example 2: Traces of fumes in the degreasing area.

Hazardous Materials and WHMIS

In an effort to provide standardized, high-quality information about hazardous materials to employers and workers, the Canadian federal and provincial governments worked together to develop WHMIS.

Because WHMIS is an occupational health and safety initiative, it required implementation at the workplace by means of a provincial law. However, because it also involves the sale and import of hazardous materials, it enters into the federal legislative domain as well. Thus, the enactment of WHMIS into law was accomplished by the passage of complementary federal and provincial legislation.

WHMIS was developed in support of the right of workers to know about the hazards of chemicals and other materials used in the workplace. Exposure to hazardous materials can cause or contribute to many serious health problems, such as, effects on the nervous system, kidney or lung damage, sterility, cancer, burns, and rashes. Some hazardous materials are safety hazards and can cause fires or explosions. WHMIS was created to help stop the injuries, illnesses, deaths, medical costs, and fires caused by hazardous materials.

The three main features of the WHMIS system are the requirement for materials safety training for workers, the requirement for warning labels on containers, and the requirement for the development and dissemination of material safety data sheets (MSDSs) by the manufacturers and distributors of hazardous materials. The WHMIS legislation also contains provisions allowing for the protection of trade secrets (for example, ingredient lists) by manufacturers, while complying with the level of disclosure necessary to allow users to protect themselves.

There are six classes of hazardous material regulated under WHMIS.

Class A: Compressed Gas

Any material that is normally a gas that is placed under pressure or chilled, and contained by a cylinder is considered to be a compressed gas. These materials are dangerous because they are under pressure. If the cylinder is broken, the container can "rocket" or "torpedo" at great speeds and this is a danger to anyone standing too close.

If the cylinder is heated (by fire or a rise in temperature) the gas may try to expand and the cylinder will explode. Leaking cylinders are also a danger because the gas that comes out is very cold and it may cause frostbite if it touches the skin (for example: carbon dioxide or propane). Common examples include compressed air, carbon dioxide (fire extinguishers), propane, oxygen, ethylene oxide, and welding gases. The hazard symbol is a picture of a cylinder or container of compressed gas surrounded by a circle shown in figure 23.4.

Additional dangers may be present if the gas has other hazardous properties. For example, propane is both a compressed gas and flammable. Propane would bear two hazard symbols: the one for a compressed gas and another to show that it is a flammable material.

Class B: Flammable and Combustible Material

Flammable means that the material will burn or catch on fire easily at normal temperatures (below 37.8 °C or 100 °F). Combustible materials must usually be heated before they will catch on fire at temperatures above normal (between 37.8 °C and 93.3 °C or 100 °F and 200 °F). Reactive flammable materials are those that may suddenly start burning when they react with other materials, such as air or water.

Flammable or combustible materials may be solids, liquids, or gases. Common examples include propane, butane, acetylene, ethanol, acetone, turpentine, toluene, kerosene, spray paints, varnish, ammonia, and chlorine. The symbol for this class is a flame with a line under it inside a circle (see figure 23.4).

Class C: Oxidizing Material

Oxygen is necessary for a fire to occur. Some chemicals can cause other materials to burn by supplying oxygen. Oxidizers do not usually burn themselves but they will either help the fire by providing more oxygen or they may cause materials that normally do not burn to suddenly catch on fire (spontaneous combustion). In some cases, a spark or flame (source of ignition) is not necessary for the material to catch on fire but only the presence of an oxidizer. Like flammable or combustible materials, oxidizers can also be in the form of gases (oxygen, ozone), liquids (nitric acid, chromic acid, sodium hypochlorite), and solids (chromates, potassium permanganate). Some oxidizers such as the organic peroxide family are extremely hazardous because they will burn (they are combustible) as well as provide oxygen for the fire. They can also have strong reactions that can result in an explosion. The symbol for oxidizing materials is shown in figure 23.4.

Class D: Poisonous and Infectious Material

Class D materials are those that can cause harm to the human body. They are divided into three major divisions.

FIGURE 23.4 WHMIS Symbols

Class A
compressed gas

Class D-2
Poisonous and infectious material causing other toxic effects

Class B
flammable and combustible material

Class D-3
biohazardous infectious material

Class C
oxidizing material

Class E
corrosive material

Class D-1
poisonous and infectious material causing immediate and serious toxic effects

Class F
dangerously reactive material

Division 1: Materials causing immediate and serious toxic effects are very poisonous and immediately dangerous to life and health. Serious health effects such as burns, loss of consciousness, coma, or death within just minutes or hours after exposure are grouped in this category. Most D-1 materials will also cause long-term effects. Examples of some D-1 materials include carbon monoxide, sodium cyanide, and sulphuric acid. The symbol for class D, division 1 (D-1) is a skull and crossed bones inside a circle (see figure 23.4).

Division 2: Materials causing other toxic effects are poisonous as well. Their effects are not always immediate, or if the effects are immediate they are only temporary. They may still have very serious consequences, however, such as: cancer, allergies, reproductive problems or harm to the baby, changes to genes, or irritation/sensitization from small exposures over a long period of time (chronic effects). Examples of this class include asbestos fibres, mercury, ammonia, acetone, benzene, propane, silica, lead, and cadmium. The symbol for materials causing other toxic effects is shown in figure 23.4.

Division 3: Biohazardous infectious material or the toxins they produce can cause diseases in people or animals. Included in this division are bacteria, viruses, fungi, and parasites. Because these organisms can live in body tissues or fluids (blood, urine), the tissues and fluids are also treated as toxic. Biohazardous infectious materials are usually found in a hospital, health care facility, laboratories, veterinary practices, and research facilities. Workers in these places do not usually know which tissues or fluids contain dangerous organisms. For this reason, the workers assume that every sample is dangerous and proper protection is used all the time. Examples of biohazardous infectious materials include the HIV virus, hepatitis B, and salmonella. The symbol for this division is shown in figure 23.4.

Class E: Corrosive Material

Corrosive is the name given to materials that can cause severe burns to skin and other human tissues, such as the eye or lung, and can attack clothes and other materials including metal. Corrosives are grouped in this special class because their effects are permanent (temporary irritants are grouped in class D-2). Common corrosives include acids such as sulphuric and nitric acids, bases such as ammonium hydroxide, caustic soda, and potassium, and other materials such as ammonium, chlorine, and nitrogen dioxide. The symbol for a corrosive is a picture of two test tubes pouring liquid on a bar (piece of metal) and a hand with lines coming off of them inside a circle (see figure 23.4).

Class F: Dangerously Reactive Material

A material is considered to be dangerously reactive if it shows one or more of the following three different properties or abilities:

- if it can react very strongly and quickly ("vigorously") with water to make a toxic gas;

- if it will react with itself when it gets shocked (bumped or dropped) or if the temperature or pressure increases; and

- if it can vigorously join to itself (polymerize), break down (decompose), or lose extra water such that it becomes a more dense material (condense).

Step Aside

Anatomy of a Material Safety Data Sheet

An MSDS must contain, at minimum, the following information:

1. product information: product identifier (name), manufacturer's and supplier's names, addresses, and emergency phone numbers;

2. hazardous ingredients;

3. physical data;

4. fire or explosion data;

5. reactivity data: information on the chemical instability of a product and the substances it may react with;

6. toxicological properties: specific health effects;

7. preventive measures;

8. first aid measures; and

9. preparation information: who is responsible for preparation and date of preparation of the MSDS.

If a material is dangerously reactive, it will most likely be described as "unstable." Most of these materials can be extremely hazardous if they are not handled properly because they can react in such a quick manner very easily. Examples of these products are ethyl acrylate, styrene, vinyl chloride, benzoyl peroxide, piric acid, and aluminum chloride. The symbol for dangerously reactive materials is a picture of a test tube with sparks or lines coming out of the tube surrounded by a letter "R" inside a circle (see figure 23.4).

For every hazardous material used in the workplace, the employer must have, and provide for review, an MSDS. The MSDS contains much more information about the material than the label and is prepared by the supplier. It is intended to

- describe the hazards of the product;

- explain how to use the product safely;

- advise what to expect if the recommendations are not followed;

- explain what to do if accidents occur;

- explain how to recognize symptoms of overexposure; and

- advise what to do if such incidents occur.

An MSDS for each hazardous material present in the workplace must be available to be read by any worker who may be exposed to a hazardous material. MSDSs are usually

- kept in a file or binder in an easily accessible place; some employers keep this binder in a materials storage area;

- stored electronically;

- available to the joint health and safety committee.

A workplace hazard is a form of energy that, when properly directed and controlled, performs a useful function, but when uncontrolled, presents a danger to workers. Several forms of energy are hazardous to workers. These are shown in figure 23.5.

Protecting workers from dangerous energy is generally accomplished through the use of energy barriers. Energy barriers can be classified as engineering controls, work practices, administrative controls, and personal protective equipment.

Engineering Controls

This form of barrier is designed as a form of built-in control. Examples include off switches, machine part guards, and ventilation systems.

Work Practices

Work practices can provide a form of barrier to individual hazards and dangers in the workplace. Examples of safe work practices include worker education and training, good housekeeping, highly visible labels, proper storage, personal hygiene, compliance with rules, and behaviour reinforcement.

Administrative Controls

This type of barrier includes the things that management can do to help avoid some workplace hazards. For example management can rotate workers to minimize their exposure to hazardous energy. They can also install warning and alarm systems to notify workers when they have received maximum allowable exposure.

FIGURE 23.5   Hazardous Energy in the Workplace

Type of hazardous energy	Example in the workplace
Gravitational	Falling from a height
Electrical	Contacting underground equipment
Mechanical	Colliding with mobile equipment
Chemical	Inhaling toxic chemicals
Noise	Working with air compressors without protective ear covering
Thermal	Contact with hot or cold objects
Radiation	Ultraviolet radiation from welding
Pressure	Uncontrolled release of pressure
Biological	Exposure to viruses
Body mechanics	Lifting heavy objects

What Would You Do?

Oh, My Aching Back

Read this scenario and answer the questions that follow.

While patrolling an automobile manufacturing plant, you spot a worker, who normally stands to perform his work at a press that moulds flat sheets of plastic into the shape of a car door interior panel sitting cross-legged on the floor. He is using a handmade L-shaped wooden lever to push the panels into position and operate the press button. You ask the worker why he is doing his job in a manner different from that prescribed—i.e., standing, and using his hands. The worker, who is very tall, complains that the work area is uncomfortably low and that his back and shoulders are constantly cramped and painful from stooping.

1. Does the worker's job modification pose a safety hazard? How would you find out?

2. If you believe the way that the worker is doing the job is unsafe, what would you do?

3. Is the worker's height a safety issue in itself?

4. Are there any other issues that may be contributing to the worker's pain (hint: consider work organization/scheduling)?

5. What might the employer do to resolve the safety issue(s)?

Personal Protective Equipment

Various forms of personal protective equipment (PPE) are used to avert danger to the worker. Examples of these are gloves, safety footwear, safety hats, splashguards, protective glasses, face shields, respirators, and aprons.

Having the responsibility for monitoring workplace safety, security officers should be aware of safety equipment, practices, and policies in place in the workplace, and they should monitor all work areas regularly to assess whether workers are taking full advantage of the protections offered them, and whether safety equipment is in proper working condition.

SUMMARY

Whether in the context of a formal, scheduled workplace safety inspection or in the course of a routine patrol, security officers are often charged with the responsibility for identifying workplace hazards.

Understanding the hazard identification process depends on the individual being able to recognize an unsafe situation before an accident or injury occurs. With practice, security personnel can make a significant contribution to the overall safety profile of a company.

Information is the key to hazard control, and thus to worker protection. WHMIS has created a system that delivers this information to employers and workers by using labels, MSDSs, and workplace training. The success of the system is measured in the number of informed workers and by the effectiveness of their contribution to improved workplace health and safety.

A key preventive step in the promotion of workplace safety is the use of energy barriers and supportive work practices. These can include anything from ventilation systems to rules with respect to smoking in the workplace. Security personnel play an important role in assuring that all safety equipment and precautions prescribed by the employer are being used and followed by the employees. The enforcement of safety rules protects everyone and can save the lives of employees and money for the employer.

KEY TERMS

hazard

Workplace Hazardous Materials Information System (WHMIS)

PERFORMANCE APPLICATION

1. List three types of workplace safety inspections.

2. Why is it useful to carry out unannounced safety "spot checks?"

3. What is the purpose of an inspection report? What sort of follow-up response should be expected?

4. List five types of hazards that might be encountered in a workplace.

5. What are some of the things a company can do to protect workers from workplace hazards?

6. Why are security officers expected to understand the role of energy barriers and how they are applied?

7. How does a security personnel's vigilance in looking out for workplace hazards protect the employer's interests?

8. What is the purpose of an MSDS? Why must these documents be made available to all employees?

PART VII EXERCISE

1. Interview a JHSC member from a company of your choice. Find out how the committee or the health and safety representative deals with worker complaints and prepare a 500-word essay for class discussion.

2. For this assignment, work in teams of four. Each team should choose one of the following areas within a facility of your choice:

   - cafeteria

   - kitchen

   - library

   - gymnasium

   - shipping and receiving area

   - parking lot

   - laboratory

   Obtain permission (where applicable) to inspect the area at a time most convenient to the users of the space before beginning the following assignment.

   Assignment: As a team, create a hazard recognition checklist based on the samples presented in this chapter and make it applicable to the area selected for inspection. Fill out the checklist and write a summary of recommendations that address the identified hazards. Be prepared to present and discuss your findings in class.

PART VIII

Emergency Response

INTRODUCTION

Fire safety is one of the most important responsibilities of the security officer. One of the most significant threats to the lives of employees and the assets of the company is fire. It is the security officer's responsibility as first responder to ensure that he or she is capable of the required response to any fire situation.

This chapter will cover the basic elements of fire safety, the composition of fire, its various sources, and basic fire response techniques.

UNDERSTANDING FIRE

Fire is a **chemical reaction** involving rapid oxidation or burning of a fuel. It needs three elements to occur: fuel, oxygen, and heat.

Fuel can be any combustible material: solid, liquid, or gas. Most solids and liquids become a vapour or gas before they will burn.

The air we breathe is about 21 percent oxygen. Fire needs only an atmosphere with at least 16 percent oxygen to burn.

Heat is the energy necessary to increase the temperature of the fuel to a point where sufficient vapours are given off for ignition to occur.

It is useful to think of the three elements of fire as a triangle. A chain reaction occurs when the three elements of fire are present in the proper conditions and proportions. When fuel is heated, fire occurs and rapid oxidation or burning takes place.

Take any one of these factors away, and a fire cannot occur or it will be extinguished if it is already burning.

Byproducts of Fire

The flame of a fire is not what kills or injures victims. It is the byproducts of a fire that are fatal. What blisters and burns a person's skin, for example, is the intense heat of the fire. As the fire burns, this heat expands the air in a building, and the expanding air generates such amazing pressure that eventually it blows doors and

> ### Chapter Objectives
> When you have completed this chapter you will
>
> - understand the importance of sound fire plans and comprehensive evacuation procedures.
>
> - be able to recognize and to understand the use of various types of fire-fighting equipment.
>
> - be able to describe the duties and responsibilities of the security officer during a fire alarm.

chemical reaction
the rapid oxidation of fuel created by fuel, oxygen, and heat

windows apart in a crushing force. Exposure to *smoke* can blind a person, and cause suffocation in very short order. Even if there is no fire present, carbon dioxide and carbon monoxide are toxic byproducts. A person exposed to these toxins will die if not rescued in time. Also, in a fire, carbon dioxide and carbon monoxide collect under pressure and as heat and pressure rise, they too combine in a lethal power that causes terrible explosions.

Classifying Fires

Fires come in five groups, and it is important to recognize each one because the type of extinguisher required to fight a fire depends on the classification of the fire. (See figure 24.1, below.)

FIRE SAFETY PLAN

Each facility should have a plan for how to deal with fire. The plan should include strategies for fire prevention, fire alarm assessment and response, fire containment/extinguishing, contacting fire fighting personnel, and evacuating people.

Once developed, a fire safety plan should be shared with the security department, who will typically act as first responders in case of a fire. (Security personnel will often be involved in the preparation of a fire safety plan.) Security personnel should receive thorough training in how to use any equipment provided, how to respond to a fire alarm, how to extinguish minor fires, and how to conduct an evacuation. In some facilities, security personnel will want to conduct occasional fire drills to educate employees about how to react in case of a fire.

Specific Responsibilities of Security Personnel

In general, in the case of a significant fire, responsibility for fire fighting lies with the fire department. Security personnel's direct role is typically limited to the discretionary use of portable fire extinguishers.

FIGURE 24.1 Fire Classifications

Fire classification	Description	Type of extinguisher
Class A	Ordinary combustibles or fibrous material, such as wood, paper, cloth, rubber, and some plastics.	Use water and dry chemicals that are flame-retardant and act as a coolant.
Class B	Flammable or combustible liquids, such as gasoline, kerosene, paint, paint thinners, and propane.	Use foam, a solution of aluminum sulphate and bicarbonate of soda or dry chemicals.
Class C	Energized electrical equipment, such as appliances, switches, panel boxes, and power tools.	Use carbon dioxide (CO_2) and a combination of water, foam, and dry chemicals.
Class D	Certain combustible metals, such as magnesium, titanium, potassium, and sodium. These metals burn at high temperatures and give off sufficient oxygen to support combustion. They may react violently with water or other chemicals and must be handled with care.	Use dry powder that smothers and coats the fire.
Class E	Vegetable and animal oils.	Use dry powder only.

However, security plays two vital indirect roles:

1. Security must ensure that the existence of the fire is promptly detected and communicated to the fire department. This is generally accomplished by the proper monitoring and maintenance of fire detection systems and communication systems.

2. Security must manage any evacuation, ensuring the safe and orderly exit of employees and the public.

One of the greatest dangers at the time of a fire emergency is the danger of panic, which can be just as deadly a threat to the welfare and safety of workers as the fire itself. Consequently, it is of vital importance that all security officers are aware of the basics of fire safety and evacuation management so that, at the time of a fire emergency, they will be able to function in a calm, orderly, and effective manner.

Under a fire safety plan, the responsibilities accorded to security personnel will likely reflect the following guidelines:

- Respond to alarm location area and take immediate control on arrival.

- Instruct the security manager to make the required announcement over the PA system to the entire facility.

- Perform first responder duties as required. (Portable fire-fighting equipment is to be used only if the attending security officer is sure that his or her safety will not be compromised.)

- Contact and consult with senior fire warden regarding the emergency.

- Stay in contact with the control operator and other patrol units.

- Liaise with fire department and any other emergency response units.

- Assist fire units as required.

- Assist with evacuation of personnel as required.

- Communicate the nature of the emergency to the affected people.

- Prepare and submit required incident reports.

- Return to scheduled duties as instructed.

Prevention and Protection

Preventing fires requires knowledge of fire hazards. Fires have many causes, and security officers should know which hazards are of particular relevance to their workplace in order to be able to monitor a developing problem.

Security departments should also have a general understanding of their facility's **fire load**. When a building is erected, furnished, and occupied, its users receive, use, store, and discard hundreds of items every day. Each of these items, when combined with the others in particular circumstances, will increase the potential for a fire to occur—that is, increase the building's fire load.

fire load
contents of a building that increase the potential for fire as items accumulate

Step Aside

Training Plan for Fire Safety

There are several essential training elements that should be addressed in any good fire-training plan.

Equipment Recognition

Security officers must become totally familiar with all forms of fire-fighting equipment so that regardless of their surroundings, they are capable of using whatever types are available.

Technical Familiarity

Security officers must be familiar with the technical specifications of each type of fire alarm system and its sensors that together make up the building system. Since officers are likely to work on several different sites, they must take the time to become familiar with each system. Lives, including their own, may depend on it.

Operational Knowledge

This form of training concentrates on the officer's knowledge of the building fire plan. The security officer must know what each person's task is. If called upon to assume the position of site supervisor in an emergency fire response, the officer must be familiar with the response duties of the supervisor.

Physical Competence

Finally, the security officer must be trained in practical fire-fighting skills. These include:

- the use of all types of fire extinguishers;
- the use of a fire blanket;
- the way to activate and hold a fire hose;
- how to check for fire at a locked door;
- evacuation procedures;
- how to assist the elderly and those with physical disabilities.

Equipment

Understanding the facility's inherent hazards and its fire load will help officers to make informd choices on protective equipment. Fire prevention and protection can be enhanced through the correct use of equipment, such as fire alarms, sprinkler systems, fire extinguishers, axes for breaking glass, fire hoses, fire doors, fire walls, smoke-proof towers, fire-resistant safes, and non-flammable rugs and furnishings.

Security officers are expected to be aware of the location and working of all the fire-protection equipment available in the workplace so that they can maintain it and to report any problems or damage.

EVACUATION PROCEDURES

The following evacuation procedures should be reviewed with all employees:

- The last person leaving a room should close, but not lock, the door. Locking the door hinders the fire department's search and rescue efforts.

- Evacuees should proceed to the nearest safe exit as outlined in an Emergency Action Plan, which should be posted on every floor of a facility.

- Elevators should never be used in a fire situation.

- When smoke or toxic gases are present (or suspected to be), evacuees should be instructed to bend over and stay low. The best air is close to the floor, so crawl if necessary.

- If possible, the mouth and nose should be covered with a damp cloth to filter the air and assist breathing.

- If the facility has multiple floors, a stairway will be the primary escape route. Most enclosed stairwells in buildings over two storeys are "rated" enclosures (which means they are more fireproof than other areas) and will provide a safe means of exit. Don't panic. Descend stairs slowly and carefully. Once in the stairwell, proceed down to the first floor. Never go up.

- Once outside the building, evacuees should report to a predetermined area so that a head count can be taken.

A person trying to escape a fire should never open a closed door without feeling it first with the back of the hand for excessive heat on the other side. If the door is hot, another exit should be used or, if none exists, the cracks around the doors and vents should be sealed with anything available.

A trapped person should use a radio or telephone to call the fire department, giving them his or her exact location. If a phone or radio is not available, the person should wave for attention at a window.

If breathing is difficult, the person should try to ventilate the room. If the fire is on an upper floor and the window is of a type that cannot be opened, the window should *never* be broken as glass will rain down on rescuers and people exiting the building.

A person on fire should stop, drop to the floor, and roll around to smother the flames. If someone else catches fire, the flames should be smothered with a blanket. Wrapping a person in a blanket or rug can save them from serious burns or even death.

Use of a Fire Extinguisher

The easiest way to remember how to use a fire extinguisher is to think of the acronym, PASS:

Pull the pin.

Aim the extinguisher nozzle at the base of the flames.

Squeeze the trigger while holding the extinguisher upright.

Sweep the extinguisher from side to side, covering the area with the extinguishing agent.

FIRE ALARM SIGNALLING SYSTEMS

There are two types of fire alarm signalling systems: local and remote.

The local alarm signal sounds only in the building. These are the red pull boxes on floors in apartment buildings or commercial buildings and are clearly identified as *local alarms only*. When one is pulled, it alerts people inside the building, but it is not connected to any outside agency.

The remote signal station signalling system is the most popular system currently in use in Canada. This system raises an audible alarm in the building, at the same time as it sends a signal through a dedicated phone line to a fire alarm monitoring station. The station in turn confirms the alarm by calling the site and then calls the fire department.

Sensors for Four Stages of a Fire

Figure 24.2 shows the four stages of a fire and the special type of sensor designed to detect each unique stage.

Fire Suppressant Systems

Several types of automatic fire suppressant systems are on the market. These systems typically react to fire, detected by sensors, to trigger the dumping of fire suppressant. The most popular and effective system is known as the dump system. The dump system uses various forms of suppressant to smother the fire inside an enclosed area within a very short reaction time. Although this system is very effective, the choice of fire suppressant used can sometimes cause more damage than the actual damage caused by the fire itself.

Some suppressant agents are halon, carbon dioxide, foam, and inergen.

Sprinkler Systems

There are two types of sprinkler systems in use: wet and dry.

A wet system has water in the pipe up to the sprinkler head. When the sensor in the sprinkler head or in the room is activated, the seal is blown and water floods out of the sprinkler head.

FIGURE 24.2   Fire Stages and Alarm Sensors

Stage of fire	Fire alarm sensor
Germinal or incipient stage	Ionization detector—Detects rise in hydrocarbons as they interfere with the electric current passing between two plates in alarm device and triggers alarm.
Smouldering stage	Photoelectric smoke detector—Sounds an alarm when smoke concentration reaches 2 percent to 4 percent.
Flame stage	Infrared flame detector—Reacts to the infrared emissions in a flame to sound an alarm.
Heat stage	Thermal detector—Senses a rapid rise in temperature. It also sounds an alarm when the thermal sensor detects a rise to a set or fixed level of temperature.

Focus on Technologies

Open Access

As part of a central fire communications project with the City of Mississauga Fire and Emergency Services, Fire Monitoring Technologies International Inc. developed an electronic direct-to-fire-department notification system known as OPEN ACCESS, which is available to all companies operating ULC-listed alarm monitoring stations. In a study by Leber/Rubes Inc., a representative sample of 95 properties was selected at random from fire department property files in Mississauga and Brampton, Ontario, for the purpose of conducting alarm response tests. All alarm tests were conducted with the assistance of fire service personnel and all times were documented through the fire department computer-aided dispatch system.

The Leber/Rubes study demonstrated that

- Conventional central station monitoring took almost five times longer than electronic notification. Reporting time took as long as 10 minutes in some cases.

- 45 (60.8 percent) of the alarms reported through central station were not reported within 90 seconds. On some occasions, an excessive amount of time was lost due to the central station operator first calling the premises and not following protocol.

- On one occasion, the operator gave the wrong address for the alarm.

- 5 (6.8 percent) of the tests were never reported to the Fire Communications Centre.

- For two of the most vulnerable population areas, hospitals and schools, the differentials between a conventional and electronic notification were 3 minutes, 35 seconds for hospitals and 2 minutes, 20.7 seconds for schools. This is much greater than the 1 minute, 54.7 second average differential for the whole study and caused the study designers great concern.

These delays and errors can be avoided with electronic notification. In virtually all cases, the fire trucks were dispatched through OPEN ACCESS before the central station contacted the fire department's communication centre.

In light of these results, Jonathan Rubes noted:

Faster response times by the fire department will result in intervention earlier in the growth of the fire. The earlier the fire department is able to take action in a fire, the greater the opportunity to save lives and reduce property damage.

The Leber/Rubes study provides a strong argument in favour of the use of direct electronic notification to fire departments.

A dry system has water in the pipe up to the sprinkler room, and a vacuum is created in the pipe up to the sprinkler head. When the sensor in the sprinkler head or in the room is activated, the seal is blown and the air leaves the vacuum. The loss in pressure triggers the water valve at the main connector and water rushes into the pipe, flooding out of the sprinkler head.

Pull stations connected to audio alarms can also activate sprinklers. For the hearing impaired, special fire signal lights flash to indicate an emergency.

The operation of sprinkler systems are supported by fire panels, detectors, lights, fire bells, and public address systems.

SUMMARY

Statistics suggest that a security officer in a typical workplace will be required to deal with a fire alarm situation about once per month. Fire can do an enormous amount of damage and can cause death or serious injury, much more quickly than most people expect. Reacting immediately and appropriately to both false alarms and real fire situations can mean the difference between life or death for people in the building.

While the actual fire-fighting responsibility lies almost exclusively with the fire department, security officers play a vital role in promoting a speedy, orderly, and effective response to a fire situation, and their assistance is crucial for evacuation management. Security officers are also expected to understand the use of fire protection equipment, to know where it is located, to report any problems with equipment, and to coordinate equipment maintenance.

KEY TERMS

chemical reaction

fire load

PERFORMANCE APPLICATION

1. In the event of a fire alarm, what actions must a security officer take immediately?

2. Explain the two most common types of fire alarm signalling systems. Which is more effective and why?

3. How does an ionization detector differ from a photoelectric, infrared, or thermal detector? Why is the ionization detector the most critical of the four sensors?

4. How do you use a fire extinguisher properly?

5. What precautions must be taken when evacuating a building during a fire?

6. What fire conditions are capable of resulting in explosion? How does one recognize the danger?

7. Why is it critical for a security officer to learn all that's possible about how fires are started, what extinguishers to use, fire safety rules, and evacuation procedures in the facility where he or she works?

INTRODUCTION

An unfortunate reality of modern security is the prospect of bomb threats. As most people know, not all bomb threats relate to the actual placement of an explosive device; some such threats are made simply as a nuisance or in an attempt to disrupt business activities.

Nevertheless, all bomb threats with some degree of credibility must be handled as if they are legitimate, which means securing the area, managing an evacuation where appropriate, and performing an exhaustive investigation, often in cooperation with public authorities, of the threat, the motives behind it, and any actual placed explosive device(s).

Chapter Objectives

When you have completed this chapter, you will

■ have a basic understanding of the duties of a security officer planning defensive strategies against, or responding to, a bomb threat.

EXPLOSIVE DEVICES

Explosive devices exist in a wide variety. An explosive device is any object containing chemical, liquid, or gas (or combination thereof) that is designed to do damage or create injury upon detonation, explosion, or chemical or physical reaction.

Bombs built by would-be criminals for the specific purpose of doing damage are sometimes called "improvised explosive devices" (IEDs). Mechanical or electrical IEDs commonly have an initiation system or fuse, explosive fill, a detonator, a power supply for the detonator, and a container.

Explosive devices can range in size from very tiny (consider, for example, the size of a grenade, or piece of plastique) to 200 kg or larger. Explosive devices can be made to look like everyday objects (particularly, small electronics) or can be hidden inside or fixed to the underside or other hidden sides of innocent objects. By the same token, harmless collections of sinister-looking materials (fuses, timers, etc.) can be assembled to look like workable explosive devices.

Explosive devices are fairly easy to create. Instructions for making bombs abound on the Internet, and many explosive devices can be made out of easily accessible materials. This means that even fairly unsophisticated would-be criminals should, in appropriate cases, not be ruled out as posing a credible security threat.

explosive device
object containing chemical, liquid, or gas (or combination thereof) that is designed to do damage or create injury upon detonation, explosion, or chemical or physical reaction

FAST FACT

How Many Threats Are Legitimate?

Using the Toronto Police Bomb Squad as an example to demonstrate the probability of a threat actually being a real event, consider the following information:

- In one year, the squad receives over 1,000 calls.

- Of these, the squad responds to an event about once every three days.

- These 100+ responses lead to the discovery of 9 or 10 real devices per year.

Thus, about 1 percent of all calls actually relate to real explosive devices.

In general, an explosive device works when an initiation system (which can be mechanical, electrical, chemical, etc.) triggers the detonation of explosive material. The resulting explosion—sudden release of energy—does damage by generating heat and/or pressure and sometimes by causing the mobilization of shrapnel or the destruction of surrounding structures or materials. Some bombs are specifically designed to trigger the release of another hazard—for example, in the case of the 1993 World Trade Center bomb, the propulsion of a canister of cyanide gas into the ventilation system. (It didn't work very well; the heat of the explosion rendered the gas harmless.)

Identifying Explosive Devices

Because of the variety of explosive devices available, training employees to identify explosives by sight is often not as effective as simply training them to identify objects that are "suspicious."

In order to be able to classify an object as suspicious, employees, including security employees, should be taught to regularly examine and observe the normal state of their working areas and the objects that surround them. When employees are familiar with what is supposed to be in the workplace, it becomes easier to note any objects that appear out of the ordinary, either because they cannot be identified or because their source or function is unknown.

When an employee notices a suspicious object in the normal course of work (i.e., not in the context of a bomb threat), security should be called. If security cannot identify the object or its origins, it may be advisable to call for appropriate outside assistance—the public Explosive Ordnance Disposal (EOD) authorities (bomb squad).

Where a suspicious object is noted in the context of a search that follows a bomb threat, the object will almost always provide cause for outside intervention.

Employees must be trained *never* to touch or move a suspicious package or object.

BOMB THREAT RESPONSE PLANNING

Any organization or facility that employs security should have a bomb threat response plan in place, no matter how remote the chance of ever receiving such a threat appears to be. The nature and level of detail of the bomb threat response plan will depend greatly on the type of organization, the size of the facility, the general risk for bomb threats, and other factors. Being prepared for a bomb threat means that, should such a threat actually materialize, security and management will have a better chance of protecting safety, minimizing disruption to business operations, and creating the impression that the workplace is safe and that security is being maintained.

Elements of a Bomb Threat Response Plan

Basic bomb threat response plans should address the following:

1. Actions on receipt of threat—the person who receives the bomb threat should know what immediate actions to take, what information to record and ask for, and whom to contact with respect to the threat.

2. The role of security—the authority and role of the security department, in the event of a bomb threat, should be described. Appropriate contact people (in larger organizations, a bomb threat team) should be identified.

3. Evacuation plans—every facility should identify evacuation routes, evacuation rules (for example, no elevator use), and a "marshalling area" to which evacuated individuals should be brought so that they can be protected and accounted for.

4. Search plan—for the purpose of searching for an explosive device, security should be trained to divide the facility into search zones. Security officers should be trained on how to perform a methodical search of a zone, and how to report their findings.

5. Plan for contacting outside authorities—security officers should know which public or other support authorities are to be contacted for support in the event of a bomb threat. Contact information should be kept in an easily accessible location, and provision should be made for orderly and accurate briefing of support authorities upon their arrival at the facility.

Larger, higher-risk, or more sophisticated organizations may also cover, in their bomb threat response plans, the following issues:

- identification of a bomb threat team;

- establishment of a bomb threat control centre;

- bomb threat response training for all employees;

- regular bomb threat drills;

- back-up communications, such as a loud hailer, in case of a bomb threat (some radio systems pose a risk of detonating explosives);

- purchase and storage of special supplies, such as bomb blankets, and letter bomb detectors;

- installation of special equipment, such as bomb-proof doors or barriers between zones;

- a policy with respect to public relations and media communications in the event of a bomb threat;

- a written/graphic search/evacuation plan that divides the facility into zones, permitting a comprehensive search and, in appropriate cases, evacuation of only at-risk parts of the facility (this is less disruptive to business activities, and minimizes risks related to panic reactions in a large facility).

BOMB THREAT RESPONSE PROCEDURE

An appropriate response to a bomb threat is critical for three key reasons (ranked in order of priority):

1. To preserve the safety of personnel, customers, and visitors, and to minimize damage to business assets.

2. To preserve the reputation of the employer/client by sending the message that the organization is prepared for and in control of the situation.

3. To minimize disruption of business activities.

All personnel, not only security, should be aware of the potential for bomb threats and should be alert to suspicious situations. At the same time, personnel should be encouraged to feel secure that there is a plan in place designed to provide for their safety and security in the event of a bomb threat.

For security personnel faced with a bomb threat, the following priorities should be observed:

- ensure personal safety at all times;

- ensure the safety of staff, contractors, visitors, and the general public;

- maintain the integrity of the site security function;

- maintain the routine operations of the site;

- obtain Explosive Ordnance Disposal (EOD) assistance when and if required.

Person Receiving the Threat

It is important to remember that bomb threats may be made to *any* employee in an organization—a bomb threat call cannot be expected to be made directly to the person best trained to handle it! For this reason, *all* employees should receive basic, well-designed training about how to respond to a threat. Simple instructions are best, as these are most easily retained.

A bomb threat can be most effectively responded to if the person taking the call can gather as much information, both objective and subjective, as possible about the threat and can later communicate that information accurately to others (for example, to security officers, or EOD staff).

Objective information about a bomb threat may include:

- the timing of the call;

- the phone number from which the call came;

- the exact wording of the threat;

- any background noise overheard.

Subjective information might include:

- the listener's perceptions of the caller's state of mind/attitude (e.g., he sounded nervous, she was trying to suppress laughter);

- perceived information about the caller (e.g., English is not his first language, she was reading from a prepared script); and

- recognition of the speaker's voice as familiar (voices are very unique).

The person who receives the threat, by listening carefully, can help security identify the seriousness of the threat. For example, most experts suggest that a threat should be perceived as valid if it is both *credible* and *specific*. Credibility might be affected by such things as the speaker's tone; for example, a person trying to suppress laughter might be rated as less credible than one speaking in a serious, even slightly nervous, tone. Specificity relates to details of the threat itself. A general threat such as "We've got the place wired to the max" might well be less valid than a specific threat such as "There's a pound of C4 explosive somewhere under the floor in the north end of Warehouse D; it will be detonated remotely at 0215 hours, or sooner if tampered with."

Because of the stress involved in receiving a bomb threat call, it can be extremely useful for employees to have a written guideline, stored near every telephone, for their reference. Figure 25.1 is an example of a form that may be used for this purpose.

Threat Response and Evacuation

Once a bomb threat has been received, it should be immediately communicated to the director of security or his or her delegate. That person, in cooperation with the bomb threat team, if any, should quickly make a determination with respect to the validity of the threat.

When a threat is deemed valid or potentially valid, and where there is some information about the location of the explosive device, the director of security may decide to evacuate all personnel, or personnel within a particular zone or zones.

Security officers will supervise the evacuation. Evacuees should be directed toward the safest possible exit route, taking into account the suspected location of the bomb. In general, employees are to be advised not to use elevators, telephones, or any other electrical devices. Cell phones, though often safe, should not be used unless security advises otherwise.

Evacuees should be advised to move quickly but not to run and to maintain quiet so that instructions can be heard (and other personnel in other areas are not alarmed unnecessarily). Line managers are to take responsibility for the employees who report to them and should account for all employees who were at work that day. Where an employee cannot be accounted for, his or her absence should be brought to the attention of security.

Evacuees should be brought to a safe marshalling area, and all personnel should be accounted for. In general, evacuees should not leave the marshalling area without express permission from security.

Where there is no reliable information about the location of an explosive device, the decision to evacuate is more complicated, because there can be no assurance of the safety of the marshalling area, or the exit route. In some cases, it may actually be safer to allow personnel to remain at their workstations. This decision should be at the discretion of the director of security, sometimes in conjunction with instructions from EOD staff.

FIGURE 25.1 Bomb Threat Checklist

Exact time of call _____

Exact words of caller _____

_____

_____

QUESTIONS TO ASK

1. When is the bomb going to explode? _____

2. Where is the bomb? _____

3. What does it look like? _____

4. What kind of bomb is it? _____

5. What will cause it to explode? _____

6. Did you place the bomb? _____

7. Why? _____

8. Where are you calling from? _____

9. What is your address? _____

10. What is your name? _____

CALLER'S VOICE (circle)

Accent	Crying	Giggling	Nasal	Sincere
Angry	Deep	High-pitched	Nervous	Slow
Broken	Disguised	Lisp	Normal	Slurred
Calm	Excited	Loud	Rapid	Stutter

If voice is familiar, whom did it sound like? _____

Were there any background noises? _____

Remarks _____

_____

Person receiving call _____

Telephone number call received at _____

Date _____

Report call immediately to _____
(Refer to bomb incident plan)

Search Procedure

Once the facility, or the affected zone of it, is secured (usually after an evacuation is complete; although in some sophisticated settings, after bomb-proof barriers are set in place), a search can be performed. Unless the risk is deemed to be certain or very high, the initial search is conducted by security officers and/or other employees, and not by an external response force.

Where possible, all parts of the facility should be searched by individuals already familiar with those areas; for example, security guards should search areas falling within their normal patrol routes.

Searchers should work systematically, according to a search plan. Useful strategies include:

- stopping to look, listen, smell, etc., upon entering a new room before moving around;

- dividing the room vertically into search zones, to ensure that the whole room is searched, not just the floor space;

- walking in a set sweep pattern;

- overlapping with another searcher;

- paying attention to hidden surfaces (undersides, topsides, backs of furnishings, doors, etc.); and

- noting damage to surfaces (e.g., marks or smudges on a false ceiling tile).

Security officers should pay special attention to stairwells, washrooms, lobby areas, vacant offices, corridors, elevators, receiving areas, garbage areas, the parking garage, and the mail room.

When a suspicious item is found in the course of a search, no one should touch it. Efforts should be made to determine its source (where it came from/who brought it there) and how long it has been in place. In most cases, an immediate call for support should be made to the appropriate authorities. If there has been no evacuation, a decision may be made to evacuate in light of the discovery of the item; however, it is important to remember that there is a possibility that there may be more than one device. In appropriate cases, the search of other areas should continue while awaiting support.

Coordination with External Response Force

When a call is made to an external response force, security should provide any available information pertaining to the incident over the phone. This information will assist in the determination of the size of the team to be dispatched and what equipment might be required.

The director of security (or his or her delegate) should be prepared to brief the external response force personnel on their arrival at the facility. Security personnel should provide ongoing support to the external response force over the course of the investigation. It is useful to have any paperwork that would assist in this task readily available—for example, a bomb threat form filled out by the person who took the call, and site plans for the facility.

SUMMARY

While only a small proportion of bomb threats relate to the actual placement of an explosive device, all such threats should be taken seriously. This means that all employees should receive basic training about how to respond to a bomb threat call.

Security departments should have a bomb threat response plan in place that addresses, at minimum, the issues of how and when to evacuate, how to search for a bomb, and whom to contact for outside support in case a device or suspected device is located.

Avoiding bomb disasters requires planning, good observation skills, and an ability to assess the credibility of bomb threats.

KEY TERMS

explosive device

PERFORMANCE APPLICATION

1. Why must bomb threats, even by apparently unsophisticated would-be criminals, be taken seriously?

2. Why is even an invalid bomb threat (i.e., one in which there is no bomb) a threat to business operations or public relations?

3. What is an IED?

4. Why should employees in most kinds of workplaces be trained simply to be alert to suspicious objects, rather than trained in how to recognize specific types of bombs?

5. How does an explosive device do damage or cause injury?

6. Why must *all* employees be trained in how to respond to a bomb threat call?

7. Why is it important to gather as much information as possible from a person delivering a bomb threat? List three kinds of objective information that should be sought. List three kinds of subjective information that should be recorded.

8. What issues are taken into consideration by a director of security in deciding whether or not to evacuate personnel and others in a facility?

9. What instructions should be given to evacuees in the event of a bomb threat?

10. List three issues that should be covered in a bomb threat response plan.

11. List three useful strategies for carrying out a search incident to a bomb threat. List three parts of a facility that should receive particular attention when conducting a bomb search.

12. What kinds of information should security personnel be prepared to share with external response force members upon their arrival at a site that has received a bomb threat?

26 Emergency Response Forces

INTRODUCTION

There is a new breed of security specialist developing in North America: emergency professionals. Particularly since the terrorist events in the United States on September 11, 2001, private companies and the public service have begun to recognize that, in addition to responding to the traditional plethora of emergencies and natural disasters, they must also build the basic tools needed to recognize and safely respond to acts of terrorism, whether these acts are nuclear, biochemical, explosive, or incendiary in origin. There is also recognition of the need to handle total infrastructure failures, wherein, because of the rapid advance of technology and greater electronic and wireless connectivity worldwide, a crisis can collapse the economies of linked nations in a split second.

While it may seem impractical to a security officer in a small residential or commercial complex to be prepared for a terrorist attack or natural disaster, there is no way to know who will and who won't be in danger if trouble strikes. The threat of terrorism changes all the rules of conventional security. Terrorist activity can and has infiltrated the streets of towns and cities all over the world. Terrorist organizations are often well funded and well organized and can afford to cripple our global economies through industrial sabotage as well as physical attack. To ignore the possibility of a terrorist attack is clearly irresponsible.

Chapter Objectives

When you have completed this chapter, you will

- be more aware of how companies and communities prepare for and respond to emergencies or disasters.

- have an understanding of work-related emergency measures and procedures as well as the integration of services from the local through to the federal level in any national emergency or disaster.

EMERGENCIES AND DISASTERS

An emergency is an urgent and/or critical situation, temporary in nature, that threatens or causes harm to people, the environment, the workplace, and/or property, or disrupts critical operations in a community, building, or organization such as hydro.

A major emergency requires coordination of support services such as police, fire, and ambulance, while a disaster includes all these services plus outside assistance including air/land/sea rescue and other military services.

What Would You Do?

The Economic Cost of Emergency Preparedness

One of the most common obstacles encountered by a security department investigating its needs for increased emergency preparedness is budget. While it is impossible to put a price on human life, many corporations resist the suggestion that their risk from terrorist activity is sufficient to justify the cost of additional security measures, whether with respect to equipment, training, or personnel.

As a security director, how would you approach the issue of requesting additional budget funds to improve security preparedness?

1. Do you think small corporations should do anything to protect themselves against terrorism? Why or why not?

2. Does the type of business affect your answer? Why or why not?

3. Does the location of the business affect your answer? Why or why not?

Examples of Emergencies and Disasters

A variety of possibilities require emergency response. They could be:

- fire, flood, earthquake, hurricane, or other type of weather disaster;
- power blackout;
- mass terrorist attack;
- airplane crash, subway accident, train derailment, or chain of highway collisions;
- toxic spills;
- bomb or bomb threat;
- building collapse;
- civil disturbance such as riot or labour strike;
- sabotage; and
- viral outbreak (such as SARS).

THE SECURITY ROLE IN AN EMERGENCY RESPONSE

In any emergency situation, security plays an active and important role. When an alarm is activated, a security officer or supervisor's first concerns are always to reduce panic, maintain order, protect life and property, and control access for emergency services. To achieve these goals, the steps to remember are as follows:

- Call police and fire department.
- Mobilize emergency response team (ERT).
- Keep order and help people stay calm.
- Activate emergency steps outlined in the organization's emergency plan.

- Assign entrances and exits that can be used.

- Direct evacuation until ERT takes over.

- Cordon off dangerous areas.

- Direct traffic to allow access for emergency services.

EMERGENCY PLANNING

To respond to an emergency effectively, a security officer must first have a plan, in writing. Organizations usually turn to their security department to prepare an emergency response plan. This plan will involve the coordination of many different services such as fire, police, paramedics, and their key directors. The elements of a good written plan include:

- an introduction;

- background information;

- definitions of important terms;

- emergency response mission;

- scope of company planning;

- potential threats;

- assumptions;

- concept of operations;

- budget for emergency response;

- company responsive capabilities;

- analysis of situation reports;

- creation of emergency operation control group (EOCG) and appointment of emergency response team;

- events or acts to activate emergency plan;

- activation of emergency plan;

- chain of command;

- conducting emergency response operation;

- command and control;

- debriefings.

IMPACT OF TERRORIST THREATS ON EMERGENCY RESPONSE

Since 9/11, Canadians have become aware of how vulnerable they are to the threat of terrorism. An arrest in the summer of 2004 of a student pilot making suspicious flights over the Pickering Nuclear Plant in Ontario drove that reality home, though the student's curiosity turned out to be innocent.

What Would You Do?

Developing a Terrorism Preparedness Plan

Read the following scenario, and answer the questions that follow:

You are a senior security officer working in a major two-tower condominium complex in the business district of a major Canadian city. Your security director has been asked to prepare a terrorism preparedness plan for the complex. While she will assume primary responsibility for the plan, she has delegated the preliminary research to you. She has asked you to prepare two things: (1) a draft list of key issues that should be addressed in the complex's plan, and (2) a list of resources she can consult in developing the plan.

1. Prepare the issue list.

2. Prepare the resource list.

Little has been publicized about Canada's efforts to develop emergency response strategies and training, but even before 9/11, many provincial organizations were already engaged in preventing and developing contingency plans for large-scale terrorist attacks on potential targets in metropolitan areas nationwide and smaller, less-populated locations across Canada. In 1990, Canada became a member of the Emergency Response Institute (ERI) International (originally formed in 1978). In creating the Emergency Response Institute Canada, all levels of government continue to invest in plans to prevent terrorism before it occurs.

EMERGENCY RESPONSE INSTITUTE CANADA

ERI Canada provides a range of services and products, including:

- training programs in emergency management and response, including diversified training programs to meet the needs of every level of emergency responder;

- textbooks, instructor manuals, and teaching kits for all courses developed by, or through, ERI;

- access to the latest disaster research documentation;

- a bookstore stocking the latest publications, research materials, and audiovisual products to aid the instructor and professional practitioner in emergency management;

- publishing capabilities to support the creation of new emergency management resources;

- consultative services for government agencies, business/industry, and private facilities, including state-of-the art emergency management program reviews, operational plan assessment, and long-range management work plan design;

- training exercises to enhance emergency response capability and training effectiveness;

- evaluation of major operational functions and plans for business and industry, fixed nuclear facilities, and other critical facilities; and

- consulting services for disaster recovery and assistance following major disasters and emergencies.

SPECIAL PERSONAL QUALIFICATIONS FOR EMERGENCY RESPONSE TEAM MEMBERS

A security officer interested in a more specialized career in emergency response must possess certain skills and traits in order to qualify. He or she must

- be in excellent health, physically fit, and able to lift 23 kg;

- have manual dexterity and excellent eye, hand, and foot coordination;

- be emotionally stable and able to perform well under stress;

- be self-confident and possess strong interpersonal and communication skills;

- be able to give and follow instructions promptly and clearly;

- be able to use good judgment under duress;

- have CPR training; and

- have a minimum of high school or, in some settings, college-level education.

DUTIES OF AN EMERGENCY RESPONSE TEAM

In an emergency situation, emergency response specialists may be required to perform duties outside the typical security mandate. For example, the first aid skills required of an emergency response specialist may include controlling bleeding, administering oxygen, giving CPR, treating shock victims, assisting with childbirth, controlling mentally disturbed persons, and treating burns or poisoning.

Emergency responders may be called upon to assist in evacuating victims trapped by fire or an accident. They may drive emergency vehicles, operate power tools, and maintain emergency equipment.

LIAISON WITH EMERGENCY MEDICAL SERVICES (EMS)

On an almost daily basis, in-house security teams and contract security officers are faced with situations that go beyond their capabilities as first responders on private property or in areas where they are responsible for the transportation of potentially dangerous or hazardous material. Examples of this would be nuclear security officers (NSOs) at one of Ontario's nuclear generating plants (NGPs) or the operational safety and security of a large interprovincial transport company. When the

Step Aside

Closeup: Office of Critical Infrastructure Protection and Emergency Preparedness (OCIPEP)

The website for Canada's Emergency Management System (CEMS) describes the role of the Office of Critical Infrastructure Protection and Emergency Preparedness of Public Safety and Emergency Preparedness Canada (PSEPC) as follows:

> Requests [for emergency/disaster response support] from the provinces to the Government of Canada are managed through the Office of Critical Infrastructure Protection and Emergency Preparedness (PSEPC), which maintains close operational links with provincial and local emergency authorities and maintains inventories of resources and experts in various fields. In practice, it can take just a few minutes for the response to move from the local to the national level and the right resources and expertise identified and triggered.
>
> PSEPC maintains the Government Emergency Operations Coordination Centre (GEOCC), which is located in Ottawa and operates 24 hours, seven days a week. During major events the GEOCC, with the help of emergency personnel from other departments, can serve as the focal point for emergency government operations.
>
> PSEPC administers two Government of Canada funding programs—the Joint Emergency Preparedness Program (JEPP) and the Disaster Financial Assistance Arrangements (DFAA). ...
>
> PSEPC also supports training and education efforts in emergency management. PSEPC's Canadian Emergency Preparedness College has been training emergency responders since 1951.
>
> The Government of Canada works continuously to refine national emergency plans and to ensure that appropriate arrangements are in place to support the response efforts of other organizations that make up Canada's emergency management system. For its part, PSEPC manages and maintains the National Support Plan, which establishes a structure and procedures for the coordination of Government of Canada support in response to assistance requests from provincial, territorial or US governments.
>
> PSEPC also plays a lead role in the National Emergency Arrangements for Public Information, the National Earthquake Support Plan, the Counter Terrorism Plan Consequence Management Arrangements as well as the Space Object Re-entry Plan.

Source: Public Safety and Emergency Preparedness Canada website, http://www.ocipep.gc.ca/info_pro/fact_sheets/general/EM_can_emerg_man_sys_e.asp.

need arises, specialized response teams are required to manage the situation and minimize the impact on people, the environment, and structures. These teams are traditionally drawn from the police, fire, and medical response communities. Security officers and supervisors must be conversant with the capabilities of these groups and practised in their role in support of these response teams when the need arises.

It is important to know that the government of Canada is leading communities in their efforts to take responsibility for their emergency response, and it has, under Canada's Emergency Management System (CEMS), an established infrastructure and a number of agencies and programs ready to go into action as needed. See "Step Aside" on page 292.

SUMMARY

No matter where you live or work, reducing risk is a growing concern at both the public and private levels. The responsibility for emergency planning and response falls squarely on private security in most of the business and industry sectors. Emergency response is an emerging specialty field for security providers, and its importance can be expected to grow rapidly in the future.

PERFORMANCE APPLICATION

1. What is an emergency?

2. What is a natural disaster?

3. Why has there been an increased interest in emergency response provision?

4. Why do emergency response specialists require additional training and special skills?

5. What kinds of additional duties might an emergency response specialist do in addition to "normal" security work?

6. For whom might an emergency response specialist work?

PART VIII **EXERCISE**

1. Search the Internet and find a copy of an emergency response plan; one example is the plan posted by the University of Western Ontario, at http://www.uwo.ca/emerg/plan133jan2001.pdf.

   a. Discuss the plan you've chosen in the context of what you've learned. Is there anything you would add? Does the plan incorporate any notable innovations or ideas?

   b. Divide into four groups. Using the UWO plan as a model, create an emergency plan for one of the facilities below. Each group should choose a different type of facility. Choose a spokesperson for your group to describe the plan to the class.

   Suggested facilities for this exercise include:

   - small manufacturing plant
   - two-storey gym in a mall
   - nursing home
   - public library
   - community centre with a pool
   - large furniture store

Glossary

A

active infrared system
volumetric motion detection device that shoots a beam of infrared light from a generator to a sensor

actus reus
act referred to as a voluntary action, omission, or state of being forbidden by the *Criminal Code*

agents
first private detectives hired by merchants and private owners to recover stolen property

allegiances
faithfulness or loyalty

ambient noise
normal background sound

analog
represented by a continuous physical variable

antenna
part of a hand-held radio for receiving transmissions

arrest
legally deprive a person of liberty by touching that person to indicate that he or she is in custody

arson
illegal act in which someone sets fire to a building or property

assault
threat of imminent harm in the mind of the intended victim

B

balance of probabilities
the ratio of likelihood to unlikelihood that a particular fact or conclusion is true, based on available evidence

battery
any unwelcome physical contact

beyond a reasonable doubt
standard of proof whereby a defendant's guilt must be proven to the extent that a reasonable person would have no choice but to conclude that the defendant committed the offence

biometrics
branch of security technology that allows access based on recognition of a person's physical attributes

bullet-resistant glass
composite of acrylic designed to withstand the impact of ammunition

burden of proof
responsibility to provide evidence to support a particular conclusion

C

Canadian Charter of Rights and Freedoms
part of the *Constitution Act, 1982* that sets out constitutionally protected rights and freedoms

capacitance sensor
detection sensor that uses an electrical field and signals an intruder when the charge is interrupted

case law
body of law based on decisions of similar cases

chemical reaction
the rapid oxidation of fuel created by fuel, oxygen, and heat

civil wrong
non-criminal wrong that can form the basis of a civil lawsuit—either a tort or a breach of contract

closed-circuit television (CCTV)
surveillance technology that allows security personnel to observe or record activity from a remote location

codes of professional conduct
policy documents prepared either by an employer, or by a body that regulates a profession that reflect the key values of either the employer or the profession and express standards of performance, integrity, and ethical behaviour for employees or association members

cognitive interview
technique developed by Ronald P. Fisher and Edward Geiselman to promote information recall by assisting the interview subject to revisit the context of the information, using four steps—reinstating the context, changing sequence, changing perspective, and retrieving specific details

colour of right
circumstances that lead to an understandable but mistaken belief that one has the right to do something

common law
rules that are formulated in judgments in case law

computer-generated image modification
use of digital printing technology to pre-print or variable-print advanced computer-generated graphic elements on identity documents

concertina wire
barbed wire extended in a spiral for use as a barrier

contaminating the evidence
destroying, altering, or depositing physical evidence at a crime scene

continuous lighting
a system that may be manually or automatically controlled to provide constant lighting

conversion
unauthorized interference with another's property that deprives the owner of its use

covert operations
investigations or observations of a suspect or a place while remaining hidden or "undercover"

criminal offence
act that contravenes a provision of criminal law

Crown attorney
lawyer who prosecutes the accused on behalf of the government

CSA International's Model Privacy Code
privacy obligations incorporated as schedule 1 of the *Personal Information Protection and Electronic Documents Act*

cybersecurity
protection of information that is vulnerable to theft, access, or corruption via the Internet or other computer networks

D

defamation
injury to a person's reputation by slander or libel

defence
denial of or justification for an act

defence counsel
the lawyer who represents the accused

detain
legally deprive a person of liberty for the purpose of asking questions

digital
represented by digits using discrete values of a physical quality

direct question
question that requests a specific piece of information

discontinuity of possession
transferring evidence from one person to another

documented research
written proof of some facts, inquiries, or investigations

Doppler effect
increase or decrease in frequency of light, sound, or other waves as the source and the observer move toward each other

due diligence
taking every reasonable precaution to avoid an undesirable consequence

E

electromagnetic cable
detection sensor that releases electromagnetic energy through tiny punctures in close intervals throughout its outer shield, producing an electric field that surrounds the cable like an aura

electromechanical sensors
vibration-detecting device in which the switches remain open until significant vibrations close the contact and trip an alarm

electronic counter-measures (ECM)
art of locating and disabling unauthorized transmission, recording, and listening devices

emergency and disaster response plans
policies or plans to maximize safety and minimize losses in the event of an emergency or disaster

emergency lighting
a system that works on auxiliary power to provide lighting when other systems fail

explosive device
object containing chemical, liquid, or gas (or combination thereof) that is designed to do damage or create injury upon detonation, explosion, or chemical or physical reaction

express authorization
admission to private roadways by invitation of the property owner

external antenna jack
part that connects an optional 50 ohms external antenna to a hand-held radio

F

false imprisonment
detention of a person without consent and without legal authority

feudalism
medieval social system based on an exchange of military protection for protection and labour

fibre optic cable
detection sensor made of fine filaments of glass that reflects light waves from a light source at one end of the fibre to a sensor at the other end

fire alarm
warning that smoke, heat, carbon monoxide, or fire has occurred

fire load
contents of a building that increase the potential for fire as items accumulate

floodlight
unit that produces a bright and broad beam of light

fluid pressure sensor
small tube sealed at one end and filled with fluid that sets off an alarm when the fluid pressure changes

fluorescent lamp
cathode-ray tube containing a gas or vapour that produces light when acted on by an electrical current

forensics
application of science to police work

form report
standardized report consisting mainly of blank spaces or check-off boxes that cover the essential data relating to specific crimes or events

four lines of defence
grounds perimeter protection, building perimeter protection, space/area protection, and object protection

frequency select switch
switch on a hand-held radio used to select the operating channel

Fresnel lens
thin optical lens consisting of concentric rings of segmental lenses

G

general occurrence report
report of the preliminary investigation prepared by the security officer who was first to encounter the incident

ghost printing
technology that adds a lighter reproduction of an image on an identity document

H

hazard
anything that might injure or harm a worker

high-risk patrol
patrol that takes place in an area known for dangerous activity or in an area that may be dangerous due to a particular situation, such as a labour dispute

hostile witness
person who may present evidence that does not support the position of the side that called the witness

human environment
personnel at the worksite

I

identity theft
misuse of another person's identity for illegal purposes

illegal activity
any action that is contrary to any federal or provincial statute

implied authorization
admission to private roadways is not prohibited by the property owner

incandescent light bulb
white-hot light caused by an electrical current flowing through the filament in a light bulb

industrial espionage
secretly accessing or collecting unauthorized manufacturing, business, or trade information from a company

interface
device that allows independent systems to interact

intrusion alarm
warning that an unauthorized person has gained entry

J

judge
court official appointed to try cases in a court of law

jurisprudence
judge-made law

jury
group of 12 people (in criminal law) or 6 people (in civil law in most provinces) who decide the case based on the evidence presented

L

laser engraving
technology that embeds data into ID cards to guard against forgery

liability
legal responsibility for a wrongful action

libel
written or recorded statement that damages a person's reputation

M

malicious prosecution
wrongful prosecution of a person without reasonable or probable cause

mens rea
deliberate intent to commit a wrongful act, with disregard for the consequence

mercury-vapour lamp
bluish light that can withstand power dips of up to 50 percent

metal halide lamp
light generated by halogen and another element or radical

microwave technology
volumetric motion detection device that relies on the Doppler effect to detect an intruder when the frequency of the microwave beam is changed

minor accidents
any incident that is non-reportable to the provincial authority and in which there are no injuries, no serious vehicle or criminal violations, and damages are under $1,000

monitor/reset switch
switch on a hand-held radio that monitors the channel for voice communication when depressed and held

N

natural barriers
features of the natural landscape that discourage access to a facility

negligence
careless conduct that causes foreseeable harm to another person

night watchmen
guards hired by merchants in the 1700s to patrol their properties at night and to protect their shops and warehouses from thieves and vandals

non-issue items
items of apparel, jewellery, hair accessories, etc., not supplied or authorized by the employer

non-stakeholders
people who do not have an interest or concern in something

O

ombudsman
public official who investigates complaints by citizens against public authorities or officials

on/off volume control
part on a hand-held radio that turns the radio on and off and adjusts the audio output level

open-ended question
question that requires an expanded answer

P

parochial police
regional guards hired by clergy in the 18th century to protect church property and parishioners within major city districts or dioceses

passive infrared system
volumetric motion detection device that floods an area with invisible low levels of infrared light

perimeter barrier
structure that defines the physical boundaries of a facility or area and restricts or impedes access

personal protective equipment
equipment or clothing, such as bulletproof vests, hard hats, and respirators, designed to protect the wearer against job hazards

physical defences
any object, structure, or piece of equipment that is designed, at least in part, to enhance the security of a facility

physical environment
surroundings or particular locations at the worksite

piezoelectric sensors
vibration-detecting device that generates an analog signal that is filtered through a process analyzer before triggering an alarm

plastique
plastic explosives

portable lighting
a battery- or generator-operated system that can be moved

press releases
written statements given to the media for publication

primary evidence
actual objects, witnesses, and documents

privacy glass
glass treated with special coating that "frosts" when subjected to an electrical impulse

professionalism
skills, integrity, ethical conduct, and competence that is expected from members of a profession

protocols
set of rules or conventions that allow sending and receiving computers to understand the messages being transmitted

PTT (push to talk) switch
switch on a hand-held radio that puts the radio in the transmit mode when depressed and held and in the receiving mode when released

public statements
comments made openly, not in private

Q

quartz lamps
a mercury-vapour lamp enclosed by an envelope made from quartz rather than glass

R

reinforced glass
two layers of plate glass with a galvanized wire screen inserted between them

reportable illegal activity
any illegal activity that is suspected or known to have taken place in the past, currently taking place, or is likely to take place in the future that is required by federal or provincial statute to be reported

ride shotgun
job of riding atop Wells Fargo stagecoaches to protect passengers and cargo from robbers during the late 1800s

S

safety glass
glass reinforced with polymer-based materials, either laminate or film

searchlights
highly focused incandescent lamps

secondary evidence
representative copy of the real evidence that is documented by a witness

security breach
any violation of a workplace policy, procedure, practice, or direction

serious or injury accidents
any incident in which there are injuries, vehicle or criminal violations, and damages are over $1,000

shrinkage
retail inventory losses attributed to shoplifting, employee theft, and administrative error

silent hours
time outside of normal business hours

situational awareness
well-developed sense of the specific patrol function being performed

slander
oral statement that damages a person's reputation

sodium-vapour lamps
soft yellow light produced by means of an electric current passing through a tube of neon and sodium vapour

solenoid
electric switch that draws power from a battery to open a lock

special-use alarm
warning that a danger, such as toxic fumes or machine malfunctions, has occurred

specialized report
flexible report used for complex and detailed investigations

standby lighting
a system equipped with searchlights that is turned on only when required

statute law
laws passed by the government

Statute of Winchester
legislation passed in 1285 that established local law enforcement in parishes throughout England

streetlights
suspended lighting that is either symmetrical (in the centre of the zone) or asymmetrical (offset for maximum distance coverage)

structural barriers
things that are created and installed for the protection of a facility

supplemental report
report that complements the general occurrence report and the specialized report

T

tailgating
to gain access by slipping in behind a person cleared to enter

taut wire sensor
detection device that operates like breaker switches on an electrical panel only in reverse order to initiate an alarm

tempered glass
glass designed to break into small regular-shaped pieces

tort
harm caused to a person or property for which the law requires a civil remedy

trespass
unlawful interference with the person, property, or rights of another

U

ultrasonic motion detector
intrusion detecting sensor that emits ultrasonic sound energy into a monitored area and reacts to a change in the reflected energy pattern

universal accessory jack
part that connects the optional external speaker-microphone or surveillance accessory to a hand-held radio

V

vassal
person who exchanged labour and loyalty for protection in feudal society

W

witness statement
formal, written record of what a witness observed, knows, and perceives

witness
person who gives evidence while under oath

Workplace Hazardous Materials Information System (WHMIS)
symbols found on hazardous products that identify the type of danger associated with the product and that provide information on safe handling

Index